THE EVERYTHING SAILING BOOK

Sail away with tons of tips, tricks, lessons, and helpful hints that cover every aspect of getting off the dock

Michael and Nikki Smorenburg

Adams Media Corporation
Holbrook, Massachusetts

An Everything Series Book.
The Everything Series is a trademark of Adams Media Corporation.

Published by Adams Media Corporation
260 Center Street, Holbrook, MA 02343

ISBN: 1-58062-187-2

Printed in the United States of America.

J I H G F E D C B

Library of Congress Cataloging-in-Publication Data
Smorenburg, Michael.
The everything sailing book / by Michael and Nikki Smorenburg.
p.   cm.
ISBN 1-58062-187-2
1. Sailing. I. Smorenburg, Nikki. II. Title.
GV811.S63   1999
797.1'24—dc21   99-16948
CIP

Some aspects of sailing are dangerous.
This book is not a substitute for expert advice or personal sailing instructions.

Illustrations by Barry Littmann and Terrel V. Broiles.

This book is available at quantity discounts for bulk purchases.
For information, call 1-800-872-5627.

Visit our home page at http://www.adamsmedia.com

Contents

PART 1: AN INTRODUCTION TO SAILING

DOCK 1: SAILING HISTORY 3

DOCK 2: TYPES OF BOATS AND BOAT ANATOMY 15

PART 2: SAILING INSTRUCTIONS FOR BEGINNERS

PART 3: RULES, ETIQUETTE, ADVICE, AND SAFETY

CONTENTS

PART 4: RACING AND INTERNATIONAL SAILING

INTRODUCTION

This book is designed to be a comprehensive guide for putting the elements of wind, water, equipment, and skill to practical use.

Of course, because sailing offers such an enormous range of activities—from tiny dinghies meandering on small and shallow lakes, to hi-tech racers competing in round-the-world competition—the hardest part has been finding a middle ground that is equally interesting and applicable to all levels of participants.

We've approached the subject from its most basic levels and will walk you through all of the most important elements, building you up with straightforward descriptions and explanations until you're armed with all of the information necessary to make you a competent student and member of the sailing community. However, don't be mistaken by our lighthearted style; water is a lady of many moods, and woe betide they who don't recognize this fact. On one day it can be a mirror barely scored by a ripple, but overnight or even within a few hours it can grow fangs of blown chop and become a fierce and hostile enemy that will ruin equipment and take lives.

No other medium in the human experience is as unpredictable and dramatic as the oceans and waterways. Newcomers to the sport of sailing are therefore well advised to gain their apprenticeship at the side of an experienced sailor or instructor.

On the other hand, we do recognize that it's precisely nature's many moods—the powerful allure of challenge, and the sheer adrenaline boost—that will keep you coming back for more. But it remains vital that you always keep in mind that the water is not our natural element, and only through skill and practiced judgment can we hope to visit it for any length of time.

This book describes the passions, the history, the rules, the peculiarities, the humor, and the many pleasures of a noble sport and pastime. While it's a fun book about a serious subject, it takes a serious look at fun.

Pirates

In the common perception, swashbuckling pirates have gained a romantic status in the annals of the collective mind. The term pirate loosely refers to all of the various sea-going rogues who made their living by pillaging other vessels. Hollywood images aside, the strict definition of the word "pirate" are people who rob or plunder on the sea for their own account. And, as such, their barbarous and thieving ways were both feared and summarily dealt with by authorities without mercy.

Pirates were traditionally hanged at the low-tide mark (above that mark the civil courts took over), to point out that the crimes had been committed within the jurisdiction of the Admiralty.

When we play so close to the edge and take the choice to challenge the unforgiving fury of nature, then we'd better be fore-armed with the collective knowledge past experience can offer and present technology can deliver.

When all is said and done, if you live anywhere near a body of water, and have blood in your veins, then this book is for you.

Sailing puts us land-dwelling humans in an environment that is both exciting and potentially hazardous. If we're to survive and enjoy our experience out on the water, we will rely heavily on our equipment and knowledge of how to use it under every condition. Therefore, to get started, we'll go right to basics and get a quick overview of the boat, its various parts, how everything works together, and other practical information to orient you to this exciting sport and way of life.

Today's sailboats are the result of a long process of development, trial, and error. The basic configuration of bringing a stream-lined hull, a mast draped with fabric sails, and some kind of steering mechanism together, is thousands of years old. Beyond being an interesting study, a quick review of the history of boats will give you an appreciation for the various modern disciplines. And, by understanding their origins, you'll be better able to judge the level at which you'd like to become involved with sailing as a lifestyle.

Environment

By definition, sailing is at its most exhilarating and rewarding when undertaken in windy conditions. Without wind, a sailboat becomes becalmed and cannot progress in any direction unless powered by motor or other mechanical means such as paddles.

However, for anyone who's ever been on water when the wind is blowing, the experience can be unpleasant without the right equipment and knowledge of how to put the wind to work for a desired outcome such as sailing from point A to point B.

The most important factor in sailing is the strength, and direction from which, the wind is blowing. With nothing more than a glance, these two factors will tell the experienced sailor everything he or she needs to know about which sails to set, how to set them, what tack or direction to sail the boat, and what precautions to take.

Of course there are a host of low- and high-tech pieces of equipment that can be employed to get the most out of the wind and its relative direction of movement to the ultimate desired direction of travel.

Low-tech equipment or observation includes such mundane elements as distant smoke blowing from a chimney, spray blown across the water, or telltale pieces of fabric or flags fixed to the mast. High-tech indicators come from such instruments and observations as wind vanes, barometers, weather reports, etc.

With experience, the savvy sailor can put the readings from these various measurement devices to work and make a judgment as to how the current wind conditions might change over the short and medium term.

The downside of wind is that the inexperienced sailor is at the whim of the direction the wind is blowing. And, if that happens to be toward a reef of breaking waves, the boat and crew could be doomed. Of course, wind also brings with it something called "wind chill." As the term implies, movement of air causes heat loss from the human body. Therefore, though it might be a warm and balmy day ashore, experienced sailors pack and dress to stay warm for their jaunt on the water.

Beyond the direct effects of wind, water is greatly affected by wind. If the wind blows long and hard enough, it gets the surface of the water to move in the direction of its travel. Eventually small ripples turn into chop, and then into waves which present their own challenges to sailors.

We could also stretch the term "environment" to include factors such as balancing the boat. The smaller the boat, the more critical this factor becomes. Sailboats are sensitive to the placement of crew and cargo. Sailors can use this placement to their advantage and compensate for a wind's strength from one direction by placing the bulk of weight in the hull so that it counterbalances the wind's force. Of course, as soon as the boat turns to travel in the opposite direction, the

weight will have to be redistributed or its formerly compensatory placement will no longer cancel the wind's force out but add to it—possibly causing a dangerous list, or leaning over of the vessel.

Then, beyond the placement of weight laterally, the placement of weight in the length of the boat can be a factor that forces either the bow or stern to ride too deeply. If such an imbalance is caused by weight distribution, a potentially dangerous situation could be caused if the sailboat encounters the slightest ripple or gust of wind.

Boat Anatomy

Regardless of its size, every sailboat is made up of four basic parts, designed to work together to keep the crew and cargo afloat, stable, and moving in the desired direction. As such, each part has a significant influence on each other, and the interaction between these parts must be understood and put to work under the guidance of an experienced skipper's skill.

Sailboats are differentiated from one another depending upon the configuration of their parts and the way in which they must be handled.

The Hull

The hull is the basic tub or shell that makes flotation possible. Historically, hulls were made of materials such as wood that had flotation properties in their own right. Modern hulls might be constructed from a variety of materials, including steel, concrete, and various composites or compounds such as carbon or glass fibers and resins.

The shape of the hull is always governed by a tradeoff between forward speed and lateral stability. The width and length of the hull, together with the shape of the hull below the waterline will greatly affect speed and stability. Long streamlined hulls with a flattened underside offer less resistance through which they must push the water than a wide, short hull with a deep "V" profile. The depth of the "V" effectively brings the boat's center of gravity closer to the water, making it stable from side to side, but also creates much resistance to forward motion.

Racing hulls tend to be of the long, slim, flat-bottomed type that emphasize light construction at the expense of durability. Family and leisure hulls tend to be more tubby and wide with a deeply rounded or "V'd" shape, and are constructed of durable materials that do not excessively add to costs; fiberglass being the most common as it is cheap to buy, work with, maintain, and repair.

Sails

Sails form the main "engine" of a sailboat. Though skilled sailors can use the sail to back the boat up, sails are designed to drive the boat in a forward direction.

More than a simple fabric bag to catch wind and pull the boat in the general direction the wind is blowing, modern sails are the result of a long evolution in studying the science of wind energy. The science of designing sails to do specific jobs under given wind conditions and circumstances has given rise to a host of different sail types, each with its specific application.

Like garment design, flat sail fabric is cut into panels and then sewn together in such a way that a three-dimensional wing shape is created. When the sail is hoisted up the mast and tensioned, the wing profile puts physics to work and converts the energy of the passing air into forward motion of the hull through the water.

For simplicity of handling, most small and beginner boats have just one sail. Large boats need to capture a lot more of the wind's energy and consequently sport several sails. These multi-sail vessels have sails that are divided into two main groups: Sails that allow the boat to sail at various angles across or even almost into the wind's direction—such as mainsails and jibs, and sails that are used when the boat is moving in generally the same direction as the wind is blowing—spinnakers.

Sails are hoisted vertically toward the top of a mast and held in place by a system of restraining ropes, wires, battens, and pulleys. By adding or loosening the tension on these restraints, sailors are

Sailor Talk

Holystone

The last Navy ships with teak decks were the battleships, long-since decommissioned. Teak, and other wooden decks were scrubbed with a piece of sandstone, nicknamed at one time by an anonymous witty sailor as the "holystone." It was so named because since its use always brought a man to his knees, it must be holy!

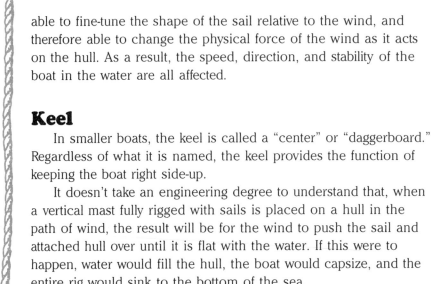

able to fine-tune the shape of the sail relative to the wind, and therefore able to change the physical force of the wind as it acts on the hull. As a result, the speed, direction, and stability of the boat in the water are all affected.

Keel

In smaller boats, the keel is called a "center" or "daggerboard." Regardless of what it is named, the keel provides the function of keeping the boat right side-up.

It doesn't take an engineering degree to understand that, when a vertical mast fully rigged with sails is placed on a hull in the path of wind, the result will be for the wind to push the sail and attached hull over until it is flat with the water. If this were to happen, water would fill the hull, the boat would capsize, and the entire rig would sink to the bottom of the sea.

The keel solves this problem by being an effective counterbalance below the water level, to the mast and sail standing above the water level. Large vessels have keels that are made from heavy material such as concrete or lead. The sheer weight of the keel is sufficient to keep the hull right side up.

Smaller vessels and racing craft rely on the lateral resistance of the water and the shape of the keel or centerboard to keep the hull from being pushed over by the wind.

Whether by its weight or by leveraging itself against the surrounding water, when the wind huffs and puffs and tries to push the boat over, it is the keel that causes the opposite equal reaction of bringing the boat's mast and hull back to a vertical orientation. Of course, the stronger the wind, the more it begins to win its fight to push the sail flat with the surface of the water. Hence, we see boats leaning or heeling ever more over as whitecaps increasingly fleck the water's surface. In such strong wind conditions, although the keel appears to be losing its battle with the wind, the wind defeats itself by pushing the sail out of its path and thereby having ever-less surface area to act upon.

Ultimately, even if the wind manages to push the mast and hull through 90-degrees and on the verge of capsize, providing the hull is sealed and no water rushes inside to fill it, a weighted keel will patiently wait till the gust is over—and up the mast will pop until the next gust hits.

Because smaller boats don't have a weighted keel, but rather rely on the lateral leverage of the water acting in opposition to the wind, the crew must compensate against the wind by leaning as far as they can into the direction that the wind is blowing. The crew tethers themselves to the mast by wires and hang, or "fly," out over the side of the boat in a harness. By so doing they use the principle of leverage to put their own body weight to work as a kind of temporary weighted keel.

Of course, having a keel sticking deeply below a hull's bottom is not a great idea in shallow water conditions or if the boat is designed to periodically be brought out of the water and moved on a trailer. Larger sailboats are therefore forced to stick to open water sailing and deep-water moorings. The fact that centerboards can be lifted allows small sailboats to enter the shallows and be loaded onto a trailer for easy transport.

The only sailboats that do not have keels are certain multi-hull designs such as Hobie Cats. These craft overcome the problem of lateral wind force by having a very wide lateral profile (from side to side) and by having deep rudders. Even so, with relatively slow wind speeds, the crew is forced into the harnesses and to "fly" out over the side to compensate.

Rudder

The rudder appears to be a second keel that extends vertically below the stern of a vessel. The difference between the rudder and a keel is the rudder is hinged and can therefore rotate. This rotation is critical because it allows the vessel to change its course or direction.

Although the job they do is a very big one, most rudders are quite small and almost insignificant when compared with the bulk of the hull and sails.

Again, whereas large vessels have rudders that are permanently fixed in place through the hull, smaller sailboats have rudders that can be raised or "kicked-up" when sailing in shallow water or encountering an obstruction.

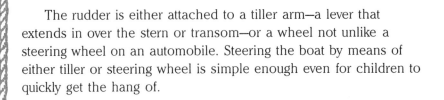

The rudder is either attached to a tiller arm—a lever that extends in over the stern or transom—or a wheel not unlike a steering wheel on an automobile. Steering the boat by means of either tiller or steering wheel is simple enough even for children to quickly get the hang of.

Equipment

Beyond the boat with all its hardware and fixed paraphernalia, there is a wide variety of equipment that will make sailing both a safe and fun-filled experience.

Almost every sailboat should be equipped with bailing apparatus, paddles, anchors, buckets, sponges, and clothing and area maps kept in a watertight container.

Safety

The number of potential injuries or disasters that one can encounter while sailing is almost limitless.

Adequately warm and dry clothing is the most obvious and primary safety precaution that every skipper and sailor must consider every time before climbing aboard.

The next most important piece of equipment includes all forms of flotation and rescue devices such as life jackets.

Depending upon the type of sailing and how far from land it will take one, various auxiliary equipment such as flares, navigational aids, radios, fire-fighting equipment, spares for critical parts, tool kits, emergency rations, first aid equipment, foul weather gear, adequate footwear, harnesses, rescue craft, bilge pumps, and a host of additional incidental items could literally mean the difference between life and death.

Skills

To be a sailor, it's not enough to simply buy a boat and equipment. It is vital that you acquire your skills and learn to apply them under the guidance of an experienced sailor.

Beyond a comprehension of sailing and safety skills, the competent sailor needs to learn how to read every situation and understand what its result might be and how to both control the environment or cope with problems before or as they arise. Fortunately, a host of state and federal laws govern the licensing of skippers and their competence to sail various classes of boat. The onus is therefore placed on the would-be sailor to research which authority governs the level of sailing they intend to partake in, and what licensing procedures they must follow before attempting to participate.

Where no laws specify minimum standards, it is wise for skippers and crews to develop skills that are at the very least equal to any eventuality that the type of sailing and region they're sailing in might present them with.

With all of the hi-tech equipment available, it becomes tempting to ignore rudimentary skills built up over generations of sailing. The old skill that some modern sailors feel they can dispense with, in this age of satellites and electronics, is navigation. However, expecting that that equipment will continue to work and never fail is a foolhardy gamble on which to stake the lives of those aboard and those who must execute the inevitable rescue. Ocean sailors need to develop the navigational skills of dead reckoning and chart plotting to augment the possibility of some future equipment failure.

Of course, the aim of sailing is to be able to reach a given destination regardless of wind direction and strength. Only practice in controlled environments can guarantee the sailor and his or her crew that a safe and enjoyable result will be the happy ending to every trip undertaken.

Rules

Beyond the rules that governing authorities might place on their jurisdiction of sailing, there are the rules of nature.

Sailing laws cover all of the do's and don'ts, tell you where and when you must sail, how to conduct yourself, and what procedures to follow.

Nature's laws include all of the actions and reactions that occur when the forces of wind, water, gravity, and solar power culminate.

Sailors in History

Leif Ericson (975–1020)
An Icelandic explorer—AKA Viking, replete with war ax and horns—Leif is believed to have landed in North America. The second son of Eric the Red—who established the first European settlement on Greenland—Leif voyaged from Greenland to Norway shortly before 1000. Tradition says Leif lost his way and happened upon North America's shore. A more reliable source claims that an Icelandic trader by name of Bjarni Herjólfsson was the first to sight North America. The Vikings called the American landmass "Vinland." Steeped in controversy and long disputed as groundless speculation, remnant Viking settlements in Newfoundland, Nova Scotia and New England are today accepted historical and archaeological fact.

Whereas defying human rules might attract interpretation of circumstance and reasonable penalty, nature either doesn't allow its rules to be broken, or imposes a severe penalty against transgressors. Fortunately, the rules of both man and nature have been well tested and documented.

Besides the laws stipulated by either authority or nature, there are laws that just make common or sociable sense. When one puts to sea in a vessel, many lives are placed in the hands of the skipper. Telling someone ashore where you're headed and when you'll be back could vastly accelerate the rescue effort in the event that a problem occurs and you cannot communicate it to potential saviors. On the other hand, taking precautions such as not littering, kicking up a big wake, or making excessive noise, will all go a long way to allowing other sailors to enjoy their time on the water too.

This book contains the most important rules and how to deal with them, or indicates where they can be found. In either case, sailing is not the pastime for the habitual rule-breaker. The penalties are much too severe.

Once you're satisfied with all of the tangible elements of sailing and how they interact, this book will help you utilize them at both a beginner and intermediate level.

The Sailing Past, Present, and Future

The first sailor to set sail probably did so in his log dugout during a howling offshore wind, and utterly by accident. Never to be seen again, the unfortunate soul was unlikely to appreciate what a trend he had started. But, wind-driven sailing proved to be a technological skill, and growth of its popularity was to unfold in direct proportion to a sailor's ability to arrive where he pointed his bow. The billowing sail can take enormous credit for shaping the modern world we live in. Who could argue that those who mastered wind were influential in molding today's social, economic, and political climate.

With the collective knowledge of our ancestors, it's relatively easy for anyone today to comprehend the dynamics of wind-driven propulsion. But, for the ancients whose frame of reference was cluttered by magic and witchcraft, designing a craft that exploited the elements was very much a trial-and-error affair. On this note, for *error*, read *death by drowning*.

Even given these dire dangers, history displays a rich tapestry of developments with wind and water that took vessels and their crews to every corner of the globe.

Like most human endeavors, economic forces shaped sailing; commodities could be transported in larger quantities for less cost by water than by land. Once the cargo routes were established, the sources of commodities had to be secured by the shipment of armies.

In addition, along with cargo came opportunity for theft, and sea piracy developed. With hostility on the high seas came a need for speed and defense systems. Then, once these elements had been developed to the maximum level of available resources, a need to sail out of sight of land for fame and profit made the refinement of navigation a necessity.

From Freight to Fun

Because humans possess a natural appetite for play, the advent of steam- and combustion-driven watercraft did not scuttle our wish to sail. On the contrary, motorized power brought a boost to the sailing equation. Remember, it's all about getting to your destination alive and intact. When the chips are down and the surf is up, the ability to furl in the sheets and beat against the weather with a motor is a far superior option than remaining at the whim of the elements.

Future Perfect?

Where to from here? We humans are always tempted to imagine that everything that can be developed, has been developed, yet we're fairly certain that the Egyptian, Viking, and Clipper designers had pretty much the same sentiments when they respectively ruled the waves.

Sure, everything has its limitations, but we firmly believe that there's a lot of excitement yet to come.

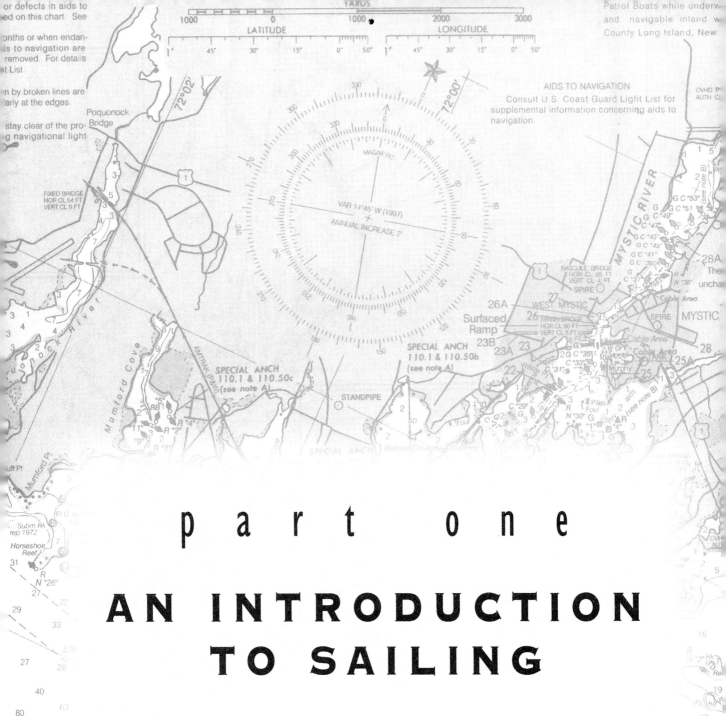

part one

AN INTRODUCTION TO SAILING

DOCK 1

Sailing History

A History Painted in Flotsam and Jetsam

Had so many of our unfortunate ancestors not gone to the bottom of the sea with their cargoes, our understanding of the origin and progress of sailing would be all the poorer. Again, it was the profit incentive to reap the rewards of lost treasure that gave birth to the first industry of salvage—and later the study of marine archaeology.

The first efforts were haphazard, disorganized, and outright dangerous. But the development of scuba delivered the pastime into the popular imagination.

Since that time we've recovered priceless artifacts and established much of humankind's rich sailing history.

Trade

It was not long ago that sailing boats of the world could be given a regional label with a single glance. Craft were developed in response to local conditions, tradition, available material, and motivation. Because these factors differed so greatly over the centuries and from one place to another, a broad variety of coastal and oceangoing vessels developed. Bear in mind that we're talking about a time when sail drove everything, from fishing to slaving, from plundering to hauling.

Available materials greatly influenced design. Wood was the material of choice among most seafaring nations, but where there was little wood—as with the Inca civilization living around the high elevations of Lake Titicaca—reeds proved a reasonable alternative.

But wood has its limitations, most notably construction costs and upkeep. As soon as it became possible, boat builders began experimenting with a host of other media including various metals, concrete, and composite fibers.

Arab dhows and Chinese junks still ply their trade in tightly defined corridors, but for the most part localized design has given way to more uniformity in hull design. In short, the market for pleasure-oriented sailing craft is far stronger than working craft. Because pleasure falls into only a few narrowly defined categories, the broad diversity of function has given way to variations on distinct themes.

War

The great sea battles and the warring parties using sailing craft are long gone. But, to get a glimpse of what has been, consider that in the year 1156 a Viking armada numbering 40,000 warriors laid siege to Paris by sailing up the Seine. It's an awe-inspiring thought to imagine how many of these relatively flimsy ships had to sail such great distances over quite hostile seas to achieve their plunder. It's a testament to the human spirit and how much can be achieved with elementary equipment.

Historic Breakthroughs

Since many aspects of hull form and rigging have been absorbed into modern designs, in order to truly appreciate the designs of modern sailing craft it's important to know something about their ancestors—the working boats of yore.

As is now the case, one of the key criteria for boat designers was the craft's speed. History proves that it didn't take long for designers to figure out the correlation between sail size and power delivery. The more sheet they could put to the wind, the more speed could be attained. On the other hand, the larger the sail grew, the heavier and more unmanageable it became, and the more crew would be needed to operate the craft. But crews required living space and investors required returns, hence boats grew to accommodate both sets of needs.

Where labor costs were low, as was the case in Arabia and the dhow, boats with massive sails were constructed, which resulted in exceptional speed and vigorous trade.

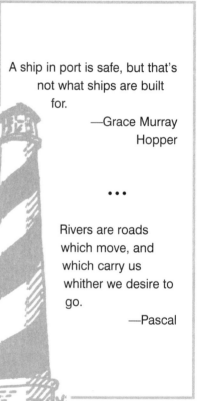

A ship in port is safe, but that's not what ships are built for.
—Grace Murray Hopper

• • •

Rivers are roads which move, and which carry us whither we desire to go.
—Pascal

In the West

By contrast, Western designers faced higher crewing costs and subsequently discovered that their solution lay in using smaller work teams. Instead of heaping yardage onto a single mast, they opted for multiple masts sporting many smaller sails.

From this design concept we see the beautiful clippers of the late nineteenth century, some with as many as seven masts, each billowing with thousands of feet of canvas. These square-riggers, as they were called because of the shape of each square sail that bagged out before the wind like a miniature balloon or spinnaker, were particularly suited for downwind sailing. They exploited the steady trade winds to shuttle their cargoes back and forth across the open ocean.

But designers found that square rigging, which basically bags the wind blowing from behind to provide forward motion, was not efficient for coastal sailing where wind direction and speed are variable. In response they developed fore and aft rigs, which set sails in the length of the vessel that could work in conjunction with a square-rigged system. The physical dynamics of this type of sail setting allowed the brigs and brigantines, barques and barquentines, snows, schooners, ketches, and yawls to navigate the coastlines.

Sailing is almost always a slave to compromise, and each design exploited its particular advantages. Some strove for speed, others for ease of handling. There was the necessity for large cargo-carrying capacity and the need for maneuverability through narrow channels.

Around the World

Designers in other parts of the world found different solutions. The Chinese junk or lugsail can be easily and cheaply repaired and is remarkably efficient sailing to windward or on a reach.

Although the junk design as been long recognized as having many advantages, it has only recently been adapted for use in what can be termed modern sailing vessels.

In some of the world's less-developed regions, traders, fishermen, and fortune seekers are still sailing the traditional way of their forebears. But neither in material nor outstanding design do any of these local examples of our human quest to sail have much impact on the world of sailing as it exists in the industrialized world.

The First Pleasure Boats

The cutter, ketch, yawl, and schooner survived the advent of steam and diesel by virtue of their suitability for recreational sailing. Many old pilot cutters or fishing smacks and most present-day yachts with their fore and aft rigs are converted adaptations to cruising boats.

Though each rig may vary a little, all fore and aft rigs consist of a main mast with a mainsail set behind it and a headsail or jib set in front of it. The sloop rig—probably the most popular boat in the West and the one you are most likely to be familiar with—has a single headsail and a mainsail.

The cutter has one mast with two or more headsails and a gaff or Marconi mainsail.

Ketches and yawls carry an additional mast. Known as the mizzenmast, it's erected toward the stern of the boat. The ketch mizzen is stepped forward of the rudderpost, while on the yawl it's stepped behind it.

A Modern Lifestyle and Culture Develops

Prior to the mid-1800s, a sheer lack of knowledge and efficient equipment had always kept sailing so risky and chore-filled a business that no private citizen would ever have imagined that there could be leisure in it. As the twentieth century was about to dawn, all of the past developments in design, seamanship, and navigational technique came together. Suddenly an individual could choose and enjoy the solitude or camaraderie of leisurely cruising for the sheer pleasure of the experience.

At first considered an eccentric pastime, the various types and venues for cruising are only limited by an individual's taste for leisure. We modern sailors now thrill to the joys of balmy tropical seas, the challenge of the tempests of icy gales, or the placid discovery of deserted coastlines.

During the twentieth century, recreational sailing has spread around the globe. Throughout the Americas, Europe, Australia, and elsewhere, privately owned sailing boats partake in every aspect of waterborne recreation.

Sailors in History

Prince Henry the Navigator (1394–1460)

Although he was a confirmed landlubber himself, the good Prince etched his legacy into sailing history as the far-sighted benefactor and sponsor of navigation. As prince of Portugal, Henry established an observatory and school of navigation and directed voyages that spurred the growth of his motherland's extensive colonial empire that would reach as far east as Japan, by way of the infamous Cape of Storms (AKA Cape of Good Hope).

Boat designers cater to all sorts of individual needs—from budgetary constraints to no-penny-spared luxury. In backyards, makeshift warehouses, and factories, professionals and hobbyists alike, building for pleasure or profit, construct rigs that they believe will suit specific tastes. Today there are a host of entire industry specialists who cater to a gamut of sailing needs—from brokerage to repair, from global shipping freight agents to parts and equipment sales.

A Sport Is Born

Whenever humans do anything, it's not long before they start competing. The moment two boats appeared on the water, the sport of racing was born. Whether they show it or not, sailors' attention to their relative progress sharpens the moment they have a reference point to judge themselves against. These informal skirmishes of the clock between vessels ultimately led to more serious racing.

Racing quickly became a game of tactics, skill, design, and big money. From this combination of factors we can see why there's a distinct difference between making a boat go fast and winning a race. Some boats are just faster, while some sailors just have a knack of cranking that extra bit of wind into their forward motion. When you're running level with them, they effortlessly leave you floundering in their wake, wondering how you squandered the same puffs of wind that drove them ahead. Then, not far down the track, they make a strategic blunder and you suddenly find yourself out in front. On the other hand, there are those whose knowledge and theory astound you, but out on the water they just can't get it together and make the boat hop.

Pride, profit, and desperation have all motivated sailors to push themselves, their crews, and their vessels to the absolute limit. The competition has been good for us all. Virtually all of modern sailing technique, equipment, and strategy are the direct result of a skipper trying to reach his or her goal ahead of schedule. Without the competition of sport there would have been little incentive to push what began as mere transport into the great leisure activity that it has become.

Regattas

In 1720 the Water Club of Cork Harbor staged the first regatta on record. At that time, thanks to the dogged determination of the maritime wanderlust of the Irish, the Brits maintained an empire on which the sun never set. Within thirty years the Duke of Cumberland seized the lead and established a fleet of small and bulky open cutters with deep keels that raced on the Thames.

Racing for no more than a few hours and remaining within sight of land, the end of the day would bring racers all the comforts of shore life. As late as the mid 1800s nobody had considered anything beyond day races, as they still believed that small boats could not be made seaworthy enough for a long haul. Overnight races were therefore not yet imagined. Perception began to rapidly change as the wanderlust of intrepid yachtsmen developed and they cruised ever further from the European coast and out into the open ocean. Design, competence, and confidence quickly gave rise to the next logical step in our competitive nature.

Ocean Races

Economics dictated that ocean racing would be separated from the common man and become the true sport of kings. In October 1661, King Charles II and the Duke of York wagered one hundred pounds sterling on their respective vessels, which raced a loop from Greenwich to Gravesend, returning up the River Thames. The Duke took the first leg but the King took the prize on the home run.

During the 1800s, transatlantic passage became the most dominant ocean racecourse. The large ships that partook were plying trade anyway, thus racing for prize money was an added bonus to their commercial profitability. By 1866, stakes as high as $90,000 lay on the line for the fastest traverse between New York and Cowes. Vessels were soon flying across the waves in less than fourteen days—putting the 100-foot-plus cutters and schooners on par with steam-driven crossings of the same period. By today's standards, human costs were high with as many as six men lost overboard during some races. Out of reach from the gen-

Racing boat

eral public, this type of sailing made little immediate impact on the general sailing fraternity.

The crossover from large to small boat ocean racing can be traced to one Thomas Fleming Day who, at that time, was editor of the American magazine *Rudder*. Though short by today's standards, on a mission to disprove the skeptics who believed it foolhardy for small boats to take on an overnight haul, in 1904 he organized a 300-mile race from Brooklyn to Marblehead via Cape Cod. Day brought up the rear of the fleet by crossing the line last, but with all boats having completed the haul, his point was proven and he had his victory.

Buoyed by that success, three years later Day organized a 660-mile Bermuda race to which only three entries were recorded. Though not all three finished, this race became a regular annual feature until 1910. Then, in 1922, the newly formed Cruising Club of America picked up the organization. To this day, the Bermuda race continues to be sponsored by them. For the record, a bigger challenge of 1906 was a Los Angeles to Honolulu crossing.

During the same period, in 1925, across the Atlantic the British were also undertaking developments that would carry through until today. Because the Royal Cruising Club had refused support for ocean racing, British yachtsmen founded the Ocean Racing Club and launched the first Fastnet race, an event that remains one of the premier events on today's yachting calendar. Purpose-built racing craft were not yet in existence. Instead, racing fleets were made up of converted working craft. Sailing a converted cutter, George Martin, commodore of the club, took line honors from six competitors entered in the inaugural race.

By the start of World War II, ocean racing had taken its hold. The European circuit already had a host of annual courses to choose from.

After the war, the Royal Ocean Racing Clubs codified a system whereby time allowances could be adjusted to allow vessels in different classes to race against one another. Meanwhile, the sleek and purpose-built American vessels that had enjoyed much triumph over the traditional cruise-designed European entrants since before the war were still creating controversy with regard to their seaworthiness.

The racing features that we take for granted today first appeared in 1947 in a British boat designed by Laurent Giles. Its long waterline to relatively short overall length was achieved by squaring off the bow and stern. Together with a light construction and shallow draft, the *Myth of Malham* presented little drag through the water and more efficiency for the wind its sails had bagged.

Naturally, the modern vessel is extremely sophisticated in the design of rigging and the complexity of deck equipment. Although today's interiors are stripped to a Spartan minimum and a host of innovative and lightweight materials have replaced wood, the thoroughbred racer is built along the same basic philosophy as the *Myth of Malham*.

Long-Haul Racing

The number of long-haul, transoceanic, and circumnavigation races that have developed over the years is almost too numerous to mention. With dozens, if not hundreds, of private citizens and their small families crisscrossing the globe and cruising at will, what fifty years ago would have seemed the demented ranting of a madman is today almost commonplace—single-handed, round the world racing.

Of all the events that have been proposed and undertaken—either as outright races or cruises—perhaps Whitbread's Round the World Race is the most notorious and punishing. Alone, these grizzled salts take on some of the world's most treacherous and awesome challenges of nature as they fly sheets to the wind through becalmed tropical waters and mountainous arctic waters, all in a single event. With high technology as their only link to civilization, they test the cutting edge of possibility for us all.

Modern Environment

Few buyers or builders of boats can spend without being subject to a budget. And what a budget will buy all comes down to the order of priorities at hand. If it's racing, then the main priority might be outright speed. If the aim is cruising, then it becomes a little more

Sailor Talk

Gun Salutes

Gun salutes were first fired as an act of good faith. In the days when it took so long to reload a gun, it was a proof of friendly intention when the ship's cannon were discharged upon entering port and thereby proving that the weapons were not cocked and ready to fire.

Pea Coat

Sailors who have to endure pea-soup weather often don their pea coats but the coat's name isn't derived from the weather.

The heavy topcoat worn in cold and miserable weather by seafaring men was once tailored from pilot cloth—a heavy, coarse, stout kind of twilled blue cloth with the nap on one side. The cloth was sometimes called P-cloth for the initial letter of "pilot" and the garment made from it was called a p-jacket—later, a pea coat. The term has been used since 1723 to denote coats made from that cloth.

complicated, with nuances of luxury measured against practical necessity.

Safety

Either way, race or leisure, expenditure on safety requirements will need to be one of the key issues in any budget. Beyond the obvious emergency equipment will be the kind of navigational and instrument investments that will help the sailor from encountering hazards. Satellite and digitized technologies have been a major boon for the private sailor.

Quality

Ultimately, though, with water and wind potentially hostile enemies, there is one issue that no sailor dare ignore—quality equipment. From bow to stern, from keel to mast, if our history of putting to sea has taught sailors anything, let it be that no penny should be spared on choosing lesser quality equipment—especially if the choice is between structural and safety over luxury.

Weekend Warriors

Racing the oceans and cruising the world are the extremes of the sport, undertaken by a relatively small minority. Aimless day tripping is certainly the single most popular sailing pastime, but it's not without a need for preparation. The first order of business is to check in with weather, wind, and surf reports. Based on the predictions, consider various scenarios that might occur and plan some kind of strategy to deal with them, then communicate these to your crew and passengers. If it's new territory you'll be visiting, lay your hands on the necessary documentation and maps, and familiarize yourself with all of the features that might have bearing on the trip as a whole. Know the distances you'll be covering, calculate your approximate departure and arrival times, and figure out the time parameters available for laying at anchor or exploring that will not compromise your safe passage. Log your intentions with a third party ashore—usually with harbor authorities. That way, if you do run into problems and have become incommunicado, a search plan to save you can be mounted in a timely fashion.

Always precheck equipment, and rectify any problems the day before departure. Victual the boat the day before and recheck equipment once more immediately before embarkation.

The Rich and Famous

Right at the top of the luxury pile we find the multimillionaires and billionaires who have discovered a sailing life away from the madding crowd. Their famous haunts along some of the most spectacular shores in the Mediterranean, Bahamas, and off Florida, and California raise specters of grandeur in our minds.

As these big spenders come to love the sailing life, their interests in sponsoring the sport grows, and with the huge sums they can afford to invest in research and development, we can all look forward to the spinoffs in materials and design that will trickle down into common usage.

A New Era of Design and Materials Ahead

Whether choosing between weight and strength of a material or choosing between practicality and cost of a design, sailing has always challenged us with ten thousand compromises. But, although all of the compromises will never disappear, technology does promise to deliver us better options. New fabrics, ropes, and materials, plus aerodynamic and hydrodynamic breakthroughs, will certainly have their impact.

If we had precise predictions of what the next best improvement would be, we wouldn't tell you about it—we'd go right out there and implement it and reap the very profitable rewards! Instead, the best we can offer is to look at our past to understand where the future might take us.

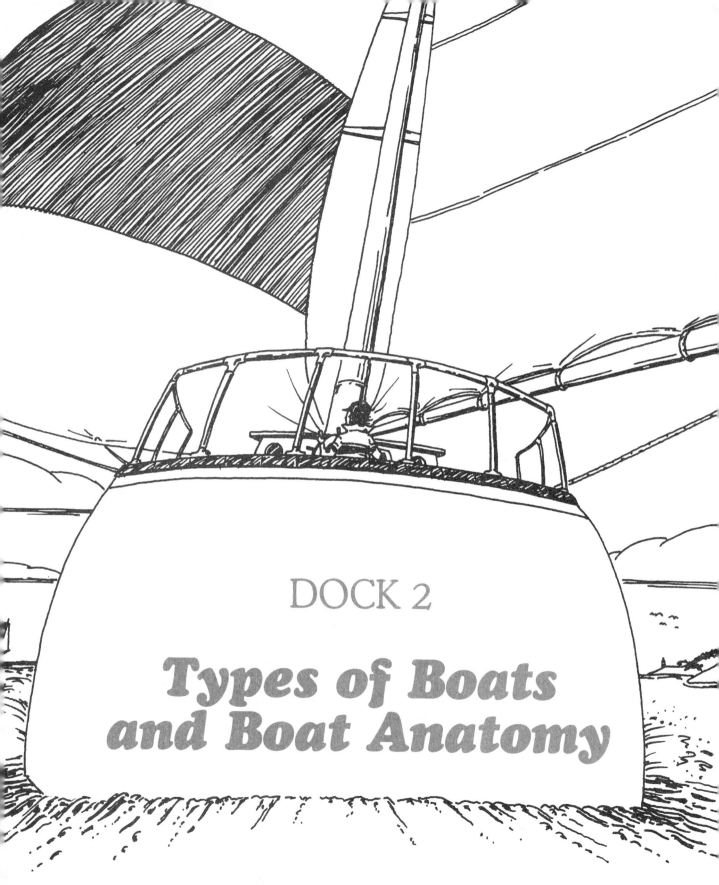

DOCK 2

Types of Boats and Boat Anatomy

In terms of classification of boats, size doesn't matter. Where the mast is positioned is the defining factor.

Modern boats come in an enormous variety of sizes and shapes—some designed for a specific task, others designed to be versatile. Each category of sailboat has taken the best elements from history and technology, and incorporated them into their design.

Whereas, historically designs changed dramatically from one geographic region to another—as in the case of Chinese junks, Arab dhows, and Western cutters—modern sailboats are fairly universal and divided by categories such as what they're used for—leisure or racing—or their application—flat water sailing, coastal sailing, ocean cruising.

Two of the most important issues in selecting a boat are cost and level of expertise. The larger the boat, the more masts, sails, and expense it will entail.

Let's begin by narrowing down the options available:

Best Beginner Options

First-time sailors are well advised to take the basic keelboat and coastal cruising classes, and spend several weeks crewing on a boat in the class of sailing they intend to sail in. These classes will teach you the fundamentals of sailing and safety, while prolonged crewing experience helps one gauge whether the intended class of sailing really holds the appeal.

A basic keelboat course generally requires you to attend between 4 and 6 hours of classroom instruction, and between 7 and 10 hours of on-the-water instruction in a moderate-sized sailboat. You will most likely learn man-overboard procedures, basic terminology, and get a feel for the boat and how to set the sails.

Your basic coastal cruising course is generally a bit more involved in sailing techniques, complex emergency procedures, and marina operations.

By taking the courses you will get a feel for how well suited the particular discipline of sailing you've chosen is to your needs.

You may get hooked and decide to buy a boat, or remain undecided as to the type of sailing you'll want to involve yourself in. If the latter is the case, we suggest you go for a dinghy class, as they're cheap and give one a really good hands-on feel for the most basic elements of wind and water.

Then, once you've got all of the necessary courses and practical experience behind you, before you buy, hire a boat that is as similar to your intended acquisition prospect as possible.

It's really a good idea to begin one's career as a boat owner with the simplest and least expensive boat in the class. In general, this means starting out with a single mast rig. Besides being a lot cheaper and simpler to sail, single-mast rigs are also much easier to sell, if you own one, when you decide it's time to graduate to bigger and better, or move to a different class.

If you're looking for a small and simple rig, consider the following:

TYPE	DESCRIPTION	LENGTH (FT)	CREW	SKILL LEVEL
International Optimist	Youth	7' 7"	1	Basic
International Cadet	Youth	10' 6"	2	Basic
Topper	Youth	11'	1	Basic
Mirror	General	10' 10"	2	Basic
Wayfarer	General	15' 10"	3	Intermediate
International 420	Racing	13' 9"	2	Advanced
International Laser	Racing	13' 10"	1	Advanced
International 14	Racing	14'	2	Advanced
International Enterprise	Racing	13' 3"	2	Intermediate
International 505	Advanced	16' 6"	2	Very Advanced
Olympic Star	Advanced	22' 8"	2	Very Advanced
Drascombe Lugger	Family	18' 9"	2	Intermediate
Hobie 14	Catamaran	14'	2	Intermediate
International Tornado	Advanced Catamaran	20'	2	Very Advanced

Sailors in History

Americus Vespucci, 1454–1512

This Italian navigator and explorer of the South American coast was the first to comprehend the mistake that Columbus had made. America was duly named in his honor.

If your tastes run to the cruising class, consider the following designs as a good starting point:

TYPE	CREW	LENGTH (FT)	NOTES
Trailer Sailer	4	20'	Retracting centerboard allows for trailer. Good for weekends and short trips.
Small Cruiser/Racer	6	30'	Good all-round boat. Popular boat and therefore easy to buy and sell. Not good for prolonged cruising.
Long-Distance Cruiser	6+	33'+	Requires experienced skipper and crew. Good water storage and food storage facilities.
Family Cruiser	6+	38'+	Wide beam makes for spacious accommodations. Should be easy to handle for a family.

Try to stay with traditional designs from well-respected manufacturers, and look for a boat that is reasonably versatile. That way, if you start out with the idea that racing will be your ultimate focus, but discover that cruising is much more your style, you'll have a boat in which you can experience the cruising lifestyle for a time before you make up your mind to upgrade into a more specialized rig.

Most beginners start with the very simplest of sailboats that can be carried on the roof of their car or pulled on a trailer. These small rigs are quite rudimentary to control and can be launched from almost anywhere. This gives the family an opportunity to find the most suitable sailing conditions on any given day, transport the boat to the location, and spend the day or weekend playing in relatively safe conditions. Being small and manageable also means that this class of sailboat is the ideal rig for children to learn sailing from a very early age.

When it comes to choosing a full-sized ocean cruising boat for the family, the stakes go up considerably because of the financial outlay. And, because there are so many different options available, it's a very good idea for you to get expert advice to help you figure out your precise requirements.

Family cruiser

The main points you'll need to consider are your level of experience, what you will use the boat for, how much you can afford to spend, the environment in which you'll be using it, and the number of sleeping berths you'll need.

Of course, in itself, cruising covers a wide spectrum of activities from short trips with family and friends, to long off-shore legs in personally unexplored territory. In this regard, size alone is not as important as how the boat is constructed, laid out, and fitted.

Single-Mast Rigs

Most modern designs fall into this category.

Typically, single-mast rigs are easier to handle, less expensive, and smaller than multi-mast vessels. It's probable then that a single-mast rig will be the first boat you'll learn how to sail or own.

Single-mast boats are divided into several categories. These include sloops, cutters, and catboats. As mentioned, it's the location of the mast that determines the boat's category. Single-masts are built anywhere from ten to seventy-plus feet in length and span the full gamut of sailing types from ocean racing to lake cruising.

A sloop's mast is positioned slightly forward of amidships—or closer to the bow than to the stern. On the bow side of the mast we would expect to find the jib sail, while on the stern side the main sail is usually rigged to a horizontal boom that protrudes sternward from the mast.

When the mast is brought slightly closer to the stern and protrudes amidships from the deck, and it supports two sails on its bow side, the boat is labeled a cutter. By contrast, if the mast is rigged well toward the bow and only carries a main sail, we classify it as a catboat.

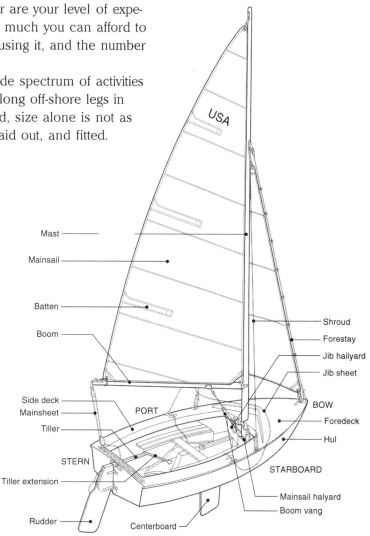

The anatomy of a single-mast sailboat

However, a single-mast doesn't mean a single sail. On a down-wind run, single mast sailboat can actually have three sails rigged at the same time: The mainsail might be set in its normal position sternward of the mast, the jib can be set toward the bow, while the spinnaker can be unfurled out over the bow.

In the hands of experienced sailors, even tiny, simply rigged, single-masted sailboats are capable of astonishing feats. There are any number of boats not much larger than the average family sedan that have repeatedly crossed the world's greatest oceans and even achieved circumnavigation single-handedly.

Although very large boats require more than one mast in order to carry the amount of sail area they require to power them, the type of boat the average family or sport sailor needs will be well served by the lower-cost, lower-maintenance, and relatively simple-to-operate single mast.

In conclusion, don't assume that single-mast sailboats are only for beginner sailors. Single-masters remain a very respectable class and the backbone of the sailing community.

Boats that are good for families fall into an enormous range. Narrowing the categories down really depends on the main activity a family intends using the boat for—sport, camping, fishing, cruising, racing, training, etc.

Of course, like selecting any craft, the primary questions to be answered relate to price, what category of water conditions will be encountered, whether or not a cabin is necessary, whether sleeping aboard will be a requirement, and so on.

Most family boats are built to traditional design, use a simple rig, and are constructed of low-maintenance and durable materials such as fiberglass.

Multi-hull sailboats are becoming ever more popular for families as they provide a lot of deck area, good accommodations, and are very stable even in relatively rough water.

Because the secondhand market for family-type boats is well developed, finding a boat to buy, and then selling it once you decide to upgrade, is relatively easy. However, because maintenance costs of a used boat can be quite high, do have an expert check out any prospective rig you're thinking of acquiring.

Besides the cost of the boat, do consider where you will berth it. If you're choosing a boat that is taken out of the water between uses, consider the local slip conditions and whether your towing vehicle will be able to handle the job of getting the boat in and out. If your boat will remain permanently in the water, consider the berthing fees and elements such as prevailing climatic conditions that might create a high level of mildew.

In short, choose your family boat according to the effort and costs that it will incur during its lifetime. Make sure that your family understands ahead of time what you'll expect of them in terms of ongoing maintenance of the boat.

Two-Mast Sailing

It stands to reason that the longer and larger a boat, the more power it will require to make it perform. For obvious reasons of stress and leverage, it's not appropriate to design excessively tall masts and massive sails. Rather, when a boat's length exceeds forty feet, it makes more sense to gain additional square footage of sail area by erecting additional masts either fore or aft of the main mast.

The larger ocean cruisers use this configuration and gain the additional safety feature of remaining mobile in the event of losing a mast out in the vastness. Two-masters might well exceed one hundred feet, and the sight of one of these majestic vessels can be breathtaking.

Again, it's the way the masts are positioned and rigged that creates the subdivisions of this category. Two-masted sailboats include schooners, ketches, and yawls.

Once the most popular arrangement for larger boats and traders, the schooner's main mast is set well to the stern and is always taller than either the single or multiple masts that are positioned closer to the bow.

Ketch rigs are two-masted vessels that have a taller main mast toward the bow, and a mizzen or smaller mast toward the stern and in front of the wheel or tiller. Though a rare configuration these days, a variation of this rig is the yawl, where the mizzenmast is located behind the wheel or tiller.

Cruisers and Day Sailers

Larger sailing boats, usually with full-length ballast keels for stability, are called cruisers. These are generally fitted for comfort and usually include facilities for overnight accommodation below decks that might be bare and Spartan or sport all the plush trimmings of home, including carpets, television, stereo, and these days even computers.

By contrast, although they may be up to thirty feet in length and require a crew of six, the more popular and affordable day sailers have no accommodation facilities. As a concession to the hardships of exposure, day sailers might have a recessed cockpit for the crew to shelter them from heavy weather.

Ocean Racers

What Formula One cars are to automobiles, these performance animals are to sailing. With no penny saved on go-fast equipment and instrumentation, these incredibly costly, extremely Spartan flat-bottomed craft have short, deep keels. The average person would be familiar with this category from seeing them in the America's Cup race.

Number of Hulls

Traditionally, because the vast majority of boats are mono- or single-hulled, we tend to think suspiciously of any variation. From the perspective of many people, catamarans or "cats" (two hulls—not to be confused with catboats) and trimarans (three hulls) seem somewhat experimental and not really an option to own. However, depending on your needs, these alternative designs might well be just what you're looking for.

Although, length for length they are more expensive to build and buy than monohulls, cats and trimarans are becoming increasingly popular. Admittedly, their wider beam can create more strife when trailing and storing, but in the water that broadness translates

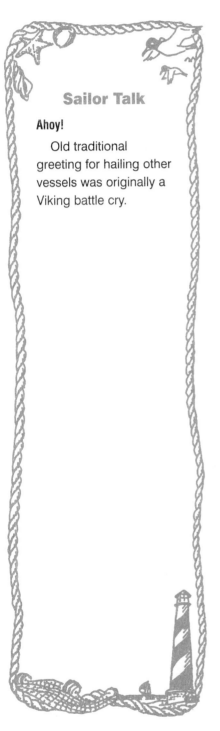

Sailor Talk

Ahoy!

Old traditional greeting for hailing other vessels was originally a Viking battle cry.

into much more deck room for relaxing and much more stability in waves and chop.

Below decks, multihulls also offer enormous space advantages. We once had the good fortune to sail on a seventy-foot cat that must have been around forty feet in its beam. On the foredeck it had a Jacuzzi and fixed garden furniture. In the saloon it had a twelve-seat mahogany dining table and a leather lounge suite that would have seated fifteen around a large-screen television. A full galley was down in one hull, and the luxury of the four cabins with queen-sized beds was only overshadowed by the main cabin with its king-sized bed. Bristling with stereo equipment and tropical plants, this little mistress was like no monohull arrangement of similar length that one could ever imagine.

In spite of an erroneous label of being unseaworthy and even dangerous in rough weather, cats offer a soft ride through heavy conditions. They also tend to require less energy to drive them; therefore they are more efficient on both wind and fuel consumption.

All told, cats are excellent cruising vessels. Personally, the cat is a fond favorite of ours. However, some don't like their lines, so it comes down to what you want out of your craft.

Catamaran

Sport Cats

Many a sailing world speed record has been set by this class of craft. These are the catamarans we see pulled up on the beaches of tropical islands. Best known in this industry is the Hobie Cat. In fact, "Hobie" has pretty much been coined as the generic name for the entire class.

With their incredible acceleration and excellent maneuverability in breezes that are barely more than a puff, these cats can get up on the plane like a powerboat and race in and out through waves. With no solid structure other than some rigging and a trampoline made from mesh fabric connecting the two lightweight hulls, they offer little resistance to the water and are exhilarating to play with.

Again, it's the broad beam of the cat that allows for more sail area and more transference into speed. In addition, because the hulls can be kept extremely narrow, they have an extremely slim profile to the water and can attain remarkable performance, even in high winds. By standing out on the windward hull, the crew can leverage their weight and keep the boat from capsizing. Often these cats can be seen riding or "flying" up on one hull with the experienced crew keeping their balance by finely adjusting their weight, the amount of wind spilled from the sail, and the rudder direction.

Sport cats are highly affordable playthings that can be trailed and launched easily. Because they draw a very shallow draft, they can get in and out through sandbars and reefs. Although they offer little in the way of comfort, they are ideally suited to young *families* and those competitive in nature.

The largest of the class are in the eighteen- to twenty-foot region. These often have centerboards or daggerboards that help the trailing rudder keels to maintain stability and direction.

Of course, sailing being sailing, there are two subcategories that refer to the type of mast rig. Where a jib system is set up, we call it a sloop-rigged catamaran. However, smaller catamarans won't have a jib and are termed cat-rigged catamarans.

All About Sails
Shapes and Dimensions

You guessed it. There are also different types of sails, each with their own identity and name. Knowing which one is which will help you understand the total sailing concept, and save you from embarrassment in front of more experienced sailors.

The cut of your jib

In the same way flat fabric is cut into panels and then sewn into a three-dimensional garment such as a shirt, so too is flat sail-cloth turned from pieces of odd-shaped fabric into a usable wing-shaped foil. A "foil" is a part or surface, such as a wing, propeller blade, or rudder, whose shape and orientation control stability, direction, lift, thrust, or propulsion. A sail dynamic is effectively a wing. Whereas we think of an airplane's wing as providing vertical "lift" that pulls the airplane "up," a sail's "lift" is horizontal and the sailboat is pulled forward. Of course, it takes great skill on the tailor or designer's part to get the curve precisely right so that the garment has form and curves with a fashionable panache, and in this way, not all sail makers are born equal. Like their tailoring cousins, they all seek to optimize the flow of wind over their creations.

- *Marconi sail.* By way of a complex set of visual association with radio mast shrouds and stays, this triangular mainsail evidently gets its name from the Italian inventor. It's the most common of all types and, as such, is the primary sheet that drives most modern boats.

- *Lateen sails.* This rig utilizes two spars to spread the sheet. The lower boom extends beyond the mast while the second runs diagonally from the top of the mast to the front end of the boom. A rarity on modern boats, mainly used on traditional sailboats and square riggers. Small vessels, such as sloops and schooners, were rigged mainly with fore-and-aft sails. Square sails were four-sided in shape. When unfurled, they flew crosswise, i.e., parallel to the width of the ship. Larger vessels, such as clippers, frigates, and naval ships of the line, were mainly square-rigged.

- *Gaff rigs.* You'll immediately recognize this rig by the gaff or spar that extends along the upper edge of the sail from two-thirds of the way up the mast. Not too common these days, it's a rig that you might still find on some classic catboats and cruising sailboats.

Sail Care

Fabric construction

Times have changed some since organic fibers such as hemp and canvas were widely used as sail fabric. The improved durability and resistance to rot and stresses aside, sails are still pretty expensive investments and need to be treated with plenty of care.

Today, most sails are constructed out of Dacron or some other tough and low-stretch synthetic weave. By the standards of the past these modern marvels are just about tear resistant, and their ability to withstand foul weather would probably outstrip yours. But, like rust on steel, salt and mildew still have an impact.

Washing and cleaning

Sails need frequent washing with fresh water. Wherever possible, dry them thoroughly before stowing them—especially for extended stowage such as over the winter months.

Though it might not be possible or practical to wash the sail that is in daily use, try to brush away debris—especially sand—as the abrasion that this can cause will quickly make even the toughest fabric threadbare.

Stowage

All types of sails need protection when not in use. At day's end you'll need to haul the sail down and either lash it inside of a protective sheet or fold it into its bag.

Larger boat sails fold down from the top of the mast onto themselves on the boom where they are secured with a cover. This technique is called flanking, and it's designed to keep the sail from overstressing the fibers by bending them excessively.

Smaller sails that are removed from the rigging should be folded neatly from the foot and worked toward the head.

After you've stowed the sail in its protective cover to assure its long life, keep it away from excessive heat. Better yet, get it into an air-conditioned environment where humidity is reduced.

The Anatomy of a Sail

Because the sail is your primary source of power, it deserves to be understood. Besides, it's not always a bad idea to hoist it aloft in the fashion it was designed, and knowing which corner goes where is a good place to start.

- *Head.* This is the topmost corner of a sail. It's important to note that in maritime terms "heads" are also toilets, and you certainly should not confuse one for the other.
- *Tack.* This is the bottom fore corner of a sail closest to the mast. To tack is also a nautical verb that applies to a manner of maneuvering, which will be covered later.
- *Clew.* I'll give you a hint (to have said "clue" would be corny, don't you think?): We've already named two of the

three corners to a triangular sail, so the clew is the bottom aft corner of a sail, furthermost from the mast.

- *Foot.* You guessed it; foot is the bottom edge of a sail.
- *Leech.* The leech refers to the back edge of a sail, furthest from the mast.
- *Luff.* The forward or leading edge of a sail that buts up against the mast. The term "luffing" applies to a sail that is not tensioned against the wind, which results in the sail flapping loosely without capturing power from the wind.
- *Roach.* The outward curve in the leech of a sail.
- *Battens.* As we learned earlier, the closer a sail can conform to a wing or foil design, the more efficient it'll be. Ideally, we'd have a solid sail the shape and size of an airplane wing jutting into the sky, but this would be impractical for the most part. A compromise is to stiffen the fabric sail in such a way that it takes on similar properties to a solid object. To do this, sail manufacturers sew pockets into a sail that will accept flattened rods. With the rods inserted on the horizontal plane, the sail has a skeleton that will transform it from a simple cloth bag into the wing required.

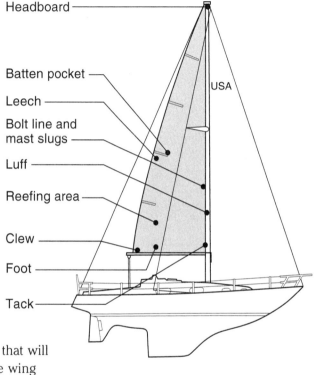

Anatomy of a sail

Sailboat Anatomy

So far, so good. But before we tell you how to hoist the sail and careen into the blue yonder, let's get a few more facts straight and establish how things work and interact.

Mast and Boom

- Mast. A pole mounted vertically by which the sail sheet and related rigging are supported.
- Boom. A pole to which the lower, horizontal edge of the sail is attached—perpendicular to the mast.

Tiller and Rudder

- Tiller. A steering lever mechanically attached to the directional rudder.
- Rudder. A vertically hinged plate mounted at the stern of a vessel used for directing its course.

Standing Rigging

The collective of all the various semi-fixed stays and shrouds that help maintain the mast in an upright posture.

- Stays. Wire cable rigging used to support the mast from stern and bow.
- Shrouds. Cable wire supports that attach to the mast from the sides of the boat.
- Spreaders. Any of various devices and bars that keep wires or stays apart.
- Winches. Any of various fixed and movable circular drums used to haul cable and rope by providing a mechanical leverage.
- Life lines. Cable strung around the edge of the boat's deck as a guardrail to prevent crew from falling overboard.
- Cleats. A piece of metal or wood having projecting arms or ends on which a rope can be wound or secured.
- Cam cleats. These are cleats that depend on eccentric or off-center wheels to lock lines in place. Faster to use than conventional cleats, they are favored for sheets.
- Fairleads. A device such as a ring or block of wood with a hole in it through which rigging is passed to hold it in place or prevent it from snagging or chafing.

- Running rigging. A collective for all of the additional lines and gear used to raise and tension sails. Running rigging needs to be frequently adjusted to suit the changing wind and course direction changes.
- Cunningham. The line used to control tension along a sail's luff.
- Boom vang. This line sits snug to the mast and is used to control boom position vertically. The primary function of the boom vang on most boats is to control the shape of the mainsail leech.

The Leech

The leech is the back of a sail toward the stern and is the last part of the sail the wind meets. Because it is not attached to anything on either the jib or the mainsail, to stop it flapping about, battens are inserted into pockets perpendicular to the leech.

1. Either vertical edge of a square sail.
2. The after edge of a fore-and-aft sail.

When the vang is tensioned, the leech gets tighter, and when released, the leech loosens and "twists" off to leeward on or toward the side to which the wind is blowing. If pulled in too much, there will be excess drag. If left loose, too much power is lost out the back of the sail.

Jib Leads

The jib does not have as many controls as does the main. One important element to remember is to keep the slot between the jib and main fairly open to allow the correct flow to form. The jib leech should also be kept mostly parallel with the closest part of the main. That slot should be maintained uniform for the entire length.

If the slot is too broad at the top, if the leech of the jib is too open, too much air will escape without imparting thrust. If it's too narrow, the flow will choke. You control the slot through the jib leads.

Famous Pirates: William Kidd (1645–1701)

Scottish-born privateer, Captain Kidd, was neither particularly ruthless nor successful. As a New York merchant, he'd previously served as a privateer against the French in the West Indies. In 1696 he was commissioned to hunt pirates but, after a series of misfortunes, he began to raid vessels in the Indian Ocean.

He was arrested on his return to America in 1699 and sent to England to stand trial for piracy.

He was hanged at Execution Dock and his body suspended in an iron cage of Tilbury Point for years as a warning to other seamen against piracy.

- Main sheet and jib sheets. These are the most interactive controls of all, and their primary function is to control the angle of attack on, or the sail's orientation to, the wind.

     When the sail is brought or sheeted in, the angle increases and this in turn increases the available power. Conversely, if the angle of attack is too large and the sail is pulled in too tight, the sail will "stall" and the lift will be destroyed. It might appear to look the same, but it won't react in the right fashion. If the angle is too small and the sail isn't tensioned in enough, the sail will begin to luff and generate zero lift.

     To get a good visual on what is going on with the wind and its flow, use the telltales on the sail. Bear in mind that the flow can either be created or destroyed by simply altering the angle of attack.
- Outhaul. The line used to horizontally tension the foot of a sail along a boom.
- Main sheet. The line used to control the mainsail via the boom.
- Jib sheet. The line used to control the jib sail.

Other Handy Terms and Concepts to Grasp

You thought this sailing thing would be a nice way to relax, but there are some more things to learn before you get to wile a few lazy hours away on your hammock.

- *Apparent wind.* Imagine it's a calm day without a breeze in sight. Wind your car window down at 40 mph, and you've suddenly got 40 mph of wind in your face. Has the wind come up? Of course not, this is apparent wind—wind created as a result of, and from, the direction of your movement.

     By contrast, on a windy day with a wind speed of 20 mph, if you drive at 40 mph in the same direction the wind is blowing, 20 mph of the apparent wind you'd nor-

Important Sailing Terms

What follows is a minimum of sailing terms that will be vital for you to know in order to sail safely and proficiently.

- **Port.** Facing the bow, this is the left side of the boat and everything to the left side of the bow or stern. The color associated with port is red. An easy way to remember this is that *left* has four letters, as does *port,* and the alcoholic beverage *port* is red in color.

  The origins of port come from Viking ships where the steering oar protruded from the starboard side of the boat, therefore, the boat always had to draw its left side up to the port.
- **Starboard.** Facing the bow, this is the right side of the boat and everything to the right side of the bow or stern. The color associated with starboard is green.

  As with the origins of port, starboard derives from the Norse word for "steer-boord," the position from which the steering oar traditionally protruded.
- **Mainsail.** The large sail aft of the main mast.
- **Jib.** The sail set on the bow side of the mast.
- **Jib sheet.** The line used to control the jib sail.

- **Halyards.** Lines used to hoist sails vertically up the mast.
- **Backstay.** A tensioned support cable that runs from the top of the mast to the stern of the boat.
- **Forestay.** A tensioned support cable that runs from the top of the mast to the bow of the boat.
- **Keel or centerboard.** The fin on the bottom of the sailboat that keeps the boat from slipping sideways. Heavy ballast or weight helps prevent the boat from capsizing. On smaller boats, an unballasted board serves the same purpose and can be swung or lifted out of the way to reduce the boat's draft and make it easier to trail.
- **Sheet-in.** To pull on the sheet line and thereby add tension to the sail sheet, i.e., to tension the sail and thereby cause amount of power to be harnessed.
- **Tensioned in.** The same as sheet-in, i.e., by pulling in on, or recovering, the sheet line, the sail has tension applied to it.
- **Luff.** The sail flaps with no power on it, i.e., begins to flap and has no wind power in it.
- **Zero lift.** Because a sail relies on the same principles as an airplane wing, "lift" is a word that describes the wind power that pushes the boat forward.

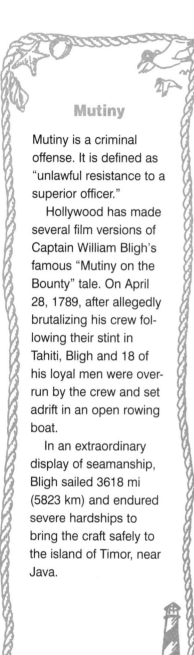

Mutiny

Mutiny is a criminal offense. It is defined as "unlawful resistance to a superior officer."

Hollywood has made several film versions of Captain William Bligh's famous "Mutiny on the Bounty" tale. On April 28, 1789, after allegedly brutalizing his crew following their stint in Tahiti, Bligh and 18 of his loyal men were overrun by the crew and set adrift in an open rowing boat.

In an extraordinary display of seamanship, Bligh sailed 3618 mi (5823 km) and endured severe hardships to bring the craft safely to the island of Timor, near Java.

mally feel will be canceled out by the 20 mph of tailwind. The purpose of this experiment is to understand that your apparent wind is still 40 mph, and the fact that the wind is blowing from behind is just a complicating factor.

This is more than an academic reality. Consider you're on your extraordinarily efficient craft and achieving a speed of 10 knots on a westerly heading from a 10-knot southerly wind. Between the apparent wind blowing into your face out of the west and the true wind blowing out of the south, you've really got southwesterly wind acting on your sails. In this instance, to attain the optimum efficiency from sail trim you'll have to understand the concept in order to trim accordingly.

- *Coming about.* To change direction or change tacks.
- *Genoa.* A large jib sail that overlaps the mast.
- *Heeling.* Leaning to one side, preferably from the force of the wind on the sails and not from water in the hull.
- *In irons.* Besides being something that many a captain longs to slap insolent crew into, when a boat points directly into the wind and the sails are unable to fill with wind and are luffing, the boat is said to be *in irons*.
- *Leeward.* Away from the wind—contrary to windward.
- *Windward.* Toward the wind—contrary to leeward.
- *Reefing.* To reduce the sail area by partially lowering the sail and rolling or tying the excess to the boom. You'd typically use this technique when confronted with heavy winds that would otherwise create strife if the sail were allowed to fully unfurl.
- *Roller furling.* A system of storing sails by winding them on a rotating spool—very often applied to jibs.
- *Slot.* The space between the headsail and the mainsail, where much of the propelling force is generated.
- *Spinnaker.* A lightweight, three-cornered sail with a parachute-like shape used for adding speed on downwind runs.
- *Telltales.* Small bits of yarn or other lightweight materials that are attached by one end to the sail to indicate true wind direction and flow. If the telltale were to be blown

horizontally toward the bow, it would mean that the wind was passing in the wrong direction over the sail. In other words, the boat would effectively be receiving a reverse thrust.

Coming to Grips with the Wind

This section outlines the major indicators and controls that you'll need in order to make intelligent and informed decisions regarding the sail shape changes you've just read about. For a beginner it's not necessarily obvious why and how you'll change the shape, size, location, or draft in your sails. This takes a little practice and possibly an apprenticeship at the side of an experienced sailor.

Wind Indicators

With experience will come a good instinct for trimming your sails, but certainly as a beginner, without an idea of what the wind is really doing in your sails, making arbitrary changes to their shape and hoping for the best is little more than relying on blind luck. To help you establish the facts, the following instruments and appendages will be invaluable.

- *Windex*. Like the rooster atop the church steeple, the Windex is a small weather vane, usually attached to the top of the mast, that indicates wind direction. If you remember the earlier note on apparent wind, you'll realize that it doesn't always tell you where the wind is coming from but rather where the wind is coming from relative to your direction and speed.
- *Sidestay telltales*. Sidestay telltales accomplish the same task as the Windex.
- *Jib telltales*. The jib telltales are the most sensitive, accurate, and useful of all. You use these to see how well the wind is attaching to the sail. On an upwind tack, ensure that the outside telltale streams backward.

Tips for Sailing with Children

- Choose a boat that can be sailed by half the adults, leaving other adults to watch over the children.
- Choose an area where the weather and sea conditions are suitable for your experience and abilities.
- Bring your own life jackets, and if the children don't swim, bring harnesses and/or lifeline netting.
- Have children bring their books, crayons, games, etc.—anything that will keep them entertained.
- To make it a fun experience, let them choose some of their own favorite clothes and food

- *Mainsail telltales.* With the jib up, these indicators are less important. On smaller boats you'll be able to trim the sail by feel.
- *Draft telltales.* As with the jib, if they're flowing straight backward, there is attachment and, if not, you've got separation.
- *Leech telltales.* These are attached to the leech of the sail, the batten inserts. When the air leaves smoothly over the leech, these will flow straight back, as they do on the surface of the sails. Your goal is to have them lifting or floating 50 percent of the time. If you spot them lifting more than 50 percent of the time, you've got too much air flowing freely off the leech, and you'll need to trim the sail in order to capture more. Tightening the vang will also achieve this. If the telltales lift less than 50 percent, the leech is too tight, and you should slightly slacken the mainsheet or the vang.

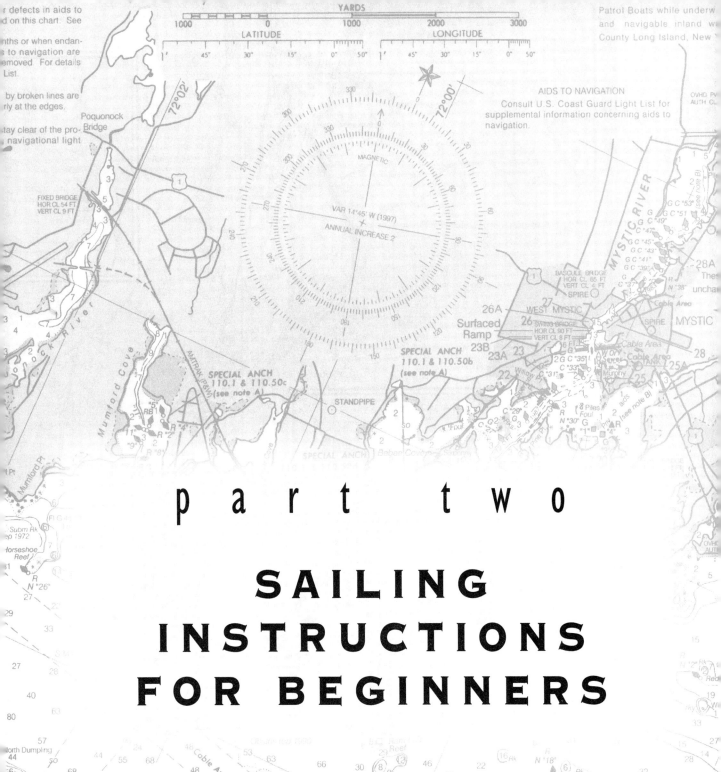

part two

SAILING
INSTRUCTIONS
FOR BEGINNERS

DOCK 3

Understanding the Boat and the Wind

Once you've got all of the theory of sailing behind you, like learning to drive a car, or learning to fly, it is vital for the beginner sailor to learn to apply this knowledge practically, under the watchful guidance of a professional and seasoned instructor.

Although this book will certainly provide you with thorough instructions and help orient you with the concepts, terminology, and potential circumstances in which you could someday find yourself, it is only in the practical and hands-on environment that you'll really get a sense of all the nuances and critical details that are vital to a long and safe sailing career.

In the section that follows, we'll assume that you've heeded our advice and gained much experience as a crew member and under the tutelage of a sailing instructor. Therefore, what follows is written from the point of view that you have already gained the necessary experience to undertake the graduation to skipper your own vessel.

What follows is a very brief overview of how tackle and nature are brought together for our edification and delight. If you're someone who revels in the theory of wind, please consult our referenced Further Reading section at the back of the book. Otherwise, get your hands on *The Art and Science of Sails* by Tom Whidden and Michael Levitt.

To keep you on your toes and to avoid burdening you with each element that makes up sailing, we'll hop around a bit between equipment and technique. However, fear not, brave soul—in the final analysis, all will be revealed and everything will gel.

Points of Sailing

As we saw with the example of apparent wind, a sailboat's heading in relation to the wind is vital if we are to comprehend the dynamics at play in sailing. Without auxiliary power, no boat can sail directly into the wind. More surprisingly than this is the fact that sailing directly downwind with no spinnaker out is not the most efficient course.

The terms that follow will decode what sailors mean when they toss around strange-sounding terminology:

- *Run.* A downwind leg, usually sailed with the main and the jib on opposite sides of the mast and the spinnaker unfurled.
- *Reach.* To sail across the wind at any angle.
- *Broad reach.* To sail downwind at an angle greater than 90 degrees to the wind direction.
- *Beam reach.* To sail across the wind at 90 degrees.
- *Close reach.* To sail upwind at an angle less than 90 degrees but not directly into the wind.
- *Close-hauled.* To sail as nearly into the wind as the boat will allow.
- *Beating.* There's nothing abusive about this term. It's the name given when you sail at an angle of as little as 45 degrees into the wind. Of course, no sailboat will beat directly into a wind.
- *Tacking.* Sometimes you have to reach a destination directly upwind, and the only way to get there is to wend through a series of zigzags, with each new close reach tack bringing you closer to the goal. Tacking is the name given to this series of maneuvers.
- *Changing tack.* This is the term given to the maneuver of *coming about.*
- *Port tack.* A boat on a port tack is bearing to the right of the wind direction, and has the wind coming in over the port side.
- *Starboard tack.* On a starboard tack, the boat is steered to the left of the wind direction so that the wind comes from the starboard or right side.

Physics of Sailing
Wind and Sail Interaction

We've got wind, and we've got an idea of how to predict its moods, but how do we use it?

If you hold up a sheet or beach towel and catch wind with it, you'll be pulled in the direction the wind is blowing. This is obvious and it doesn't take a Ph.D. to figure out. Spinnaker-type sails apply this principle.

Sailors in History

Magellan, Ferdinand (1480–1521)

A Portuguese navigator who, while trying to find a western route to the Moluccas (1519), wound up being blown by storms into the strait at the southern tip of South America that still bears his name (1520). Becalmed shortly thereafter in a great body of water that seemed so "passive" he named it Pacific, Ferdinand sailed onward to reach the Marianas and the Philippines (1521). He was then killed while fighting for a friendly native king. One of his ships did, however, return to Spain (1522) and thereby completed the first circumnavigation of the globe—minus one captain.

What is less obvious is the dynamic of fore and aft rigs. Keep in mind that these rigs set the sails in the *length* of the vessel, and intuition would tell us that any wind should simply blow the boat over and onto its side. So how does such a sail convert the power of a wind blowing out of the south into forward motion for a boat wishing to make headway on all other bearings except directly south (into the wind)?

The answer lies in aerodynamics. Consider how an aircraft's wing operates: The lower wing surface is flat, whereas the upper surface is convex. If you measured the distance over the top of the convex, you'd find that it's much longer than the straight distance below the wing. So, physically, as the plane is thrust forward, apparent wind is forced to either rush above or below the wing surface. Because the air molecules traveling over the top of the wing must cover a greater distance than the ones traveling below the wing, the molecules must accelerate rapidly and more space develops between individual molecules. When there is relatively little space between molecules of air, we call it a vacuum, and physics dictates that the plane's wing—and all that is attached to it—is pulled toward that vacuum.

Basic Sail Theory

The two themes to understand are *lift* and *flow*. Lift is the force that provides propulsion, while flow describes how the air is moving over the sails and generating that lift. However, the movement of air also causes drag, and, like friction, this tends to slow the boat down. The trick therefore is to get as much lift with the optimum in flow—which does not cause excessive drag.

In practice

Imagine you're aboard a boat with its course perpendicular to the wind direction. Take a look at how the sail's design forces the sail to have a shape that is very much like an aircraft wing—a convex shape being created on the leeward side. As with the aircraft, when air molecules are forced to travel around this convex, a vacuum develops and the sail, mast, and all that are attached to them are pulled into that vacuum. Provided the wind's direction remains constant, the sail's design causes that vacuum to always form toward the front edge of the sail, causing the sail to "lift," except that the lift is not vertical as with a wing but horizontal.

Therefore, caught between the resistant force of its weighted keel and directional rudder in the water—which stops the boat from blowing sideways or upside-down—the boat will keep moving forward until the sail's shape no longer offers the wind direction a longer convex shape to rush around.

Now, don't blame us for this complicated set of circumstances. We're only reporting what is called the Bernoulli effect.

Upwind and downwind sailing

Of course, the Bernoulli effect does not apply strictly to downwind sailing. Comprehending what follows is particularly important if you wish to use the Bernoulli effect to your best advantage.

Sail draft

In order to shape the sail to the absolute optimum foil profile, we need to be able to label the variable that creates the lift. In sailing terms we call the depth that the sail is distorted to, or amount of convex it attains, the sail's *draft*. In other words, you've allowed the sail to bag somewhat.

However, it's not as simple as setting the sail's draft and then never attending to it again. Particularly on a smaller craft, due to various factors of aerodynamics, maintaining the optimum draft is an ongoing task of monitoring the wind and adjusting accordingly. The general rule is that the bigger the draft, the more power you'll have, and the flatter the sail, the more speed you'll have. It's a little like the gearing in a car with a large draft being a first gear, and a near-flat sail being a top gear.

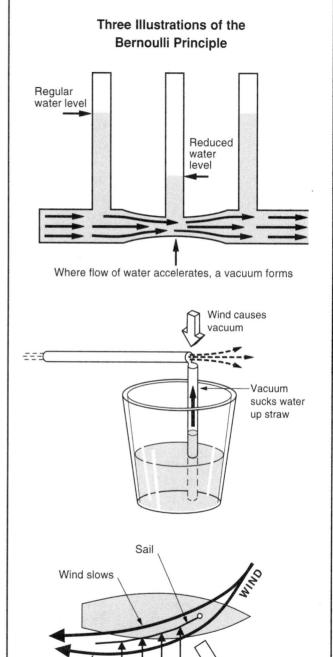

Three Illustrations of the Bernoulli Principle

Regular water level

Reduced water level

Where flow of water accelerates, a vacuum forms

Wind causes vacuum

Vacuum sucks water up straw

Sail

Wind slows

WIND

Wind accelerates

Vacuum

Boat is pulled into vacuum

The Wind's Reaction

Light winds

By definition, light winds do not carry nearly the same potential for energy as strong winds. Like water, wind tries to take the line of least resistance, and when it encounters the barrier that a sail forms, if the draft is too large and the wind is too weak, it simply gives up.

To compensate, you *flatten* the sail and allow the wind to move around the sail. If you're sailing near other craft and the wind picks up, you'll notice their deeper draft pushing them farther ahead of you. At this point you've got to decide whether the wind is going to increase or whether that puff was just a rough gust.

Moderate winds

You'll follow the rule that the larger the draft, the more power—the smaller the draft, the more speed. Once you're an advanced sailor, in a competitive environment where top speed and acceleration are important, you'll use your experience to judge whether the wind is likely to tend toward stronger or weaker. You'll also consider the length of each run between tacks, and then set your sail draft accordingly.

Heavy winds

There is a point at which too much power in the sail is no longer an advantage and actually starts to become dangerous. Apart from reefing the sail in, what can you do about this? Of course, if you flatten the sail, you'll "squeeze" the power out of the sail—and hopefully attain a more manageable situation. However, even with all that square footage exposed to the wind, you'll feel the boat is uncharacteristically sluggish in its acceleration, but it will make up for it in speed.

Wind Flow

It doesn't end with wind strength. To make the most of your equipment and prevailing conditions, you've got to know how the wind flows across the fabric that makes up the sail.

If you've ever seen wind-tunnel tests where they funnel smoke wisps over automobiles to see their drag coefficient, you'll have a good mental picture of the swirls and eddies that are created along the surface. In sailing terms, although we can't physically see the wind as it flows over the sail's surface, we can imagine that the same thing is happening, and we've got telltales to assist us in this task—but more on this in a moment.

What you're looking to do is to eliminate swirls and keep the air running smoothly along the sail. This air running smoothly across the surface is called *attached* air. By contrast, when air begins to swirl it's termed *unattached*.

Attached air makes the most efficient use out of the wind's power potential by generating the most lift with the least drag. And, because the air starts to swirl when it's forced to make sudden turns, to reduce the drag in light winds, flatten the sail.

Drag

Let's get a better handle on this phenomenon. There are two types of drag that will be important to understand if you are to eliminate them.

- *Friction drag.* Friction drag is probably the most obvious kind of drag. Any surface that opposes the wind will cause a degree of drag. These include the stays that hold the mast up, the seams on the sail, and human beings just standing around.
- *Induced drag.* Induced drag is formed when the air tumbles around from the high into the low pressure zone, it swirls back onto itself, canceling out a large portion of the thrust that would otherwise be converted into the forward motion of the vessel. Various attempts are made to reduce this effect. Sailboard design has eliminated this phenomenon at the foot of the sail by allowing the mast to be tilted all the way back so that the foot of the sail effectively seals the "leakage" of pressures against the deck of the board. More limited design success has been achieved in larger vessels.

Another area in which drag can reduce efficiency is at the trailing edge of the sail's surface. Without a smooth exit off of the sail, the wind begins to tumble. To eliminate this phenomenon as

Famous Pirates

Blackbeard, (real name Edward Teach) 1680–1718

The most notorious of English pirates, Blackbeard was probably born in Bristol. He was widely known and feared for his robberies and atrocities throughout the West Indies and along the coast of the North Carolina and Virginia colonies. In 1718 the governor of Virginia dispatched two British ships to attack Blackbeard. They attacked him as he spent the winter in a North Carolina inlet. Mortally wounded, Blackbeard is reputed to have said, "I've buried my treasure where none but Satan and myself can find it." So far, his boast has proved valid.

much as possible, don't let the draft migrate too far back in the sail where it will allow the wind to come swirling off.

Keeping from Capsizing

And, while on the subject and just to complicate the entire issue, to help prevent a boat from capsizing, the rounded design of the keel creates a *hydrofoil* effect that works with the water in the same way a sail works with air.

In larger boats, in the event that a gust does knock the boat over and it capsizes, the ballast weight of the keel causes the boat to be bottom-heavy, which makes it self-righting. When smaller boats capsize, it takes the crew's weight to lever the boat upright.

Summary

You've now got a basic idea of sailing dynamics. Of course, nothing is as simple as it seems and there are many nuances that come into play, but these aren't in the test, so you can relax.

Initial Preparations

Your sailing clothing can a wide variety of options. It really all comes down to the type of sailing you'll be embarking on; the prevailing weather conditions and likely changes in conditions; club, fashion, or other etiquette requirements; and personal preference.

As a rule of thumb, staying dry, warm, and not wearing fabrics that will snag equipment or become waterlogged in the unlucky event you fell overboard, are all good commonsense issues to observe.

Of course you can sail in any fabric, style, or design—or nothing at all—that's your prerogative. The list below is simply an overview of some of the apparel options you might wish to consider. You'll find them available in a wide variety of sailing-specific designs. If it's parting with a whole lot of money that turns you on, there are no end of designer labels who will happily help you fulfill your ambition in that department. Sailing clothing has become such an industry in its own right that it has graduated into the mass market. Without a doubt, there are

An optimist is someone who goes after Moby Dick in a rowboat and takes the tartar sauce with him.
—Zig Ziglar

The Bernoulli Principle

The Bernoulli Principle states that as the velocity of air increases, its pressure (or density) decreases. In other words, the distance between individual molecules increases. A decrease in pressure is called a (relative) vacuum.

A sail is designed to be a highly efficient obstruction in the way of the wind. As it splits the moving air, it allows some molecules to travel a straight and unhindered path. However, adjacent molecules must travel a much greater distance around the sail's perimeter, so the sail creates a relatively high pressure on the side of the low-speed molecules and a low pressure on the side of the high-speed molecules (that have accelerated in order to reach the far side of the obstruction at the same time).

In the same way that champagne corks fly away from the relatively high pressure of their contents toward the relatively low pressure of the outside world, boats that are attached to sails fly "away" from the high pressure of their sail's windward side and "toward" the low pressure of their sail's leeward side.

Of course, not just any shape will do. If this were so, then you could put a log, or a box, or a computer monitor on deck to obstruct the wind and hope to get somewhere. Centuries of trial and error with sail cut and rigging have been augmented by developments in flying to design the optimum shape that offers greatest efficiency of *Bernoulli's Principle* without creating too much unnecessary turbulence that reduces efficiency.

The result is a sail that possesses all the attributes of an airplane wing and is called an airfoil. Of course, planes extend their wings horizontally and consequently fly on the vertical plane, or fly relative to vertical height. Therefore, because sails are set on the vertical plane, even in the lightest breeze you can claim to have "flown along" on the horizontal plane, and nobody will dare contradict you.

Now, what happens if you place foils on both the horizontal and vertical planes on a single vessel? Good question. You begin to fly in three dimensions. Commercially available vessels of this sort are just making their way onto the market in the form of high-performance, though relatively small and sporty, catamarans.

clothing and apparel retailers situated five hundred miles from the nearest navigable waterway who carry Dockers and Bermuda shorts.

Fashionable design and brand naming aside, the items you choose for your sailing need to fulfill the basic requirements for which they're ostensibly designed.

Wear a Hat

Always wear a hat. On the water you are exposed to the sun from above and reflection from every other angle.

Wear Shoes

A yacht is not a construction site, but there's still sufficient toe-damaging equipment to warrant this caution. When you choose footwear, be sure that it's non-slip and purpose-designed.

Shirt with a Collar

For the same reason you wear a hat and bathe in sunblock, the shirt and collar protect against exposure to sun, wind, and cold. The collar is of course to protect your delicate neck and not necessarily or even intended for a tie!

Wear Sunglasses

If you don't want cataracts, slip a good set of shades on and ensure that they're really cool looking.

Dressing for Cold Weather

When sailing in a colder climate, a windbreaker, gloves, and pants made of Gore-Tex are a must for every crew member.

Long Polypropylene Underwear

We don't mean to meddle with your private choice of lingerie, but good underwear can really save your butt—if you get our drift.

Lighter Gloves

Some weekend warriors might be surgeons or have a job where extending a paw full of gnarly calluses in their professional environment would be a no-no. Specifically, to protect their delicate digits from the rubbing of rough lines, they may well want to glove up with light leather gym gloves before touching anything rough aboard.

Besides being a great fashion accessory to the wraparound mirrored shades, the fingerless variety—as seen in the early *Rocky* movies—will give you the best of both worlds: plenty of dexterity with protection where you need it most.

Hoods with a Broad Stiff Brim and Earmuffs

In the event you're swept away into the deep arctic reaches, don't say that we didn't suggest you have a couple of sets of these aboard.

Brrrrr...Happy sailing!

Wear UV Sunblock

Apply the highest level of UV protection you can lay your hands on, and slap it on liberally.

UV Rays/Brightness of Sun Reflected on Water

A word again about UV rays. Severe sunburns are a notorious hazard of sailing. This is because, apart from being bombarded by harmful UV rays from above, reflection off of the water's undulating surface multiplies the harmful ray's effects by several fold.

For the best protection, wear long shirt sleeves, long pants, wide brim hats, and sun block with a sun protection factor of 30 or better.

The National Weather Service (NWS), the Environmental Protection Agency (EPA), and the Centers for Disease Control and

Clothing Essentials Checklist

- Foul-weather gear
- Change of clothing
- Light polypropylene top(s) and leggings (avoid cotton and denim)
- A polyester fleece (also known as "pile") pullover
- Polyester fleece neck gaiter (protect your neck)
- Two basic layers of clothing: an insulating layer and water-and-windproof clothing over it
- Thermal underwear
- Wool polyester hat
- Scarf
- Gloves (polypropylene gloves)
- Non-slip sailing boots or shoes
- Sunglasses
- Vest
- Close-fitting wet suit, for the racing enthusiasts who may capsize
- Buoyancy aids and lifejackets
- Sunscreen

Prevention (CDC) developed the UV Index in an effort to raise the visibility of the risks associated with prolonged exposure to ultraviolet radiation. The NWS, EPA, and CDC began offering an experimental UV index on a limited basis on June 28, 1994, in response to increasing incidence of skin cancer, cataracts, and other effects from exposure to the sun's harmful rays. The NWS UV Index is now a regular element of atmospheric forecasts. Listen for them and heed their cautions.

UV Index Number and Forecast

The UV Index number, ranging between 0 and 10+, is an indication of the amount of UV radiation reaching the earth's surface over the one-hour period around noon. The lower the number, the less the amount of UV radiation. The UV Index forecast is produced by the NWS Climate Analysis Center, Camp Springs, MD, about a day in advance of the time for which the forecast is effective. The forecast is based on several factors: latitude, day of year, time of day, total ozone in the atmosphere, elevation, and predicted cloud conditions at solar noon time. A forecast is given for 58 listed cities. The index is valid for a radius of about 30 miles around a listed city; however, adjustments should be made for a number of factors.

Ozone

Total ozone is measured by a NOAA polar orbiting satellite. This measurement is combined with the aforementioned factors to help determine how much atmosphere the UV rays must pass through to reach the surface; the greater the distance and more ozone, the lower the UV radiation at the surface.

Cloudiness

Rapid changes in cloud amount can alter the predicted UV Index. Increased cloudiness will lower the index number.

Latitude

The closer one ventures toward the equator, the higher the UV radiation level becomes. It therefore makes good sense to cover exposed areas of skin and to wear sunglasses when traveling in tropical regions. (A person can suffer a bad sunburn in the Tropics even during winter.)

DOCK 4

Finally Aboard

Before You Set Sail

You must be tired of all the cautions—the if's, the but's, and the maybes—but there's really no way to make your sailing career a happy and safe one without first preparing you for every eventuality. In addition, beyond your reading this all-encompassing book on sailing, you should take some professional lessons where you'll get some hands-on practice with a tutor standing by. At the end of the book we list a few of the schools available. Check with local authorities for a more extensive list in your area.

Before you can set sail, you must first rig the boat. Rigging the boat entails attaching all of the equipment that is normally removed at the end of the previous day's sailing. This means preparing and attaching the sails, the rudder, and other loose equipment that might be lost, damaged, or stolen if left in place overnight or while the boat is at its mooring.

In smaller boats that are placed on a trailer for transport, the mast is often removed and must therefore be erected before you can hoist the sail.

Stepping Aboard

Do:

- Make sure you're holding onto something strong, stable, and solid enough to help keep you balanced and support your weight in the event you fall
- Bend your knees and keep your center of gravity low
- Step to the centerline of the boat, i.e., over the keel line
- Look for wet areas that may be slippery
- Test your footing before putting all your weight onto a leg
- Look out for obstructions in your path
- Watch the general vicinity for wakes, waves, wind gusts, or any swinging object such as a boom that is threatening to cause the boat to tip or bump into you
- Do move between boat and shore, or boat and boat, with reasonable haste—since the two objects might move apart or close together without much warning

Don't:
- Overextend your balance
- Place your weight on a foot until you've tested the deck/floor for slipperiness
- Block the path of others behind you

Because boats have a tendency to move rather easily in the direction a force heaves them, the smaller the boat and the bigger you are, the tougher getting aboard becomes. And, when conditions deteriorate or the landing is wet and slippery, bridging the short gap can be positively dangerous.

When stepping aboard, be careful but decisive. Don't hurry, and don't hesitate with one foot on shore and the other on the boat—both of these scenarios are bound to drop you in the water. The boat's rising and falling motion relative to the shore could make it a very dangerous place to be.

With smaller boats, try to keep your weight over the keel line to prevent accidental heeling over the side.

Bigger keelboats don't present as big a hazard to climb aboard, but the penalties for falling into the water between boat and dock rise.

In order to maintain your balance and the boat's balance, never carry equipment aboard; hand it across or lift it across.

Elementary Skipper Responsibilities

The captain gets to bark the orders, but this is not the navy, and there's no guarantee that everyone aboard has boating experience or has a clue what sailing jargon means. When you're learning, be sure to ask questions if terms or instructions are unfamiliar. And once you become the captain, remember that your crew can't read your mind, so try to be specific with your instructions, acting them out whenever necessary. In short, don't expect anyone aboard to second-guess your wishes.

In addition, those aboard may not have the benefit of well-practiced skills, so besides avoiding fancy sailor's language, get an idea of who knows what before you dish out responsibilities. Remember that

Sailor Talk

Crow's Nest

The raven, or crow, was an essential part of the Vikings' navigation equipment. These land-lubbing birds were carried aboard to help the ship's navigator determine where the closest land lay when weather prevented sighting the shore. In cases of poor visibility, a crow was released and the navigator plotted a course corresponding to the bird's flight path because the crow invariably headed toward land.

The Norsemen carried the birds in a cage secured to the top of the mast. Later on, as ships grew and the lookout stood his watch in a tub located high on the main mast, the name "crow's nest" was given to this tub.

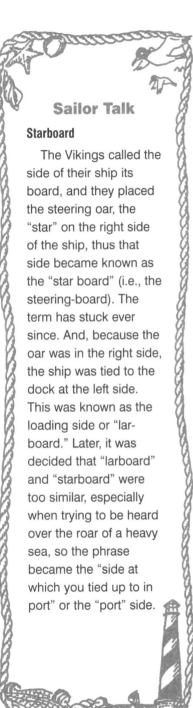

a well-meaning passenger might think they've tied the right knot or steered the right heading, but you could be on the rocks if they've overestimated their own abilities and were too proud to admit it.

Beyond these cautions above and below, we'll keep coming back to your responsibilities as they apply to the various issues under discussion. At this stage, let's set up a foundation.

- Review emergency equipment and procedures. You've seen how the airline flight crews do it—now it's your turn on the pantomime stage—what fun you'll have.
- Be sure that at least one member aboard knows how to operate the vessel in your absence.
- Speed postings or other restrictions need to be observed with respect.

Knowing who's boss

No boat can be run by a committee, and there can't be any fuzziness as to who *El Capitan* is.

In smaller craft, the type you'll probably be sailing in, the boss is usually the one with his or her hands on the wheel or tiller arm. This person is generally the vessel's owner and the individual aboard with the most experience who can therefore make rapid and accurate decisions.

Like any leadership role, you don't have to be Captain Bligh to make things happen, but you do need to have everyone understand that your decisions and orders need to be followed precisely as you give them. Get this message across before you cast off and you shouldn't have a problem. Experienced crews will expect you to take this role, while inexperienced crews will probably appreciate the security of knowing that someone's taking charge.

By all means give everyone a speech and include the following elements:

- When you make the initial arrangement and invite guests, be sure to advise them to bring sufficient clothing appropriate to the anticipated conditions. In addition, even if you're on the equator and it's midsummer, ensure that they have foul weather gear along—just in case.

- Explain the course you'll be following and what you'll be expecting from everyone in general and certain individuals in specific.
- Elect the person who you identified as being able to operate the boat as second in command. In the event you're not able to be skipper for a period, your commander will take over.
- After this, run through the rudiments of the boat's operation with everyone else.
- On smaller boats that might be disturbed by crew movement, remind everyone to remain seated as much as possible and to move with caution. On larger boats, remind them to be aware of the pitch and roll in the swells.
- Run through a short list of emergency equipment and procedures, including proper use of radio equipment. Point out the PFDs and have everyone try them on and adjust to fit. Do ensure that those who can't swim keep theirs on *at all times*.
- Tell everyone where the heads (toilets) are.
- Insist on a no-smoking policy anywhere near fuel—particularly while filling.
- Explain good conduct and courtesy.

Caution guests

Surfaces can be very slippery on and around boats, particularly during the morning after a sprinkling of dew. Always test your footing before putting weight onto it, and then apply the weight slowly and evenly.

As mentioned, never step aboard with arms full. Both hands should be free to use in balancing and bracing as the guest transitions from land to boat.

Guests, but particularly children, have an uncanny knack of getting extremities between the boat and the dock, so be especially careful about cautioning them and keep especially observant watch of them.

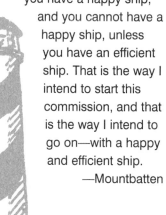

In my experience I have always found that you cannot have an efficient ship, unless you have a happy ship, and you cannot have a happy ship, unless you have an efficient ship. That is the way I intend to start this commission, and that is the way I intend to go on—with a happy and efficient ship.
—Mountbatten

A common sense?

Sometimes you've just got to wonder: Is this really the most common of the senses? More common than eyesight, touch, or hearing?

The clue here is to pause a moment before making rash decisions. Are there consequences and how can I reduce them?

You'll find passengers who delight in hanging over the bow—*Titanic* style—perhaps feeling they're monarchs of the world. Do they ever pause a moment and consider how equally exhilarating it would be to pull the same stunt on the hood of their car?

You get the point, no doubt? Be sure to make clear to everyone on board the risks and consequences of potentially dangerous behavior.

Positive sailing attitude

Why are you sailing? Let's face it, wind and water are not the greatest combinations for feeble creatures such as we.

Whether you're racing, cruising, traveling, or just getting your kicks in your unique way, we'll wager that it comes down to one word—*enjoyment*. You enjoy sailing, so smile. Remember the song, ". . . even the bad times are good . . . ," and take it to sea with you. When all hell breaks loose, hum it to yourself; you're developing a new coping skill.

Sailors are a community who share a strong tradition of kinship. How many people do you wave to while driving down the road or greet in the middle of the city? Out on the water you'll receive plenty of greetings and always find buddies at any club you visit. More than a sport or convenience, sailing is a lifestyle. Never forget why you became a sailor and sustain the positive experience for others. Happiness like love is just one of those things that you tend to get more of when you give it away.

Tips You Can Use

Congratulations, you've made it through orientation. Now for some fun, let's put this baby to work.

Quite obviously, today—and for the next few trips—you'll probably want to limit yourself to a day trip. Also, you'll want to pick your crew with some caution until you have some experience and confidence. Ensure you've got enough experienced members aboard, equal to the passage you are setting yourself up for.

Before Unfurling the Sails

It's imperative that you run through this short safety inspection:

- Conduct an inventory of equipment and spares. Produce a checklist for this task and always use this list as your basis—not your memory.
- Check the rigging. Go aloft yourself or send the most experienced of the crew up into the rigging to inspect that everything is well secured and in good condition.
- Stow personal belongings to ensure they're not underfoot when you break out the equipment.

Strategy vs. Tactics

In life, but especially in sailing, you'll hear the words strategy and tactics constantly being repeated. Just to be sure that you understand, here is a brief definition of each term:

- *Strategy:* A plan of action intended to accomplish a specific goal.
- *Tactic:* An expedient for achieving a goal; a maneuver.

Let's say you're racing from A to B. Your strategy is your broad plan, your overview and instructions you'll give to your crew. Then, out on the water, as a fast-moving boat begins to encroach on your windward side and threatens to steal the wind from your sails, you'll employ cunning tactics to avoid the challenge.

Beyond racing, knowing the difference between strategy and tactics will still be important—if only in terms of managing your crew efficiently. You'll devise a strategy of how they'll work most efficiently to give everyone a safe and enjoyable ride, and you'll employ various tactics to execute these ideas.

Rigging the Rig

For a change of pace, let's do it by the numbers. But please bear in mind that rigs might differ, and this description is meant to be generic in nature and simply give you an overview of the procedure you'll go through:

Sailors in History

Tsunenaga Hasekura (early seventeenth century)

Samurai commander of the first Japanese-built Western-style ship, undertook a 90-day voyage to Acapulco in New Spain. The 120-ton schooner was built with technical advice from a Spaniard and carries Don Rodrigo de Vivero, Spanish governor of Luzon, who was stranded in Japan by a shipwreck.

Sail and Rigging Anatomy

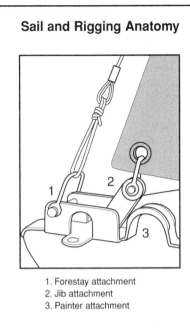

1. Forestay attachment
2. Jib attachment
3. Painter attachment

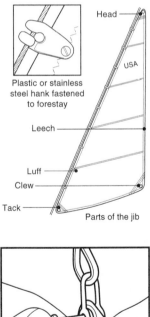

Plastic or stainless
steel hank fastened
to forestay

Head

USA

Leech

Luff

Clew

Tack

Parts of the jib

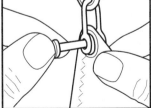

Eye and shackle pin attachment

1. With the boat at its mooring, lay the mainsail on deck next to the boom.
2. Locate the clew and feed it into the track that runs along the top of the boom, or into the groove designed to hold it. Get a buddy to help, as this is far more simple when one feeds and the other slides the clew along toward the outer end.
3. It the sail has batten pockets, slip in the battens. You'll probably notice they're tapered and of different length. Generally, the longest are near the foot and shortest near the head, so sort them into descending length, then hold them against each pocket to get an idea if they'll fit. Now, insert the thinner end first, and don't forget to secure them with the clip or pocket provided.
4. Straighten the sail's luff and remove any twists, then secure the tack to the fitting on the boom close to where it attaches to the mast.
5. Attach the clew to the outhaul at the other end of the boom. With the foot of the sail secured, gently increase tension on the line to stretch it out, then cleat the outhaul.
6. Inspect the main halyard and ensure it's not snagged or twisted around any stays. Now, attach the halyard's shackle to the head of the sail.
7. Attach the luff to the mast via the slide attachments spaced along its edge.
8. Ensure the rudder is functioning and lower the centerboard if you have one and be sure that the water is deep enough.
9. You don't want to sail until you're ready, so, before raising the sails, point the boat upwind so that they luff and the boat is in irons. Double check that the rope that controls the mainsail is slack so that the sail cannot fill with wind even if the boat drifts perpendicular to the wind.
10. Begin hoisting the sail, all the while feeding the slide into the groove in the back of the mast.

11. When the head reaches the top of its extent, cleat the halyard off on the mast, coil the remaining line neatly, and hang it below the cleat.

12. Although your very first trip should be with mainsail only, if your boat has a jib, first priority is to locate its tack. With your own sails it's not a bad idea to indelibly mark this corner, as sorting through bundles of sheet can be frustrating and all corners look pretty much the same at first. A hint with the jib is that the angle this corner forms is wider than the clew.

13. Now, approach the bow and, adjacent to the forestay, you'll find a fitting that can support the jib in the same way the mast supports the mainsail.

14. With the jib attached to the forestay with the hanks or snaps along its luff, begin at the bottom of the sail up—not vice versa—that way the bottom section will be easier to attach.

15. Next, find the jib's clew. The best way to find the tack is to look for the corner where the bolt ropes that attach to the boom and the mast meet. If there's only one rope, it's the clew.

16. Using a bowline or shackles, attach the jib sheets and run the sheets through the pulleys (blocks) provided back to the cockpit. One goes to each side. Put a figure-eight stopper knot in the end of each so they don't run back through the blocks.

17. Attach the jib halyard to the head of the jib. On a windy day, it's very easy for the jib to be blown off the front deck, so have a crewperson sit on the jib until you're ready to hoist it.

That's it, you're finally ready to go.

Final Preparations

By now you're probably feeling completely calm without a care in the world. Of course you are, there's nothing much to be stressed about. If she sinks, she sinks—you've got all that

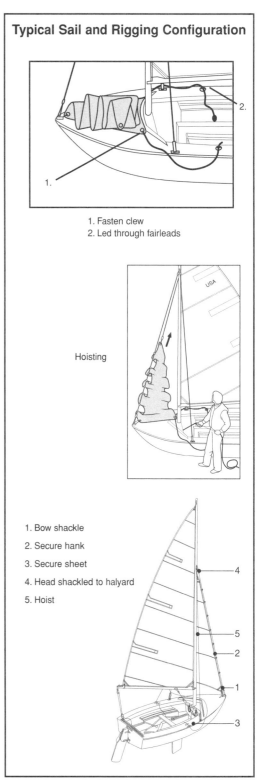

Typical Sail and Rigging Configuration

1. Fasten clew
2. Led through fairleads

Hoisting

1. Bow shackle
2. Secure hank
3. Secure sheet
4. Head shackled to halyard
5. Hoist

safety equipment on board, remember? Besides, you'd never be crazy enough to put to sea without an instructor—would you?

First, clue in the passengers and crew. Give them a rough idea of where you're heading and what they can anticipate. A skipper might caution his or her crew in the following way: "As we pass the headland, the wind out of the south will most likely become fairly gusty. Be careful of the boom swinging violently and unexpectedly. Also, the currents and cliffs in that area can cause a lot of wave chop that could cause the boat to rock violently. If you're prone to seasickness, stay on deck, try to sit as close to the waterline and toward the center of the boat as possible, keep your eyes on the horizon, and, if you do move about, be aware of wet areas on the deck as they may be slippery, and watch out for any obstructions that might trip you up. Dress warmly and make sure you've got sunscreen on all exposed areas of your skin. The bay we're headed to is very protected from the wind and untouched by humans. Noise carries a long way, so try to keep it to a minimum. Also, don't throw any garbage overboard."

Run a radio check, ensure you've got plenty of fuel, and give the engine a turn and let it idle up to operating temperature—just to be sure.

Instruct the crew to first cast off spring lines or other tethers before casting off the bow and stern lines. "Cast off bow line, cast off stern line." The boat is probably secured with four lines. In addition to the main bow and stern lines that secure the boat to the dock that you wanted cast off, an additional spring line at both bow and stern are used to reduce fore and aft movement.

Line Handling, Knots, and Marlinespike

Assuming that the last time the boat was used, it was secured with a proper sailing knot that will not overtighten, the job of untying and casting off the lines will be simple. However, in the event that knots have binded tightly and the crew struggles to untie them, use a marlinespike to leverage the knot loose. A marlinespike is a pointed metal spike that can be purchased at any sailing equipment supplier. It is designed to separate strands of rope in splicing or to unbind knots that have overtightened.

The five knots you'll find most important to know are easy to tie, yet can take incredible strain to untie. Practice your knot-tying techniques so that you can tie them in your sleep. Then, never let just anybody tie important knots—especially if you intend to undo them at some time in the future.

In case you do end up with an impossible knot and a solidly fouled line, there's no need to pillage the cutlery drawer looking for the carving knife. In the marlinespike we've got a bona fide tool designed for the job. Its pointed metal spike and heavy construction make it a fine lever to wedge into an uncooperative knot and massage the bundle loose. Alternatively, it's used to separate strands of rope when splicing.

Getting Knotted

The following knots are pretty much all you'll need to get you going:

Cleat Hitch

This is the most common knot for securing a boat to the dock or for securing a line to a boat. See illustration below. First take the line to the ear of the cleat furthest from where the line originates, i.e., the load. Then make one wrap around the base of the cleat. Next start a figure eight across the top of the opposite ear. Finish with a half hitch turned under so that the line comes away from the cleat in the opposite direction from which it came in, and—*voilà*—it's done.

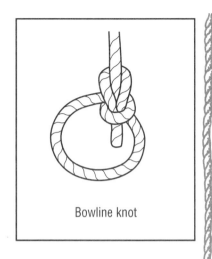

Bowline knot

Bowline

This is used to create a temporary loop in a line which is then used to hook over a cleat or piling—hence the "bow" element in its name. This king of knots is extremely versatile and will neither slip nor jam. (The word itself is pronounced bo-lin.)

Start by making an overhand loop, which looks like a six. With the end of the line, come up through the hole in the six, around the back of the line you're holding, and back down through the hole in the six. Grab the part of the line that went up through the hole and the part of the line that came back down through the hole in one hand, and the top of the line you were holding in the other, and pull—*presto*—it's done.

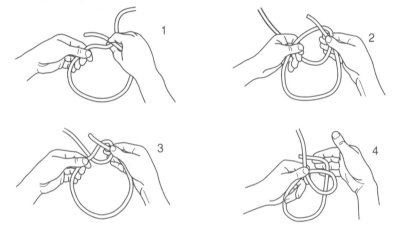

Round Turn and Two Half Hitches

When a permanent knot is required for a mooring or ring, this is the one to go for. Simply take a full turn around the object being tied up to, and take two half hitches around the line itself. Over and up, through and under, and down through. Did you follow that? Sure, it was simple.

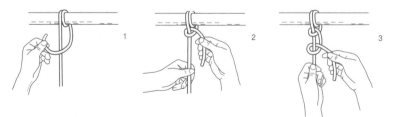

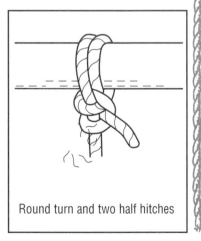

Round turn and two half hitches

Square Knot (Reef Knot)

Probably the simplest of all knots, the square knot is used for a wide variety of light duties. It's a variation of the granny knot—the first one you use when tying your shoe laces, before you make the bow.

Start with one granny knot as though you're beginning to tie your shoelace. Loop the left cord over the right, now make a second identical loop with the cords, but this time loop right over left. (Alternatively, tie right over left first, and follow this by a left over right.) If you don't alternate the cord going over the top, you'll end up with a true granny knot that will jam when pressure is applied. You'll recognize the reef knot because it forms a neat crushed-down figure eight, which resembles a cube in shape. *Bingo*—you're done—we're running out of silly exclamations and there's still one knot to go.

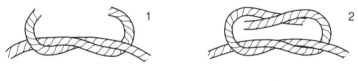

Clove Hitch

This is used in a variety of temporary situations, such as mooring. However, to counteract its tendency to loosen, add a couple of half hitches above the clove hitch to make it more permanent. The knot is simply two loops with an end tucked under.

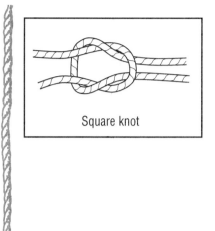

Square knot

Clove hitch

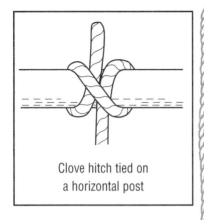

Clove hitch tied on
a horizontal post

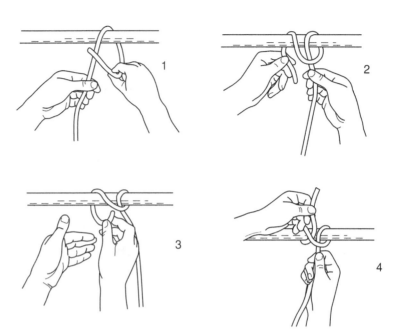

Safety Aboard

Now that you reckon you know all there is to know about sailing, it's almost time to climb aboard and put it all into action. But something always has to crop up to spoil all the fun as you've got one foot in the air about to step aboard. Let's spoil your fun and take another quick journey into yet more paraphernalia and jargon.

It's fully understandable that the Coast Guard is becoming a little irritated at having to play fetch with boats and crews that are ill-equipped to sail the seas. Consequently, whether in a dinghy or two-master, whether crossing an ocean or a bay, federal regulations require a minimum of safety equipment to be maintained aboard and in good working condition.

PFDs

We all know what happened with the *Titanic*, so at the top of the list are personal flotation devices (PFD), otherwise known as life jackets. You need at least one PFD for every human being aboard.

Extinguisher

Federal regulators don't think it's a particularly smart idea to rely on scuttling your boat in the unlikely event of a fire. In fact, they take such a dim view at such a crazy notion that they require at least one regularly charged extinguisher to be on board.

Boat Registration

It won't save your life, but this one's also the law. All boats in U.S. waters must be registered, licensed yearly, and numbered.

Distress Equipment

- A horn or other device to create sound
- Equipment capable of venting your engine compartment
- Distress signaling equipment as prescribed by each state

Additional Safeguards

A few inexpensive and low-tech items we think you might consider are:

- A steel bucket—which won't break or melt and which you can clang with any object to attract attention in emergency situations.
- Several lightweight space blankets—besides folding to nothing, being ultra-light, and providing emergency insulation—when held fully extended or wrapped on a makeshift frame they make wonderful radar targets during search and rescue efforts.
- A handheld compass and waterproof, portable two-way radio.

DOCK 5

Getting Under Way

Undocking Plan

You're ready to launch! Before taking another step, don't forget to unplug and recover any electrical or telephone cables that might be linked to the shore. The first order of business is to consider what currents are in the immediate area of your slip. By the way, in this context, slip is not a form of accident, it's the name given to the home your boat occupies along the dock. Check the depth of water on your anticipated exit path, the current wind direction and level, and whether there is any traffic that could possibly be a hazard or factor. The more eyes and hands you've got on these various tasks the better, so enlist the help of your crew and passengers.

Water Depth

In all shallow water maneuvers, a skipper should post lookouts on the deck closest to the direction of movement. In other words, if backing up, place lookouts on the stern; if proceeding forward, place lookouts on the bow.

Ensure that sails are either not hoisted, or are allowed to luff. If not under engine power, give lookouts boat hooks, paddles, or poles to enable them to leverage the boat away from obstructions under the surface.

If the water's reasonably clear, the lookouts should watch for any obstructions under the surface and the boat should move as slowly as possible until the water is deep enough.

If the water is murky, either use electronic depth sounding equipment such as-depth or fish finder, or use a rope with a weight attached to it. Repeatedly throw the rope out, letting the weight sink to the bottom, and recover it. Be careful not to run over the line and entangle it in the propeller.

These methods are equally important for all types of boats. However, with small boats that have retractable centerboards and rudders, lift these out of the way as an extra precaution.

Wind

Judging wind direction is fairly obvious. One can generally feel which way the wind is blowing. Alternatively, watch for wave ripples and water spray, flags or windsocks that are nearby, or smoke from a funnel or chimney in the distance.

If you are having trouble figuring out the wind direction, watch the birds—they always know the wind direction and will land and stand facing into wind.

Currents

Currents may be a little more difficult to judge, but by spending a few minutes observing the direction in which flotsam or drifting debris is moving, a sailor can get a reasonable idea of local current direction and speed. Do note that, because currents are greatly affected by local topography and obstructions, the skipper needs to consider the entire course and note how the currents in various regions are causing debris to float.

A good indicator for current direction is boats at anchor. They are usually anchored from their bows, making their stern trail down the current with the bow point up the current.

Negligent, Careless, or Reckless Sailing

We assume you know the difference between apathy ("I don't care") and ignorance ("I don't know"). Besides removing the "I don't know" element of this statement, this book aims to equally dispel any notions of "and I don't care" from the world of sailing. We can't change the world, but we do hope we can assist you, and that you'll pass the sentiment along.

It's also the responsibility of the operator to refrain from careless, reckless, or negligent operations on the water. Failure to operate a boat in a safe manner could endanger life or property of other persons. Again, be courteous and exercise caution.

Privateer

A privateer, as opposed to a pirate, refers to an armed vessel, captain, or crew authorized by a commission or a letter of marquee issued by their government to capture the merchant vessels of hostile nations. As such, privateers could not be charged with piracy.

General Conduct

Courtesy

The waterways of the free world that are neither private nor restricted are like the shade of a tree—they belong to everyone, yet they belong to no one. Everybody has a right to enjoy the tranquillity of the shore or open reaches in their own way, providing their enjoyment does not encroach on the rights of others.

We all hate rules, particularly when they restrict our recreational time, but they are necessary for a civilized community to interact. As skipper, you're responsible for your passengers and crew and how they conduct themselves.

If you want to have a good time, as a responsible sailor, the onus is on you to uphold your end of the bargain. Keep in mind that your wake is a very tangible impact that you leave behind. It might be fun to scream around in your motor-powered tender, but please control it. Along this line is sound pollution. Sound travels far over water, so try to keep your engine noise and general revelry to a minimum even when you are quite far from other people.

- Besides being illegal, physical pollution and littering is offensive and unnecessary. Please respect nature and the rights of those who will follow you. Don't dump waste overboard or allow your beaten-up old engine to leak gas or oil into the drink.
- Private docks are like private or reserved parking bays and need to be respected.

Some slips are like parking bays in that the boat is backed into its spot. In this instance, simply edge slowly out.

However, other slips are more like cars parked along a street parallel with the sidewalk. Like parking and exiting a car in this kind of circumstance, it can be a little trickier than simply pulling away. Follow these instructions and you'll find it's all very logical.

Unlike a car, boats can move laterally. This is both good and bad news. On the one hand, wind and current can push you in directions you don't want to go. On the other hand, with fenders, lines, and brute strength you can force the boat in directions you do want to go.

Ideal Conditions

If wind and current are your friends today, pushing you gently away from the dock, all you'll need to do is cast off the lines and retrieve the fenders. A fender is a cushioning device, such as a bundle of rope or an inflatable bladder that is used on the side of a vessel or dock to absorb impact or friction between the boat and the dock when wave motion causes rocking and movement. Then, as the boat drifts gently and safely into open water, make one last inspection that no lines are overboard that the propeller could foul. Once you're satisfied that it is safe to begin moving, shift the motor into forward gear and edge the boat forward with minimum speed. Make sure that the rudder is working and that the boat responds to steering that you do with the tiller or wheel. Stay aware of your surroundings and make sure that you don't swing into the dock or run over any submerged obstructions.

You'll immediately notice that this boat does not steer like a car. A car pivots at the point over its front wheels, but most boats pivot about a third of the way back from the bow. Get a feel for this as soon as you safely can. To do so, serpentine (serpentining is a snaking movement that swings left and right, and left and right) very gently.

What more can we say? You're a natural.

Difficult Conditions

Dockward winds

When the elements of wind and current conspire against you by shoving you toward the dock, you'll have to do a little more preparation and thinking.

First, as described earlier, do everything you otherwise would up to the point of casting off lines. Then, cast off all lines except the bow spring line. You want the stern to pivot out and away from the dock, so get a fender doown over the bow to cushion you in case you touch the dock.

Get your steering mechanism into a direction that will push the stern away from the dock when you shift the motor to forward idle speed. This done, shift into forward and let the boat pivot very slowly around that line. Once the stern is clear of all obstacles,

Famous Pirates: The Corsairs

Historically, these were pirates who occupied the Mediterranean. The *Barbary Corsairs* from the Barbary Coast of North Africa were the most notorious and feared as they had the authorization of their governments to attack the shipping of Christian countries.

The *Maltese Corsairs* who led the fight against the Turks were less well known. They were authorized by Knights of St. John to carry out their plundering.

cast off the spring line and back slowly away from the dock, then shift into forward once more and idle into open water.

Quickly stow all lines and fenders to ensure they're not hazards anyone would trip on. Keep a lookout for flotsam or submerged obstacles—particularly swimmers and divers who tend to become a little testy when run through a prop.

Parallel winds

When winds blow parallel to the dock, simply cast off the line that is upwind and the boat will pivot around the downwind line. As soon as either the bow or stern point into clear water, cast away the restraining line and power away from the dock gently.

The caution here is that things don't get out of hand and the boat wraps entirely around the pivot and slams its other side into the dock or some other object or person!

The trick here is to judge the wind speed. In light wind conditions, either the bow or stern that is upwind and allowed to swing out will move quite slowly. The only time that this maneuver might "get out of hand" is when the wind is excessively strong. In this instance, be prepared to power away from the dock just as soon as the boat begins to point toward open water.

Maneuvering

As the head honcho aboard, you have a tremendous obligation and responsibility toward your crew and all other people or things that your boat might encounter. Lives are quite literally in your hands, and you'll be solely accountable to any and all for personal or property damage that might occur. Before we wax lyrical about the dynamics of sailing, here are a few pointers that will govern your actions and help you immeasurably:

- Become familiar with the handling characteristics of your boat. Know how it responds to the controls at your fingertips. Understand its turning circle—both to port and starboard—its idling speed, cruising speed, top speed, and its reverse speed under power and how quickly you can reverse halt and reverse the direction of your travel. To do so, get

Bermuda Triangle

The Bermuda Triangle is a region of the western Atlantic Ocean that has become legendary in popular imagination for mysterious maritime and even air disasters. Also known as the Devil's Triangle, the triangular-shaped area covers about 1,140,000 sq km (about 440,000 sq mi). The points of the triangle are defined by the island of Bermuda, the coast of southern Florida, and Puerto Rico.

The reputation of the Bermuda Triangle can be traced to reports made in the late fifteenth century by Christopher Columbus concerning the Sargasso Sea. Other reports date the notoriety of the area from the mid-nineteenth century, following a host of logged reports concerning unexplained disappearances.

The incident that cemented the reputation of the Bermuda Triangle was the disappearance in 1945 of Flight 19, a training squadron of five United States Navy planes.

Since then, at least four other significant reports of missing aircraft or boats have been made. However, some disappearances actually occurred beyond the defined triangle, in inclement weather conditions, or in darkness, and some can be traced to mechanical or equipment problems.

Scientific evaluations have concluded that the number of disappearances in the region is not abnormal and that most of the disappearances have logical explanations.

Sound explanation and statistical analyses aside, sail the triangle at your own peril . . .

About Flares

- Read and understand the instructions.
- Note expiration date and replace as necessary.
- Hold lighted flares downwind and away from the boat.
- Do not point them at anyone and hold away from your body.
- Store in a watertight container such as a resealable plastic bag.
- Store where readily accessible and ready to use.
- Use only in case of an emergency.

out into open water and pick up a reference point—perhaps a piece of floating debris that would not cause damage in the event you make a mistake and have a collision.

- Diligently study the charts for any area you might visit and pick your course with care, avoiding any risks that might endanger people or property.
- In the event of an emergency, the most vital information you'll have to give rescuers is where you are. Therefore, know your precise location at all times and keep a constant lookout for unexpected dangers that suddenly loom in your vicinity. Use landmarks, navigational aides, and any other means possible to keep a running point of reference as to your progress.
- Before you leave the safety of the mooring area, everyone aboard should have checked the fit and condition of their lifejacket, and stow it where it can be retrieved in an instant. Also, check the function of all peripheral equipment such as whistles, lights, and clips.
- Alongside, guard rails and stanchions always seem that much more secure. Now that you're sailing free, but not yet exposed to extreme dangers, recheck their soundness and ensure that lifelines are properly secured with enough length and play to make them function as they should.
- The sea has many moods and reserves the right to change them without warning. Watch out for changes in wind, weather, current, buildups of cloud, and mist. Understand how these will affect your course heading, destination arrival time, and ability to maintain a visual picture of your immediate and extended environment.
- Beyond abiding by the immediate laws of any given area, such as speed limits and off-limits areas, be courteous and handle your boat defensively—assuming that any other person potentially in your path really doesn't know what they're doing and will probably make mistakes. Give others a wide berth and control your speed.
- Boating is a community, and the laws of the waves dictate that you are obliged to lend your assistance to anyone in distress or in danger. Don't wait to be called to help; keep

an eye out for any signs of your fellow sailors having problems, and give them a hail to see if they want assistance.

- Systematically test all the sails and understand what combinations work best together under different circumstances. Also, check that your reefing lines (the lines used to reef the sail, in other words, to reduce the size of a sail by tucking in a part and tying it or rolling it) are sufficient.

- Purposefully make limited mistakes under controlled conditions to understand where the limits of your boat are and see what degree of compensation and margin for error exists.

- Power gives way to sail. Back in the seventies, *Mad* magazine ran a quaint rhyme with a very serious message. In typically zany fashion, a cartoon character in his bathtub yacht is defiantly sailing under the bow of a steaming supertanker, holding the course that maritime law guarantees him. The caption below read:

    Here lies the body of John Day,
    who died maintaining his right of way.
    He was right, quite right, as he sailed along,
    but he's just as dead as if he were wrong.

- Conduct man-overboard trials and practice retrieval.

- In doing so, become intimately familiar with your safety and recovery equipment and again make limited errors to develop methods of overcoming potential glitches.

- Drop anchor in a safe area to check whether the anchor equipment and recovery system are in good condition and properly stowed.

More on all of your duties later, but first, let's take a look at other dynamics.

Beating Upwind

Let's face it, although they might not win any races, anyone could sit in a bathtub, hold up a towel on a stick, and set out on the ocean. We couldn't deny that they'd be sailing, but we'd also have a pretty good idea that they'll either be heading on a one-way

> **James Cook (Known as "Captain Cook" 1728–1779)**
> Born in Yorkshire, England, Captain Cook became one of the most famous sailors of all time. He commanded three major voyages of discovery, charting and naming many islands of the Pacific Ocean. He also sailed along the coast of North America as far north as the Bering Strait. Following an incident in which one of his lieutenants shot and killed a native Hawaiian Islander, Captain Cook was later killed by an islander.

journey over the horizon or onto the rocks somewhere downwind. We put it to you that, of every skill that sailing encompasses, perhaps the most important skill is the ability to travel against the direction the wind is blowing. In fact, legend has it that the first Viking who got this feat right was burned at the stake for being a witch.

In this section, as in all others, we'll assume that although you're not necessarily racing, you do want to go from point A to point B in the least amount of time. Consequently, this section is all about efficiency.

Answers in the Wake

The bigger and more turbulent your wake, the more water you're disturbing—and disturbing water costs precious energy that should rather be spent in forward motion. An oversized wake may be the result of your hull's shape, your load distribution, or your boat's displacement. Try to do whatever you can to reduce the size of your wake.

Boat Trim

Of course, in the same way we commonly refer to the sun as setting even though we know it's the earth that is rotating, when we refer to the water rushing toward the boat, we do understand that the water is not necessarily moving but rather that the boat is moving through it. Nevertheless, we'll continue to describe the water as rushing by.

Trimming your boat refers to the actions you take to affect the relative balance of the boat within the water and the consequent shape that it offers the water rushing toward it. To trim a boat, you therefore redistribute this angle by moving ballast or by some other mechanical means such as trimming the sails or adding hydrofoils. A boat has hydrofoils when it has foils or skis under its hull onto which it rises to plane across the water surface at high speed. When a boat planes, it rises slightly out of the water so that it is gliding over the water rather than plowing through it. Because simple body weight adjustments make a big difference, trimming on smaller boats will be both more noticeable and easily adjustable. Regardless of this fact, the point needs to be made that the greatest resistance your boat comes up against is the water rushing toward it.

Trimming fore and aft

The water drag that affects the hull is often difficult to detect, but there are ways to find and reduce it. With more weight in the stern, the bow obviously rises as the stern falls, and large swirls will begin to form in your wake. These are not good. They tell you the same thing that leech telltales would tell you—the hull is dragging through the water and the water is not flowing in an even pattern under it.

To solve the problem, try to get some weight toward the front or mechanically alter the boat's dynamics so that the stern is allowed to rise.

Heel in the beam

If you watch a yacht race, you'll see the crew hiking out over the side of the boat and hanging in harnesses, desperately trying to leverage the boat onto an even keel. They're not panicking, they're simply following this rule.

Sure it's fun—although pretty terrifying for landlubbers—to heel over to the side, but it's not necessarily the most efficient way to sail. Your quest is to keep the boat as flat as possible as though it's at rest.

You need to keep your keel as deep as possible in order to stop yourself from slipping sideways through the water. Using boats with a removable centerboard you can demonstrate this quite easily by rigging them similarly and then simply lifting one boat's board half way out. The one with the deeper keel will certainly be faster.

Of course, if we consider two extremes, we'll have another clear picture of why you'd want to flatten the boat. With the mast vertical it presents the largest possible area to the wind. If you were to push the boat right over so that the mast lay parallel with the water, absolutely no wind would be in the sails. It follows that you need as vertical a mast as possible in order to grab a bunch of wind.

Famous Privateers

Sir Francis Drake (English admiral privateer, 1543–1596)

A legendary sea captain, Sir Francis was also a privateer. Between 1577 and 1580 he became the first Englishman to circumnavigate the world and returned with a cargo of splendid plunder taken from Spanish galleons and raids upon the coasts of Chile and Peru.

In 1581 Francis Drake captured the richest prize ever taken on the high seas. His plunder of gold, silver, and gemstones was worth as much as the Crown's total revenue for a year. The Spanish ambassador demanded restitution; instead Elizabeth I knighted England's hero.

Of course, if a gust does strike, the boat will naturally heel. The onus is then on the skipper to spill sufficient wind to bring the mast back to an optimum pitch.

On the other hand, if you hauled down all of your sails, the boat would sit quite nicely on the water's surface, but it wouldn't go to any destination. Therefore, the balance between boat heeling and maximum efficiency is a delicate one and needs to be experienced to be understood.

Judging the Edge

Wind doesn't always blow evenly with uniform strength, and there will be times when you need to know that a gust is about to hit you. Experienced sailors know precisely the moment that such a squall will hit and take the appropriate action at the critical moment. They might tell you it's like a voodoo that they can't explain. Athough it gives them a critical advantage in both the departments of safety and competitiveness, they're not necessarily holding out on you. It's just that they've been doing it so long that they've forgotten the intricacies. You, too, will develop this sense with experience.

Watching the Telltales

Those little telltales on your sail will offer you a lot of feedback on precisely what is happening to the wind high above the water's surface.

Your goal is to ensure that the leeward tale flows directly backward, while the windward tale lifts occasionally. This occasional lifting means air is getting to it in puffs. With lifting, err on the side of too often, because it's better to have excessive airflow than not enough.

By diligently watching the telltales, you'll see the wind's gust before you feel its response when the boat heels or surges. Eventually, with hundreds and thousands of hours on the water, you'll barely need to use your eyes anymore as you'll begin to hear the change and sense it a moment before it hits.

But the principal failing
  occurred in the Sailing,
And the Bellman,
  perplexed and
  distressed,
Said he had hoped, at
  least, when
The wind blew due
  East.
That the ship would
  not travel
due West!
      —Lewis Carroll

Why is this important?

In light winds this is important if you're looking to eke the last ounce of energy out of every breath of wind. In heavy weather, sudden gusts can be devastating to life and limb and can rip your rigging to pieces.

How to react

You're trying to maintain an even speed through the water. When the gust hits, you'll want to make the most out of it while not running risks of capsizing.

React to the blast's strength by swinging your bow upwind and maintaining that course for as long as the blast continues, then bearing off as the blast diminishes. In light conditions you'll maintain the same speed but gain a little extra ground against the wind that you can later afford when you need to run out in a lull. In heavy weather you'll instantly spill the surplus power from the sail while maintaining your speed.

In dangerous situations, you can supplement this action by sheeting out and losing the draft from your sail.

Use Wind and Sails to Steer the Boat

If you take a look at a sailboard, you'll notice that there's no rudder for steering. Of course there's a fin, but that only serves the same purpose as the keel or centerboard; it's a pivot. In order to turn the board you need to use your weight displacement and the power of the wind in your sails.

On larger boats it's a little difficult to significantly shift weight efficiently enough to steer the entire vessel, but the principle of using sail power is a possibility.

Of course, when you think about it, your rudder turns the boat by dragging at an awkward angle through the water. Now, we know that anything dragged through the water costs you precious energy and forward motion. It follows then that the less you can steer by dragging and the more you can steer by applying productive power, the better.

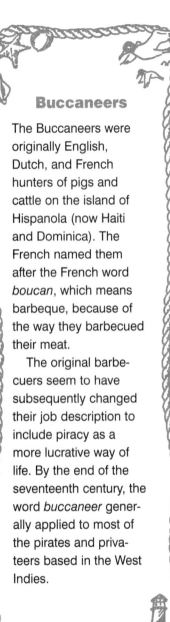

Technique

The more you shift the wind's center of effort ahead of the boat's keel or pivot, the more the boat will want to point downwind. Conversely, the more you slack off on sail power fore and apply sail power aft, the more the boat will pivot and bring its bow up to windward.

The bigger the boat, the more complex constant adjustments would become, but it's important to set the sails appropriately so that your average rudder compensation is at an absolute minimum.

Sailing without a rudder—small vessels only

As with sailboards, we can see that you might refine this technique to such a degree that you can actually sail the boat without the need for a rudder.

If you want to practice, here is a step-by-step procedure to achieve this:

- Only attempt this if you have plenty of sailing experience and are prepared to make mistakes that could capsize you.
- Pick a day with light to moderate wind.
- Get out into clear and open water with no chance of dinging anything or anyone.
- Remove the rudder completely.
- Get the boat moving on a beam reach.

To head up
- Trim the main.
- Ease the jib.
- Heel the boat to leeward.

To bear off
- Trim the jib.
- Ease the main.
- Heel the boat to windward.

Seeing results

To see just how successful this technique is, arrange to sail alongside someone with a similar rig who's not using the technique. Besides the competition making a better sailor of you, you'll have a point of reference to see precisely how to make improvements to your technique.

Tacking

Tacking is the act of changing from one position or direction to another. If you've ever watched car racing, you'll notice that cornering is where races are won or lost and that the cars that consistently pick the best line into the corner make fewer mistakes and come out of the corner at higher speeds than those who have not set themselves up correctly. Tacking is essentially the same maneuver as cornering, with similar dynamics at work. As such, it's a vital transition where ground and momentum can either be gained or lost very quickly if your approach is not correct.

Again, this is an area in which experience will be your best teacher. Experimenting with making your tacks long and smooth or fast and choppy will give you an idea of the most appropriate decision under each condition, and for your vessel. On this note, one of the keys is to maintain momentum throughout the maneuver.

Maintaining momentum

Obviously, because the wind direction will remain constant and your relative sail position will be altering, there will be a period when you are actually decelerating. This requires your momentum to shift you through the eye of the tack where your boat will momentarily run the risk of being in-irons.

The less momentum you have coming into the tack, the more you allow your rudder to be dragging through the water. And the

Tacking to Sail Upwind

Tacking—steering your boat into the wind on a zigzag course—is what you do when the wind is blowing toward you from the direction of your destination.

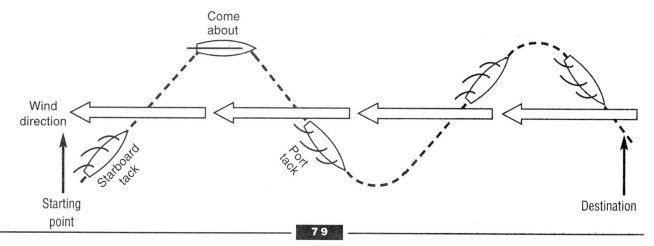

Come about

Wind direction

Starting point

Starboard tack

Port tack

Destination

longer you remain on an upwind heading, the more risk you'll have of actualizing an in-irons condition.

Jamming the tack

On the other extreme, if you jam your boat through the tack—apart from jarring your crew, turning the swinging boom into a violently swinging weapon, and placing excessive strain on your entire rig—you'll also decelerate very suddenly and face the prospect of a delayed acceleration on your new heading.

Post-tack acceleration

Going into the tack you have a given speed, coming through the tack you decelerate, and coming out onto the other heading you'll logically be traveling relatively slower—or practically stalled. Again, as with a cornering car coming through a sharp bend, you'll have to shift gears in order to accelerate back to cruising speed. Sure, you could remain in top gear and you'd eventually get to top speed, but this would hardly be an optimum way of doing so. Treat your sails the same way you'd treat your car's transmission. Refer to the section "Physics of Sailing" and the subsection "The wind's reaction" earlier in this text.

Methods of tacking will vary to suit every vessel, its sail configuration, and circumstance. The only way to be proficient in all of these situations is to practice them by placing yourself in each. However, remember to communicate what your intentions are with your crew before executing them, or you may inadvertently find yourself conducting a search-and-rescue mission to tend to bruised, bumped, and man-overboard situations. Also, ensure that these maneuvers take place well away from anyone or anything that could pose as potential hazards.

Caution

Finally, don't be mistaken; beyond being an important and technically complex maneuver, tacking can also be a dangerous one. As you come about, the windward and leeward sides of the sail suddenly switch. The result is that the sail suddenly fills with wind coming from the opposite side and hundreds or even thousands of pounds of sail-filled power suddenly swing the solid boom through an arc defined by the mast. Because the boom is often at head height, if the skipper fails to warn passengers and crew to keep heads down, the capacity of the boom to deliver a blow will give someone a smack he or she won't forget in a hurry.

Bad Wind

Bad wind refers to your sails experiencing a disruption in the flow of the wind reaching them. If the bad air is being created by other boat sails, you'll obviously not have their same wind power and will travel relatively slower. To remedy this you'll have to find your way to clear air. To do so, your first priority is to establish the exact originator of the bad air. The following pointers will help you.

Blanketing

When there is a boat to windward, its sail blankets or stops the air from getting to your sail. It's a windless pocket of air, a form of wind shadow, that will vary in size, shape, and extent depending on various circumstances such as wind speed, direction, and consistency; sail shape and size; and relative position to the wind and your respective headings.

If you're caught in this intense doldrum, your boat will tend to decelerate until the blanket overtakes you. The wind will then snap into your sails once again, and you'll begin to accelerate once more. But, if you don't take evasive action at this point you'll just end up sailing directly back into the blanket.

What to do?

If possible, without hitting the blanketer, shift to a new tack. If you've got a fast enough vessel and rig—and you're hemmed in by other boats, objects, or course requirement—hang back enough to build enough momentum to push yourself through the blanket and on to clear air ahead. Naturally, if you don't have sufficient momentum, the best you could hope to do is to cross in the blanketer's wake and attempt to pass on the windward side.

Dinghies

Dinghies are small, fast, manageable and cheap watercraft that can be sailed or rowed. Beyond being practical toys and ferries to hitch along behind your larger boat, they can be enormous fun on small stretches of water.

Modern sailing **dinghies** have built-in buoyancy chambers to prevent them from sinking when capsized.

They are incredibly responsive and small enough to provide a real feeling of being part of the water. Because of light construction and relative sail area to weight ratios, the sensation of smooth, quiet speed can be far out of proportion to how fast you are actually moving. Be careful not to travel far in a dinghy, and be sure to bring oars if you don't have a motor.

Backwinding

Whereas the blanket is a small but intense area relatively close to the blanketer's rig, the backwind zone is a much larger area that surrounds it. Think of the umbra of the sun when the earth experiences an eclipse. Only a small portion of the earth will experience a relatively short-lived period of total darkness, whereas there is a much larger area of shadow.

The same principle is true for wind. Beyond being a large area of lowered wind intensity, it's also an area of turbulence. As if this is not enough, the *back* part of the backwind term derives its name from the wind that turns the corner around the leading edge of the sail. As it rushes into the relative vacuum caused on the leeward side of the sail, it's actually changing the wind's relative direction. Therefore, from your perspective in the zone, you'll be facing more of a headwind, with a consequent loss of power and potential for speed.

Making the Best of Circumstance

Now for some basic wind shift philosophy and appropriate tactics:

Lifts and headers

Both of these terms are wind shifts that get their names from their effect on your course.

- Header. Sailing on a close-hauled (sails trimmed flat for sailing as close to the wind as possible) course, a *header* is a shift that forces you to bear off in order to maintain the sail's power.
- Lift. A *lift* is a shift that allows your boat to head more toward the windward mark. In other words, it allows you to "lift" your course higher.

In the case of a header, you'll notice that you're suddenly not heading as tight to the windward mark as you had been. When the header is sufficiently severe, it's time to consider tacking. Besides, those on the other tack are experiencing the same shift, but from their perspective it'll be in the form of a lift.

Land was created to provide a place for boats to visit.
—Brooks Atkinson

• • •

Nowhere else than upon the sea do the days, weeks, and months fall away quicker into the past. They seem to be left astern as easily as the light air-bubbles in the swirls of the ship's wake.
—Joseph Conrad

Overlapped boats

What follows is a fairly sophisticated element of sailing and it cannot be fully exploited until you gain enough experience to judge what the wind will do next. However, it's worth noting.

If two boats are sailing alongside one another, lifts and headers become important issues. In the case of a lift, the inside boat will immediately gain an advantage. Logically, a header gives the outside boat the advantage.

Tacking lines

When a shift or header hits, it changes the dynamic of the best possible line to take in order to reach your destination. Therefore, keep a constant running evaluation of precise wind shifts in mind in order to make your course changes accordingly with a smooth transition.

Covering

Applying these principles to the racing environment, a basic rule to follow is to stay between opponents and the next tack. If you can, push to stay as close to your opponent's side of the course as you can. It may mean that you're not sailing in the optimum wind, but at least you'll be ahead of them and pick up any favorable shift or gust in the wind that they might experience.

Races like the America's Cup will quickly show even the uninitiated what a big part tacking duels can play in the final result. If you're not competitive, these tactics can still be of some importance in terms of honing your sailing technique to the optimum level—presumably the very reason you're reading this book.

Anchoring

Besides those all-important slumbers in the sun where you leisurely sip your nonalcoholic beverage or lazily haul hungry fish aboard, you will need to drop anchor in order to control the boat when hostile circumstances threaten.

The Pirate Flag

The name Jolly Roger is thought to have derived from the French name for the red flag—*Jolie Rouge*.

The Jolly Roger was designed to encourage a hasty surrender and strike fear into victims. Although the black Jolly Roger often depicted symbols of death such as skull and crossbones, it was not as greatly feared as the red flag which meant that no mercy would be shown in battle.

Safety

Every year there are far too many avoidable fatalities that occur as a result of boaters not acting responsibly. In the heat of excitement, they overload their boats and don't observe proper safety practices. They move about the boat without watching their footing or fail to read the prevailing conditions or anchor near blinder reefs or in narrow channels or shipping lanes.

As a courtesy, if you see anyone lying at anchor, but particularly if they are fishing, control your wake so as not to upset them too much. Fishermen often stand to cast and anyone on another boat who falls overboard as a result of your negligence is not going to be a happy camper.

Swimming

Whirling propellers and big or fast-moving watercraft are notoriously nasty things for our feeble bodies to meet by accident. To avoid this unpleasant and even deadly experience, always swim close to shore, avoid areas where boating is heavy, and never swim alone away from the boat.

Besides man-made nasties, there are also the lurkies and eddies to spoil our day if we're not paying attention. Beware of currents and hungry or otherwise unfriendly sea-life.

If possible, always have somebody left aboard who knows who is out swimming and approximately where they'll be swimming.

Ensure there is a ladder or some other means of climbing aboard. We've heard horror stories about revelers diving overboard with abandon only to then realize that everyone is in the water and there are several feet of vertical and slippery hull between themselves and the deck of their boat.

As a precaution against sudden emergencies, tie a line and life ring or some other flotation device to the guardrail. This could prove the difference between life and death for a tired or cramping swimmer. Retrieve the line before getting under way.

By contrast, when you're maneuvering, be alert for swimmers in the water and don't assume that they'll always restrict themselves to designated swim areas. This is particularly important whenever you approach an anchored or drifting boat or pontoons where sunbathers are lying.

Adverse Circumstances

Consider onshore gales, or engine or steering failure. Under these circumstances you've got to maintain your position and keep your bow up into any oncoming bad weather or waves.

Again, it's only practice that can ensure smooth operation under the stress of an emergency.

The first consideration is selecting an appropriate anchor for the task at hand. To the uninitiated, it comes as a surprise that all anchors are not made equal. The selection depends on a host of circumstances, but the most important are the size of the boat and the ocean floor's terrain at any given location.

Dynamics of the Anchor

Sure, a rock tied to a line would be better than nothing at all, but the size rock you'd need to hold even a small craft wouldn't be a welcome passenger aboard any self-respecting sailor's vessel. Good anchor function has a lot less to do with the weight of the anchor than its shape. The anchor works because it holds onto the terrain. If you wanted to hold all the sand you could fit in your hand, you wouldn't spread your fingers. But to hold many larger stones, you'd spread your fingers as far apart as possible to pile more on. Since the anchor is essentially doing this same job on the bottom of the ocean, it needs to be suited to either rock or sand.

Commonly, anchors consist of a shaft with a movable crosspiece called the stock at its top end and two curved arms ending in spade-like points called flukes at its bottom end. Alternatively, they are more bucket-shaped and designed to grab a sandy floor. The three most common anchors you'll encounter are flukes, danforths, and mushrooms.

It's unlikely then that you'll have just one anchor onboard. The more variety you have at your disposal to cover every eventuality, the better off you'll be. Once you've arrived at your chosen destination, try to get an idea of what kind of topography your anchor will be landing on and put down the appropriate design.

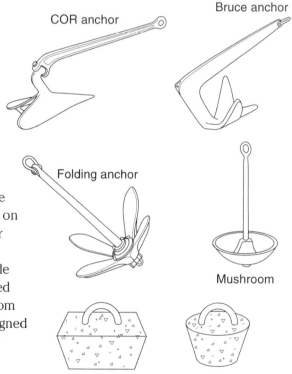

COR anchor

Bruce anchor

Folding anchor

Mushroom

Concrete anchors
with 1/2" round steel eye, hot dipped, galvanized

Anchors

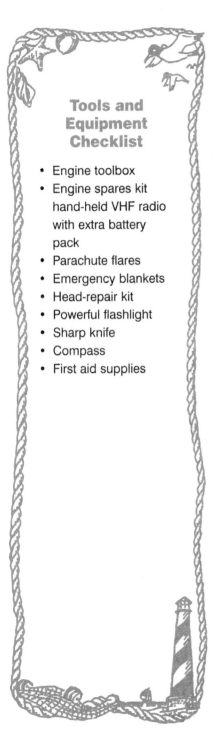

Tools and Equipment Checklist

- Engine toolbox
- Engine spares kit hand-held VHF radio with extra battery pack
- Parachute flares
- Emergency blankets
- Head-repair kit
- Powerful flashlight
- Sharp knife
- Compass
- First aid supplies

Retrieval Systems

Almost as important as having an anchor hold your position is the ability to retrieve it at will. To do so you'll obviously need to attach it with a sufficiently strong line or chain, or a combination of both.

However, there are times that anchors stick fast in rock crevices, and cutting the line is not always the smart option. Specifically for this reason, most anchors are cunningly designed with a sacrificial break loose option. When the anchor is jammed and you put enough pressure on it, the sacrificial clasp breaks free and the leverage of the anchor ropes pull is transferred to a different angle on the anchor unit. Under most conditions this allows the obstruction to be circumvented; the disabled anchor can be retrieved and then reset to its functional configuration.

Taken together, the anchor setup, including line and chain, is called ground tackle.

Scope

The amount of rope you allow overboard when at anchor is called the *scope.* The amount of scope depends on water depth and weather conditions. The deeper the water and the more severe the weather becomes, the more scope you allow.

Measure the water depth. Under normal conditions, for normal recreation you'll allow the scope to be at least five times the depth. However, if you decide to stay overnight, build in that little margin of error and bring the scope up to eight times the depth. Don't forget to add the distance your bow cleat is from the water surface to the depth before making your calculation.

An important observation to make is that the anchor might well drag a distance before it catches and holds fast, so you'll need to build in a margin for error. After you've dropped the anchor, keep an eye on a few markers to establish how long you drift before the anchor sets and you begin to hold your position.

At this stationary position there is another important concept to understand. Consider the fact that because the boat can now swing in an arc around the point that the anchor grips you will need a margin of error that allows you a sizable radius to swing around the anchor pivot. Take a good look around and estimate what objects your arc could intersect if the wind or current shifts. Also, if and when you do swing, the boat will pull on the anchor from a different position, and this may loosen the anchor and allow it to slide another distance before it finds a new hold. Take this possibility into account.

However, when mooring near other similarly moored boats, understand that the same tide and wind factors will allow them to swing in their own arc. But you'll all be doing so in unison, so the relative distances between you should remain the same unless they have more scope or either their or your anchor drags excessively.

Other Elements of Smooth Anchoring

- Select a venue that will offer you the maximum shelter from current, wind, and boat traffic.
- Don't be shy to ask others at anchor how much scope they've allowed, what kind of anchor they dropped (if it isn't plainly obvious what terrain you're over), and how well their anchor is sitting.
- Also have a look at whether they're anchored bow and stern or only anchored at the bow; then anchor in the same manner.
- Before dropping anchor, ensure that all shackles, fixtures, and fittings are in good condition and within operational specification.
- Neatly lay the total amount of anchor rope you'll be needing on the deck in such a way that it can run smoothly overboard without tangling or snarling objects or people.
- If you don't want to make a chump out of yourself and lose your anchor besides, remember to secure the rope at the point you intend it to hold *before* you drop anchor.
- Bring the boat to a position just upwind or up current of the spot you intend the anchor to find its hold, keeping the bow into the wind or current.
- Lower the anchor in a controlled fashion until it touches the ground and the rope begins to slacken. Then, use the

motor to gently back you away from that position until all of the predetermined rope is overboard and allow the motor to gently drag the anchor until you feel it has bitten. With someone's hand on the rope, this will be easy to feel as the submerged unit bumps into an obstacle. At this point, don't let the rope in the water tangle in the propeller.

- From time to time check your bearings and ensure that the anchor hasn't dragged. However, keep in mind and make compensation for the fact that your bearings will change as a result of current and wind shifts altering your relative position to the anchor. This is not just your duty, but that of everyone aboard, so make them aware of this fact and tell them to communicate with you if they assess any danger at all (never show irritation with false alarms—they're a lot less expensive than silent mistakes).

- When it's time to retrieve the anchor, reverse the procedure and gently use the motor to ride forward and help you recover rope slack. Put the motor into neutral when the rope hangs vertically from the bow. Cleat or tie the line at this point and then gently ride forward once more under motor power; thus you'll use the boat's own force to free the anchor. Apart from saving on blistered hands, it'll also save your crew from being dragged overboard or having extremities injured if the rise of the swell pulls their wayward appendages into rigging.

- Once free, bring the engine to neutral and recover the anchor, coiling the line in a neat fashion. With the anchor at the water surface, you can clean it if necessary. Stow the line only after it has dried.

Putting Your Boat Away

This is more correctly termed mooring your boat, but we'll pretend we didn't hear that—just this once.

That was a great day of fun and excitement, wasn't it? Now, back to the issue of getting home safely.

Stowing the Sails

It's a smart idea to have the sails already stowed before you enter the mooring area, as sudden gusts and confined spaces are not the best of bedfellows.

- First, loosen the sheets, vang, cunningham, and halyard.
- Remove the sails by reversing the procedure you used to put them up.
- Properly fold the sails and stow the lines. Fold the sails according to their type and the manufacturer's specifications.
- Remove the halyards, raise the boom, and coil all other lines that are not lines you'll be using in the mooring procedure.

Slip Mooring Plan

As though you haven't guessed, besides being a lot more fun, sailing's a little more complex than driving a car. It's more like flying a plane, where landings are everything. In this instance, dockings are vital. But first, there are a few preparations you have to make before you arrive at your final destination.

Ensure that the docking lines you so diligently stowed when you cast off earlier are ready for use, with one end appropriately tied to the boat and the other free and ready to be tossed ashore. Place the fenders overboard in a position that they'll buffer the boat when you come alongside.

Psychology

We're not getting weird on you; this is a really important issue. Nobody likes making mistakes, but we all like it a lot less when there's an audience.

Marinas and docks are favorite haunts for rubberneckers. As you enter the enclosure, you'll feel their eyes on you, watching as you burble by. It'll feel like everyone's watching you. The downside is that they certainly will be if you start crashing into things, so it's a really good idea that you get a little practice out of the public eye.

Famous Sailors

Sir Francis Chichester

Born in Devon in 1901, Sir Francis became a sailing legend whose achievements—including fastest voyage around the world by any small vessel—sparked many a transoceanic and circumnavigation race and series. And, beyond being a great sailor, Sir Francis also set many flight records in the late 1920s.

His many achievements earned him a knighthood from Queen Elizabeth II. Sir Francis died in 1972.

Find a backwater somewhere, a venue or various venues that provide all of the possible tide and wind variables you're likely to encounter. That way you can make mistakes to your heart's content.

Shoehorn maneuvering

With boats temporarily obstructing your path, it's best to take up a temporary mooring. If there's someone on shore to assist, come alongside and toss him or her a line. If there's no shore assistance, gently bring your bow to the dock and let a crewmember jump ashore to attach an appropriate line.

Go slow

Reduce speed well before you approach. Boats don't have brakes, and an emergency stop, even with motors slammed full astern, takes longer than you'd imagine.

The maneuver

Assess the wind direction relative to the dock. If the direction is toward the dock, steer the boat for a point that'll place you a couple of feet away, but level with the dock, and the wind will push you snugly home where you can secure the bow, stern, and spring lines.

If the wind is blowing away from the dock, approach the dock at an angle of around 25° and either have a crewmember step ashore with the bow line or pass it to a waiting dock hand.

On boats with outboard or inboard-outboard engines, turn the motors toward the dock and power the stern in. Once alongside, the stern and other lines can be secured.

Boats with inboard engines don't have this luxury, and you'll need to use a bow spring to keep the bow from moving forward. Then, using a combination of engine thrust and rudder position, leverage the boat around the restraining line, and the stern will be forced toward the dock where you can secure it. If the boat has two engines, you're in a little more luck because you can use them with opposite thrust and they'll leverage off one another.

Provision for Tides

If you're tying in an area that has a large tidal range, allow sufficient play in your lines for tidal variance.

Too little slack in a line tied at high tide could either break the line or leave the boat dangling in mid-air as the water recedes. By contrast, too much slack at low tide would allow the boat to wander around with a mind of its own when the water floods and there are fathoms of play in the line.

On the other hand, if you tie with too little play on the wharf too close to the waterline at low tide, when high water returns the boat could either be pulled under or the line could be hydraulically wrenched into the structure and cause untold damage.

Mooring Anchors

Where dock space is at a premium, permanently placed anchors are attached to buoys. Although a little inconvenient for instant and direct access to the boat, moorings are cheaper to maintain and for larger vessels less hassle to secure to than a solid quayside.

At day's start, a skeleton crew would usually take a tender to the boat, disengage it, and then bring it to the quay where the people, goods, and equipment would be loaded. At day's end this procedure would be reversed.

To moor, approach the buoy slowly. There are two main types of floats you'll find. If there are two buoys, attach to the smaller buoy by scooping it up with a boat hook (a pole with a metal point and hook at one end) and attach it to your bow cleat. It is used to maneuver by sailors as they come alongside land or another boat or object. The hook is used to pull the sailboat closer to the object, while the stiffness of the pole allows the sailor to push away from the object and thereby avert danger. If there's only a single large buoy, scoop it up, attach your anchor line to the bottom of this buoy, and then drop the buoy overboard once more and tie your line off with little scope.

Although it is a relatively simple procedure to hitch up to the mooring, there are some associated dangers such as overshooting

Sailor Talk

Log Book

In the early days of sailing ships, the ship's records were written on shingles cut from logs. These shingles were hinged and opened like a book. The record was called the "log book." Later on, when paper was readily available and bound into books, the record maintained its name.

Fenders for Every Occasion

Boat fender

Wharf fender

Bow fender

the mark and fouling the prop or having crew yanked overboard if the approach is too vigorous.

Issues of Interest

Chafing

While you're at work or restfully asleep, water movement is tirelessly working away at your boat's securing lines.

Whenever you'll be leaving a boat tied to the slip for more than a few days, ensure that you add antichafing gear to whatever surfaces run the risk of being rubbed in the wrong way.

Because boats on water relentlessly roll and move back and forth, lines are exposed to an enormous amount of wear and tear—particularly in areas where they are repeatedly pulled over or through hooks, decks, and along wharves. In order to protect the line from wearing and thus from ultimately breaking—with the resultant damage to the vessel that this will bring—antichafing gear in the form of plastic sleeves can be purchased at any sailing supply store. Antichaffing gear can take a variety of forms, and is dictated by the particular application.

Having a crush on fenders

Boat fenders are meant to be squashed, squeezed, and crushed. Usually inflated with air, they're tough customers designed to absorb the shocks and attrition of life between a rock and a hard place—to coin a phrase.

Like any other safety equipment, the price you'd expect to pay for them all depends on the replacement value of the boat you're protecting. If you figure that a piece of Styrofoam that washed up will do, then go for it, but we'd suggest a top-grade, commercially available unit designed for the task.

The larger your boat, the larger the task at hand and the more extensive and robust the fender needs to be. Usually the minimum number of fenders you'd employ would be three—one off the bow, one amidships, and one off the stern—all obviously at the most extreme parts of your vessel that are likely to come into contact with the dock or any other solid object.

Where docksides are rough or barnacle-encrusted, place a dock board on the outside of the fender to ensure that excessive abrasion or puncturing does not occur.

DOCK 6

Weathering the Conditions

Dealing with the Effects of Climatology

One of the most important parts of becoming an expert sailor is learning how to understand weather and harness its power, while protecting yourself, your crew, and your vessel from its many dangers.

Clearly, no matter how sophisticated we humans become, we cannot change the weather to our preference. The best you can do is to understand the basic climatalogical theory of weather patterns and learn how to interpret and use them to your advantage.

The section that follows will give you a good basis on which to build a solid foundation of knowledge. Before we get into the detail, here are some pointers for you to be aware of:

- Watch the local weather and tides, and plan passages to avoid heavy weather
- Have a "well-found" yacht: structurally sound, well provisioned and outfitted with proper operating, maintenance, safety and emergency gear and systems
- Prepare your crew for every weather eventuality and practice emergency procedures
- Keep your priorities in order: "safety, comfort, speed"

The section that follows briefly covers the complex and all-important external influences that any sailor needs to understand.

Weather

If there is one factor over which the sailor has no control, but is entirely at the mercy of, it's the weather. But, before we throw our hands in the air and declare this a wildcard, let's pause a moment and take a trip behind the scenes of weather prediction to glimpse what drives this all-important force. The point of this section is to give you a brief overview of the dynamics at work so that you have an appreciation for how much or how little modern prediction techniques can forewarn you of what's on the weather horizon within the coming hours and days.

Weather Information

Accurately interpreting the weather is an essential element of the sailor's art. In addition, the type of knowledge you need depends on the sort of sailing you intend to do.

If you're a weekend warrior and only sail local haunts, you'll be interested in the weather for that specific area over short periods of time. On the other hand, if you're into cruising once you gain experience, you'll be concerned with the weather projections over a period of days and its behavior in the wider areas. Those sailors who venture out in the latitudes where weather is variable rather than merely seasonal must learn to make their own meteorological maps and forecasts for themselves.

In addition, beyond the weather report you need before embarking on a journey, it's wise to constantly update the information—both from official sources as well as by personal observation.

Impending foul weather

Beyond the ideal weather you're seeking, you're most interested in the foul weather you're trying to avoid. However, the term foul weather is subjective and means different things to different people. Though you might consider even one cloud in the sky and any wind over eight knots to be foul, (solo) sailors in the doldrums think of foul weather as a glass sea with no breeze in sight!

Having stated this, there is weather that's just plain nasty to be out in. For instance, it might be great to have 25 knots in your sails when the water's calm, but if the wind were just 15 knots but the sea was lumpy with chop, we'd personally call that foul.

Hemispheric Variance

Because sailing has no global boundaries, it's important to recognize that directly opposite seasons occur in the Northern and Southern Hemispheres. This is good news for the fair-weather, northern sailor who has the budget to flip down south in January for a bit of summer sailing, or the masochistic but determined racer who wishes to experience a southern winter in August.

Sailor Talk

Between the Devil and the Deep

In wooden ships, the "devil" was the longest seam of the ship. It ran from the bow to the stern. When at sea and the "devil" had to be caulked, the sailor sat in a bo'sun's chair to do so. He was suspended between the "devil" and the sea—the "deep"—a very precarious position, especially when the ship was under way.

Why opposite weather systems?

Because the earth does not constantly sit with its equator perpendicular to the sun—but rather has a tilt of slightly more than 23 degrees—the hemisphere with angles to the sun that are closest to the perpendicular will experience more intense and longer sunshine, displaying the properties of summer. By contrast, the opposite hemisphere will simultaneously experience less sunshine with its associated winter.

However, because the earth is not stationary relative to the sun, but rotates around it every twelve months, the dynamic alternates through the solstices or high summer/winter (which occur December 21 and June 21). The midpoint of the entire cycle is called the equinox (March 21 and September 21), at which point the sun relative to the equator is perpendicular.

Wind

Where does the wind come from, and where is it going?

Do a little exercise for us, please. Pick a hot and clear summer's day, find yourself a black cast-iron manhole cover, remove your shoes and socks, and step onto the plate with your bare feet.

As the smoke poured out between your sizzling toes, did you notice your tendency to leap high into the air? That's the same reaction air has when it passes over hot surfaces. It rises rapidly, leaving a vacuum or low pressure in its wake.

If you want to cool those feet really quickly, quench them in a nearby swimming pool—don't pick a shallow dish of water that's lying in the sun; it'll be too hot.

The swimming pool is deep, light in color, and able to circulate, so it distributes the sun's temperature into its depths. The manhole cover is solid and black, and simply keeps on building concentrated heat energy right near the surface. And although the dish has water, it's shallow so the temperature distributes as much as it can, but it too quickly heats up.

The Part Pressure Plays

The earth is made up of so many different components—water, desert, rock, vegetation, etc.—each of which heat at different rates. The relative rising of heated air and falling of cooled upper air creates huge volumes of differing air pressures.

Since air is in a gaseous form, and a gas will always find its natural pressure equilibrium, air movement—or wind—rushes from regions of relatively high pressure to regions of relatively low pressure.

Gradient steepness

The greater the difference in relative pressures between adjacent high- and low-pressure zones, and the distance or proximity of these extremes to one another, the more violent will be the air movement and the higher the wind speed.

Oceanic influence

To complicate matters, because oceans differ in depth and relative origin—some flow from polar regions, while others flow from the tropics—they too carry an inherent ambient temperature that influences the air above them.

Naming the Winds

We commonly say, "The north wind is blowing again," or "Looks like we're in for a nasty southeaster." Although you've probably figured it out, it's worth noting that we name the winds according to the compass bearing they're blowing *from*. In other words, a westerly wind comes from the west (no prizes for getting that right).

However, just to be difficult, we name currents according to the direction they are traveling to.

So, if there's a current coming out of the south and a wind that picks up is also blowing from the south, what do we have?

We'd have a southerly wind and a north streaming current.

What the Wind Carries with It

Although wind in itself is one issue a sailor must consider, the amount of moisture and electric charge it carries with it is quite another.

Not all winds are the same nor do they carry similar clouds, rain, and lightning with them. Depending on where in the world you are, you'll need to consider the local conditions before judging whether an anticipated wind is good or bad news.

And, if you think no wind is great news, how often have you seen fog during windy conditions? Fog can be one of the nastiest experiences for a sailor.

Measuring Air Pressure

If air pressure is so important, you'd expect we can measure and track its changes, and you'd be right. When you look at a weather map you'll see swirling lines that trace the edges of increasing or decreasing pressure zones. At their centers they'll display either an H or an L—indicating a high-or low-pressure zone, respectively.

The numbers logged on each of these lines indicates the pressure at sea surface, at a particular time of day, and at a specific location on the earth. Not too many years ago, weather plotters who drew these maps relied on ship readings and weather outposts to report their pressure readings at certain times of day. From there they'd plot these numbers onto maps and play connect the dots until they had interpolated where the pressure lines most likely ran through areas that they had not received any hard information from.

Technology to the Fore

These days computers and satellite data have taken a lot of the guesswork out of weather prediction, but it's not yet a foolproof science, and mother nature still throws us plenty of curve balls. As data is built and computer simulation models become ever more sophisticated, we can expect the prediction of weather to become an ever more precise undertaking. For now, for the most part, no weather predictor would wager his or her salary on a precise forecast.

Common Winds and Their Temperaments

Pleasure sailors generally seek steady but strong winds and generally temperate climates. Not surprisingly then, most sailing activity takes place in a band on either side of the equator where these conditions are most prevalent.

Sailing near land

Because the vast majority of sailors rarely venture too far from land, it's worth noting that wind is generally slowed by the land and less steady than it might be further out to sea where there are no obstructions and the air can move freely.

In marinas and harbors, wind conditions might be generally light but gusty, while out on the water wind strength picks up and the feed becomes a little more constant. This fact is important for two reasons:

- Beware of sudden gusts when you're near shore.
- Beware of much more wind than you bargained for once you're out on open water.

To help you assess how much wind is really out there, systems and facilities are in place to provide you with the tools to make the correct judgments.

Firstly, weather reports generally will tell you the wind direction and speed. And, secondly, through the Beaufort scale you'll be able to equate these rather nebulous details to a very tangible image.

Land and sea breezes

Beyond prevailing wind, even on a calm day you're likely to experience some kind of breeze whenever land and sea meet. Because the land heats more quickly during the day and then cools quicker at night, light breezes tend to blow onshore by day and off-shore by night. These localized air movements are usually gentle and of little consequence apart from being useful to smaller craft.

Navy History

Cup of Joe

Josephus Daniels (1862–1948) was appointed Secretary of the Navy by President Woodrow Wilson in 1913. Among his reforms of the Navy were inaugurating the practice of making 100 Sailors from the Fleet eligible for entrance into the Naval Academy, the introduction of women into the service, and the abolishment of the officers' wine mess. From that time on, the strongest drink aboard Navy ships could only be coffee, and over the years, a cup of coffee became known as "a cup of Joe."

The Beaufort Scale

The Beaufort Scale is most commonly known as an indicator of gale and hurricane intensity. The Beaufort Scale uses open sea conditions as its base.

Beaufort Number	Wind Speed (Knots)	Description	Effect on Water
0	Less than 1	Calm	Mirror–calm surface
1	1–3	Light air	Scale–like ripples
2	4–6	Light breeze	Wavelets, no breaking
3	7–10	Gentle breeze	Crest begin to break
4	11–16	Moderate breeze	Waves 1½ –4 feet, numerous white-caps
5	17–21	Fresh breeze	Waves 4–8 feet, some spray
6	22–27	Strong wind	Waves 8–13 feet, whitecaps everywhere
7	28–33	Near gale	Waves 13–20 feet, white foam, wave streaks
8	34–40	Gale	Waves increase in length, foam blown off to sea, sea streaks white
9	41–47	Strong gale	Waves over 20 feet, limited visibility
10	48–55	Storm	Waves 20–30 feet, sea heavily streaked
11	56–63	Violent storm	Waves to 45 feet, sea nearly white
12	64–71	Hurricane or extremely violent storm	Waves over 45 feet, sea completely white, visibility near zero

Chop, Swell, and Waves

Out on the water you'll experience these three connected elements in the order named above, with each being a natural extension of the other. Whereas chop is small and localized wave motion that tosses a boat about with a high frequency, swell is its cousin.

When chop graduates to swell, it's more uniform in direction and form and has a slower frequency. It can also be much taller and has a more regular and vertical motion on the boat as opposed to chop, which tends to oscillate the boat in unpredictable directions around its center of gravity, turning everyone aboard green with sea sickness.

When swells turn angry, they then graduate into waves. These are the teeth of the sea, and you don't want to be anywhere near them. But, in order to stay out of their way and cope with them, you need to understand them.

Fetching Conditions

The wind is only half of the equation in determining when it's going to be too rough for you and your boat. The other is the fetch or the distance the wind will blow over unobstructed water. A long fetch can create big waves, even on an inland lake with 15-knot winds, while a short fetch will prevent much stronger winds from making the water too rough for comfort.

Wave Formation

As wind blows over a beach or dirt parking lot, the friction at the surface lifts particles. Depending on the strength of the wind and the distance over which it remains in contact with the dusty surface, you'd expect proportionate amount of silt to be carried.

Chop

In this same way, wind blowing over water has friction with the water surface and lifts particles that evaporate and rise into clouds, or is visible in high winds as spray along the surface. On the other hand, water is different from grit. Being a liquid, water allows a wave motion to be set up. The dynamics of wind and water allow the water particles to advance in the direction of wind movement in tumbling circles.

The first sign that swell and waves will eventually result—hours later and miles downwind—is unevenness in water surface. This is called chop and is characterized by small, irregularly shaped peaks and valleys of water that may be from inches to a few feet in height between trough and peak.

Swell

The longer and stronger the wind keeps up the friction across the surface, the greater the tumbling and advancing energy of the individual molecules and the greater the resulting wave motion of the entire mass that all the molecules constitute.

When the fetch is sufficiently long, the wave motion sorts itself out into a more regular pattern, known as a swell. These swells then "march" in long lines over the oceans of the world. In addition, if a lake or other body of water is sufficiently large to allow for a decent fetch, waves will ultimately result there too.

In deep water—water with a depth at least four units deep for every three units of wave amplitude or height—the wave motion or swells move at around fifteen knots. However, when sea bottom becomes less than four units deep for every three units of wave height, the wave motion is stalled and slowed in the bottom traverse of its oscillation, and the top of the oscillation consequently overtakes it, resulting in the swell breaking into a wave.

Breaking Waves

Swell in itself provides little more than an unpleasant elevator ride up to a broad crest, a swoop down into the following trough, then up and down, repeated hour in and hour out. Not the most pleasant experience for the uninitiated.

Wind-collapsed waves

If the swell is accompanied by strong wind—as is the case near the Arctic Circles—the tops of each crest might become unstable and roll over, creating several feet of tumbling and angry surge atop each crest. In some extreme instances this whitewater might even be several feet high and thick, and not the place to be if you don't know what you're doing and don't have the right equipment.

True waves

A true breaking wave depends on the depth of the water. If the water depth gently decreases, the break is not too dramatic, and the wave simply crumbles from the top.

On the other hand, if the sea depth suddenly shallows—as is the case with blinder reefs and submerged rocks—the wave is suddenly halted and the resulting wave pitches over and breaks violently. The common term for such a wave is a breaker. It's characterized by a hollow and air-filled chamber that makes a thudding sound.

It's for reasons of violence that you don't want to be anywhere near a blind reef when there is swell around, as there is little warning to such a dangerous and violent occurrence. A cubic yard of water weighs around a ton; therefore, a three-foot section of a three-foot high wave traveling at a dozen knots will hit you with a force capable of sweeping crew into the water, seriously damaging equipment, and even sinking the vessel.

Remember the lessons on *assessing water depth* and keep an eye out for any swirls on the surface or lumping swells that might indicate that the swell is becoming a little large to be traveling through the depth of water. Often these physical changes in the water's surface profile indicate that a reef, sandbar, or rock pinnacle will shortly be the sight of breaking waves—either as a result of dropping tide or rising swell size.

Huge Waves

For truly massive waves to develop, you need steady, strong, and extended wind blowing over a large body of water. For this reason there's not an awful lot of good surf in the Mediterranean since there simply isn't enough distance and high enough wind speeds to impart its kinetic energy to the water. On the other hand, the Pacific is a massive body of water with more than enough wind bands and therefore generates the type of surf we see in Hawaii.

Sailors in History

Vitus Jonassen Bering (1680–1741)

A Danish navigator born in Horsens who explored the water routes between Siberia and North America, in 1728 Bering sailed from Kamchatka Peninsula and passed north through the Bering Strait into the Arctic Ocean, but failed to see the North American continent due to foul weather. In a 1741 voyage Bering sailed into the Gulf of Alaska and landed on Kayak Island. While returning, he and his crew were shipwrecked on an uninhabited island, where Bering died. The island was subsequently named Bering Island. His explorations proved that the Asian and North American continents are not joined. He was therefore honored with the strait that bears his name.

Extent

Once developed, large swells can extend laterally and run on for hundreds or thousands of miles, so that a large enough storm system deep in the south Pacific might spawn large swells and waves that will race by California some days later. With the advent of better climatology predictions and satellite application, predicting waves is quickly becoming quite an accurate science.

Danger zones

Another notable region for high surf is the frigid southern oceanic waters. These are constantly thrashed by hurricane force gales that blow for weeks over thousands of miles of open sea. The waves that they build are the infamous terrors early explorers faced when they rounded Cape Horn on the southern tip of South America and the Cape of Storms off South Africa. Colossal waves, some dozens of feet tall, were the stuff of nightmares for sailors in past centuries and remain so to this day.

Hurricane surf

Contrary to intuition, hurricanes do not produce particularly large waves. Rather, they produce storm surge, where a large volume of water is forced ashore that swamps communities and carries surprisingly massive vessels up into the most unlikely terrains. The reason for this is that hurricanes, although violent, are generally fairly localized storm systems as far as wave development is concerned.

Tsunami

By contrast, another violent localized event can trigger monumentally large waves. Quite wrongly termed "tidal waves," tsunami are associated with seismic activity and rush away from the epicenter of earthquakes and volcanic eruptions, traveling at enormous speeds that might well approach 500 mph. Again, surprisingly, a tsunami might be rather small out in the open ocean, and one could pass under your boat without your even realizing it. However, because of the speed, when a tsunami slams into shallower water, that entire 500-mph wave of energy has to go somewhere, so it goes upward. Without warning the wave will suck water back from

Mary Celeste, 1872

The *Mary Celeste* was an unlucky ship. Her first captain passed away within 48 hours of her original dedication under the name *Amazon*. Her maiden voyage found the ship suffering hull damage as a result of hitting a fishing weir. Although she later survived fire and a collision in the Straits of Dover that sank the other vessel involved, her fourth captain accidentally grounded her on Cape Breton Island. Eventually, the boat was salvaged, repaired, and renamed *Mary Celeste*.

The *Mary Celeste* was found abandoned at sea in 1872. Her crew had disappeared without a trace, leaving no indication as to where they'd gone or why they'd left the ship. The disappearance of the crew from an undamaged ship remains one of the most famous maritime mysteries.

The last entry in the general log of the *Mary Celeste* was dated November 25. She had sailed without crew for some nine days and travelled 700 miles northeast during the interim.

British investigating officials suspected a plot to scuttle the *Mary Celeste* in order to claim salvage fees. Another hypothesis for the ship's condition was a crew mutiny following a night of drinking, but the Admiralty eventually concluded both outcomes were unlikely.

Subsequent attempts to solve the riddle of the missing crew have been no more successful. Alien abduction is often bandied about.

However, because the mystery of the *Mary Celeste* remains unsolved, it continues to haunt the dreams of sea-faring men and women throughout the globe. Speculation aside, the name *Mary Celeste* endures as a true and tragic tale of the sea.

Physical Oceanography

Where do the highest tides occur?

In the Bay of Fundy, Nova Scotia, Canada. The difference between high and low tide may be as high as 53 feet.

• • •

What causes sea foam?

Sea foam is made of air bubbles separated by a film of liquid.

• • •

How high was the largest tsunami?

210 feet, recorded in 1737.

the shore and turn into a tower of water anywhere from perhaps ten feet high up to one hundred feet or more.

Although that is an awfully large wave with inestimable power, it's also so very rare that it's really not worth worrying about.

True tidal waves

Dictionaries define true tidal waves as being *"an unusual rise of water along the seashore, as from a storm or a combination of wind and spring tide."* These are not waves you want to face either, but at least they're not a real tsunami.

Mastering Tides

In terms of their effect on your happy or distressed sailing, tides aren't in the same league as wind and waves, but they're still important elements of sailing. In addition, they can conspire with the waves to create more havoc than you'd otherwise experience.

Technically Speaking

What are they?

Tides are the periodic vertical rises and falls of oceans that occur with two cycles per day—two high and two low tides—each spaced approximately six hours apart.

Where do they come from?

Tides are created by the gravitational pulls of the moon and the sun, either combining their strengths or canceling one another's strength. Water is literally attracted vertically toward the two forces, leaving us with "bumps" of water that follow the heavenly bodies through the water. These bumps are experienced as more vertical water and a consequent rise in the tide. Absolute high tide is reached when the bump of water travels directly through that region of ocean.

By contrast, at 90 degrees on the earth's surface to the bumps, water is relatively diminished and a trough is formed. This is experienced as a low tide.

Tidal Ranges

For a host of factors, tidal ranges—the difference between maximum and minimum high and low tides—differ considerably from from region to region. Some regions might only experience a one-foot range, while the distant extreme might approach fifty feet! That's either fifty feet of water where solid ground was six hours previously, or fifty feet of water where terra firma will be in just six hours, time.

For the sailor, a small tidal range is of little consequence, but large ranges could quite conceivably leave the unsuspecting skipper with his or her vessel literally lying high and dry.

In addition, many of these high-ranging zones are located in bays or enclosures with tight headlands. In order to fill and empty through these heads, tremendous surges of inward- or outward-bound waters flow with the strength of a river. Such enormous movements of water can be dangerous to any boater or swimmer.

Fortunately, tidal ranges and when they will occur are about the most predictable of all the sailing phenomena and therefore pose a reduced risk to mariners.

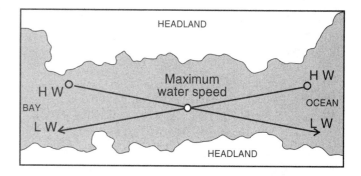

Headlands restrict water movement and cause a bay to lag behind ocean tides. Water accelerates between headlands as it rushes from relatively high to relatively low levels.

Heavenly conspiracy

Right across the gulf of space, the sun and moon's gravity causes the water of the oceans to bulge slightly toward these attracting bodies. On earth, we experience these "bulges" as high tides, and the resulting "hollows" between the bulges as low tides. When the sun and moon's pull is along the same vector, then the "bulge" or high tides—and resulting low tides—are most extreme.

A powerful moon

Although the sun's gravitational pull is several times that of the moon's, it's so very distant from us that its effect on the oceans is

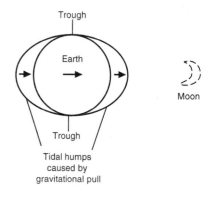

Moon Gravity Causes Tides

Boating Terminology

It's important to have an understanding of some basic boat terminology.

Aft—near or at the stern of the boat.

Beam—the width of a boat; also the direction at right angles to the centerline of a vessel.

Bilge—the lowest point of a boat's interior hull.

Bow—the forward part (toward the front) of a boat.

Draft—the vertical distance from the waterline to the lowest point of the keel; the minimum depth of water in which a vessel will float.

Forward—aboard a boat, the direction to the front, to the bow.

Freeboard—the vertical distance from the waterline to the gunwale.

Gunwale—the upper edge of the side of a boat.

Hull—the structural body of the boat; does not include superstructure, masts, or rigging.

Keel—the main structural member of a boat; its backbone; the lateral area beneath the hull that helps to provide stability and reduce the sideways drift of a boat.

PFD—personal flotation device (life jacket, vest, preserver).

Port—the left side of the boat.

Starboard—the right side of the boat.

Stern—the after (back or rear) portion of the boat.

Transom—the transverse part of the stern (where an outboard motor is attached).

Waterline—the intersection of a boat's hull and the water's surface.

USCG—the United States Coast Guard.

USPS—the United States Power Squadrons.

Types of Tides

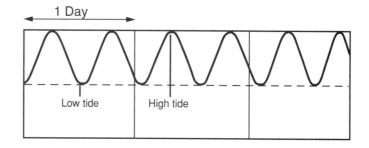

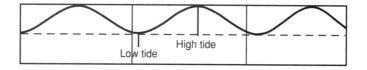

1. Semi-Diurnal Tide: Two high and two low tides every day

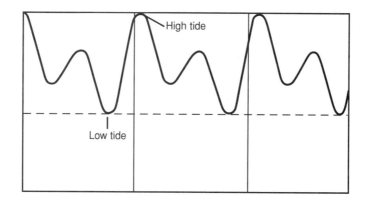

2. Diurnal Tide: One high and one low tide every day

3. Mixed Tide: Two high and two low tides per day
with great variation between them

**These tides vary from one part of the world to another
in realtion to the path the moon travels.**

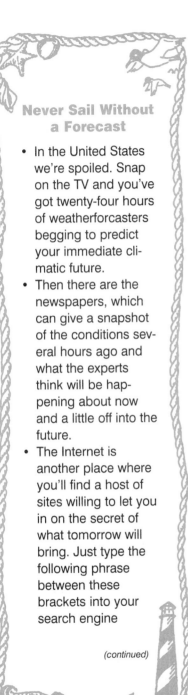

Never Sail Without a Forecast

- In the United States we're spoiled. Snap on the TV and you've got twenty-four hours of weatherforcasters begging to predict your immediate climatic future.
- Then there are the newspapers, which can give a snapshot of the conditions several hours ago and what the experts think will be happening about now and a little off into the future.
- The Internet is another place where you'll find a host of sites willing to let you in on the secret of what tomorrow will bring. Just type the following phrase between these brackets into your search engine

(continued)

relatively minimal. Consequently, the moon's gravitational pull on the oceans causes a bump that's larger than the one the sun causes, which results in a higher tide.

These days, most people are familiar with the fact that we circle the sun, while the moon circles us. The phases of the moon we observe from earth are therefore nothing but changing light and shadow effects from our perspective. To get a good image of it, view the earth as the apex of an angle defined by the sun and moon.

In practice, this is how it works

The strongest tides are during new and full moons when the sun and moon are aligned, while the weakest tides are at the moon quarter periods, when the moon is at a 90-degree angle to the gravitational vector of the sun. Because of the progression of the moon phases, today's high tide at noon will become a low tide at about noon seven days from now, and a high tide very close to noon once again fourteen days from now. The moon rotates around the earth not every twenty-four hours, but every twenty-four hours and fifty minutes. Thus the tidal periods are fifty minutes later each of our earth days.

Tidal Names

For safety sake, the extremes of tidal ranges that result from the heavenly conspiracy phenomenon need to be labeled.

Spring tides

The term spring has nothing to do with the season, since we have at least twenty-four of these tides per year—two per month. Spring tides are tides around new and full moons. They are the highest highs and lowest lows.

Neap tides

Neap tides are the least tidal range variance within the cycle. These are the tides associated with first and last quarters of the moon.

Seasonal variations

Tides do display some variation from summer to winter, but in sailing terms, this is generally not significant enough to worry about.

Wind-driven tides

As with hurricanes, wind can move water, so it does have the effect of canceling or exaggerating the natural tidal flow. Because wind occurrence and direction are unpredictable, their effect does create something of a limited wildcard to the tidal zone saga.

The predicted tides are based on the pull of the moon, sun, and earth, but they can't take into account the effect of winds. Winds can even create tides in fresh water.

Sea Level and Water Depth

With all this water height variation, it's interesting to note that altitude, as calculated against sea level, takes a mean average between high and low tides as the reference point.

Boaters rarely speak of sea level, but rather of sea surface, sea bottom, boat's draft (how much water it draws—how deeply in the water it sits and how much water depth needs to exist for it to pass safely), or sea depth—all-important concepts to relate to one another and termed *controlling depth* in combination. Controlling depth is therefore the maximum draft of a vessel that can pass over a given spot in a channel at mean low tide. For example, a vessel with a five-foot draft will go aground in a channel with a controlling depth of 4'11" at mean low tide.

Larger keelboats may require upward of five feet of controlling depth to keep their keel from grinding into the bottom. Knowledge of tide heights is thus critical for inshore navigation in all boats but especially keelboats.

Tide Tables to the Rescue

All over the world, marine authorities have long histories of tides and their ranges and continue to plot and predict their every move. In the United States, the National Ocean Service plots and

Never Sail Without a Forecast

of choice, and we guarantee you'll be swamped by the deluge of links you'll find: {+*"weather report"* +*"your region of interest"*}.

- If you're still not satisfied, consult your local telephone directory, and there's sure to be an audio weather-predicting service. And, quite possibly, you'll also find one for wind.
- Once aboard, press the WX-1, WX-2, or WX-3 buttons on your VHF to hear continuous broadcasts.

As you can see, there's really no reason you should ever be caught without some forewarning.

forecasts tidal height and current data. They also collate this information for locations around the world and make it available.

At home

If you mainly sail in your region, you'll begin to note the rhythm of the ebbs and flows, neaps and springs. To take the guesswork out of it, most bait shops, marinas, and other interested parties offer handy tidal charts for free that list local tides.

Away

When you venture far from home and cannot get ahold of local tables, the full-sized tables offer you the wonderful experience of converting data to arrive at conclusions for your region of interest.

Happily, computers are taking the torture out of the conversion process. Electronic tide charts such as *TideMaster* can take over the thankless task of pencil and calculator and predict tides well into the future to help with those all-important forays you're planning a year from now.

How to Treat the Tides

Like everything else on the water, treat tides with the utmost respect. Sure, they're generally slow and lazy, but they can also sneak up and cause the inattentive sailor plenty of anguish and discomfort.

If you must venture into shallow water, check out when high tide will be and then ride in very cautiously on the rising tide about halfway to full. To be on the safe side, check when the tide peaks and be sure that you vacate the area into deeper water not halfway to low tide, but do it a little early—at only one-third of the way to low tide.

For example: If full high is at noon, begin your approach at 9 a.m., and shift on out of the area by 2 p.m. If you do happen to run aground at 11 a.m., you'll still have an additional hour of flooding tide to refloat your little catastrophe.

Weather Proverbs

There is an awful lot of wisdom to old salt's proverbs. Learn to heed them well:

Red sky in the morning is the sailors warning.
Red sky in the night is a sailors delight.

Although a red sky at night may be a sailors delight, "orange or yellow can hurt a fellow." Clouds that turn these colors at sundown indicate excessive humidity moving in. Rain is likely and storms are possible.

Mackerel scales and mares' tails make tall ships carry low sails.

Anytime you see a black line of clouds approaching on the horizon, it's time to scuttle on home. If your craft is slow and the distance home great, the only alternative is to batten down the hatches, don your PFDs, rain gear, and life lines, and prepare for a bit of cabaret.

A low, black bank of clouds stretching from horizon to horizon is a *squall line*. They travel at up to a mile per minute, goading a gentle breeze into a tempest from one moment to the next. These can be vicious little creeps that spoil your whole day, and the nicest place to be when they bite is at home with soup on the boil.

Bridge clearance

The threats tides pose are not just from below. On a full tide, overhead obstructions become a very real danger. Apart from feeling a proper nitwit for de-masting your vessel on a bridge, it could also cost you a pretty penny.

The abbreviation BC applies to bridge clearance and indicates the vertical height between water surface and overhead obstructions.

Estuaries

Moon- and sun-induced bumps aside, water always tries to find its natural vertical equilibrium.

Naturally, because the water must physically flow in to flood the furthermost areas, it must make its way up from the opening to the sea. This has two effects:

- If the opening to the sea is narrow and the waterway inland is extensive, the volume of water passing in and out will be great and powerful, making it a dangerous place to navigate or linger.
- When measured at the mouth and at the furthermost reaches simultaneously, there can be a significant lag between high and low tide extremes with the high only reaching inland and emptying to full low long after the adjacent ocean and mouth experience their extreme.

Local publications and sources would generally inform you of the specifics of each region.

Unusual Water and Weather

Even in this day of alleged gender egalitarianism, the oceans and boats of the world retain the title "she." At the risk of offending where only amusement is intended, this is probably because these elements retain their inalienable right to change mood without too much warning. One moment you're drifting into a shallow sleep to the gentle slap of the chop against your hull, the next you're cowering under tall thunderclouds and clawing your way up a tempest-driven gargantuan swell.

Okay. So that is a little far-fetched, but you do get the picture—never, ever, put to sea unprepared for every eventuality—NEVER!

Under Pressure—Helter-Skelter for Shelter

Cast your mind back a few pages to where we discussed winds. Remember the explanations of pressure gradients and wind speeds? Well, when you spot the air pressure going south in a hurry, you're heading into a major low pressure. What does air do when it finds a low pressure? It rushes to fill it.

Rushing air is, of course, called wind, and, apart from being the stuff that makes sailing possible, excessive wind delivers some nasty by-products such as waves, rain, and storms.

Opposite to a plummeting barometer, and equally as scary, is a rocketing one. Although the worst bedfellows we associate with a low—rain and lightning—usually don't travel with a high, winds can be just as powerful. In either case, you'll probably want to skelter for shelter.

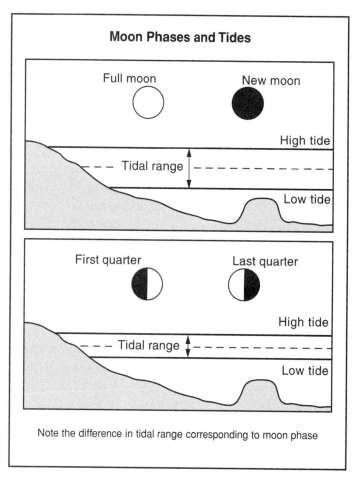

Moon Phases and Tides

Full moon

New moon

High tide

Tidal range

Low tide

First quarter

Last quarter

High tide

Tidal range

Low tide

Note the difference in tidal range corresponding to moon phase

An Instinct for Nasty Weather

Sometimes our "sixth sense" has its foundation in very real physics. You might not even realize it, but Uncle Jim's old and aching war wound that he swears by as a reliable forecaster of rain is just his injury's way of saying, "I feel the pressure changing."

If you're not blessed with a physical barometer such as a war wound to help you predict advancing lows, perhaps you should listen more carefully. You see, when clouds move in and moisture levels rise, sound travels better and further. If you hear a horn blowing miles away, you can be sure that rain is probably not far away.

Fronts

Although not unusual, fronts need to be mentioned as they can be harbingers of some nasty shifts in weather. Apart from usually being associated with dips in barometric pressure, fronts are what their name suggests—the leading edge of nasty weather that sweeps across a clear sky bringing bad weather in its wake.

Lightning

Lightning is upper air electrical charge with millions of volts looking for a way to the ground—or water, as the case may be. Lightning is typically associated with a thunderhead, an anvil-shaped cloud technically referred to as a *cumulonimbus* cloud. The direction that the anvil points will tell you the direction in which the storm is heading. These clouds can develop and move quite rapidly. Once you've spotted it on the horizon, it can be over you within an hour.

On land, we all know that a tree is a bad place to be under when lightning is possible. So, how much worse is it to be under a beautifully erected metal mast?

Not surprisingly, with little competition from the surrounding flat expanse of water, lightning can be a very unwelcome visitor that

might stretch way out from distant clouds and touch your vessel under clear skies.

The rule here is to get out of the way when thunderclouds are within five miles of you. Because this is sometimes impossible, at least get below decks and stay well away from all metals that may be grounded.

Unfortunately, the steering wheel is likely to be one of these no-no articles.

Wherever possible, haul down all vertical units such as fishing poles and antennas. Then, keep your head down. If your mast does get struck by lightning, provided you're not touching it, the charge should dissipate into the water directly through the grounding.

Waterspouts

Waterspouts are essentially tornadoes over water that can be dangerous for boats.

It doesn't need to be pointed out that taking a direct hit from one of these impressive beauties will tie your rigging in a knot. They certainly won't be hard to spot as their twenty- to hundred-foot-plus girths spiral down from low-hanging cumulonimbus clouds.

Boaters in the Keys might underestimate the dangers of waterspouts because they're so common. Waterspouts probably occur more frequently in the Florida Keys than anywhere in the world. Waters around the Keys see 400 or 500 waterspouts a year.

Many waterspouts hit the Florida Keys because the weather and geography supply two necessary ingredients. First, the islands and the shallow water around them help heat the air. During the summer (waterspout season) the air is extremely humid with temperatures from about 85°F/30°c to around 95°F/35°C. The heat causes the air to rise, and, as it rises, the air's humidity condenses into the tiny water droplets that make up clouds. As water vapor condenses, it releases more heat—making the air rise even faster. Rising air currents are needed for waterspout formation.

The second waterspout ingredient in the Keys seems to be the regular east or northeast trade winds that blow right down the islands. These winds help line up the clouds. Lines of clouds encourage waterspouts. Exactly how is one of the questions researchers are trying to answer.

Waterspouts are likely to form when the clouds are growing upward. In the Keys, waterspouts are most likely to form between 4 and 7 p.m. with a secondary maximum from 11 a.m. to 1 p.m. A few waterspouts form around sunrise.

After the Florida Keys, the next most active U.S. waterspout area is the southeast Florida Coast from around Stuart south to Homestead. Tampa Bay has the greatest number of damaging waterspouts, probably because the shores of the bay are so built up. Places around the Gulf of Mexico along with the Atlantic Coast northward to Chesapeake Bay are also likely to see waterspouts.

Waterspouts have been reported on the West Coast from Tatoohs Island, WA, south to San Diego, CA, but they tend to be weak and short-lived. Waterspouts also skip across the Great Lakes and Utah's Great Salt Lake from time to time.

Most Popular Names

According to the annual survey conducted by BOAT/U.S. (Boat Owners Association of The United States), the ten most popular boat names for 1998 were:

- Serenity
- Osprey
- Obsession
- Wind Dancer
- Therapy
- Destiny
- Fantasea
- Escape
- Odyssey
- Tide Runner

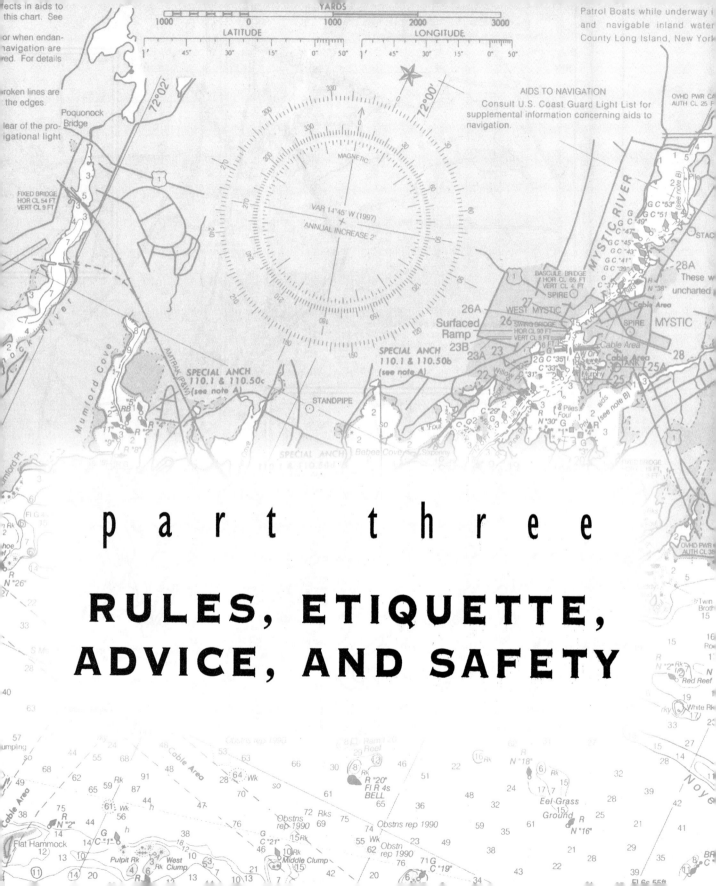

part three

RULES, ETIQUETTE, ADVICE, AND SAFETY

Now that we've had a taste of the good stuff, let's head back to the classroom and begin sweating again. Today's lesson: The Rules of the Road.

With so many boats involved in such diverse activities, the sea-lanes, byways, and estuaries could quickly become hazardous to your health and life if they were not properly managed. In response, collision avoidance regulations, or COLREGS, have been designed to set standards that everyone can understand and abide by. These are akin to DMV rules of the highway, such as keep right, obey signs, and observe speed limits.

Guess what? There are thousands of them, and they cover every eventuality the authorities could conceive of that might lead to collision. Although it's not necessary for you to commit them all to memory, you do need to have a working concept of the basic rules of safe operation.

General Observations

Good seamanship

What is good seamanship? It's a bit of a vague term, but the key issue here is that you keep one paramount goal in mind: You must keep the safety of your crew, your vessel, and all other persons or property that you might encounter foremost in your mind. Stay out of the way of other vessels and obey all stipulated laws, whether actively enforced or not.

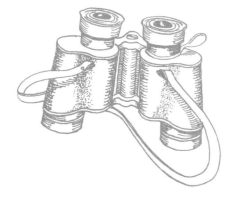

Proper lookout

Sailing is a team sport. Treat everyone aboard as members of the team and make them understand this concept.

The rules concerning lookout watch are very specific. It's a 360-degree, three-dimensional job. Watch for anything that the mast won't fit under, anything submerged that the boat and its keel won't sail over, and any object or person that the boat might hit. Also, watch out for signs that communicate restricted areas and people on shore or on another boat trying to get your attention.

Try to assign at least one but preferably two people to the task of maintaining high alert. Go so far as to split the crew and

Rules and Definitions

Again, we're in the pesky territory of nautical jargon, but, because these are governed by federal enforcement, it's necessary that you pay close attention to the official definition of terms. Every four years the International Sailing Federation (the ISAF, formerly, the International Yacht Racing Union or IYRU) revises and publishes the rules that govern the sport of sailboat racing, including the "right of way" rules.

The list that follows forms the basis of what you'll need to know:

- *Vessel*—Every craft of any description used or capable of being used on the water.
- *Power Driven Vessel (Motorboat)*—Any vessel propelled by machinery.
- *Sailing Vessel*—Any vessel under sail alone with no mechanical means of propulsion. (A sailboat propelled by machinery is a motorboat.)
- *Under way*—Not at anchor, aground, or attached to the dock or shore.
- *Danger Zone*—An arc of 112.5 degrees measured from dead ahead to just aft of the starboard beam.
- *Right-of-way*—The right and duty to maintain course and speed.
- *Stand-On Vessel*—The vessel that has the right-of-way.
- *Give-Way Vessel*—The vessel that must keep clear of the stand-on vessel.
- *Visible (when applied to lights)*—Visible on a dark, clear night.
- *Short Blast*—A blast of one to two seconds' duration.
- *Prolonged Blast*—A blast of four to six seconds' duration.

passengers into groups or watches and set periods with them whereby they understand that they'll be "on watch."

This is not an academic concept to be taken lightly. It can quite literally be the difference between life and death.

Sound Signals

Boats are required to produce sound signals at any time that they come into close quarters and believe there's a risk of collision. The law dictates that all boats less than 12 meters in length must carry an efficient sound-producing device which can be heard for one-half mile. Here again, the rules stipulate a precise procedure for signaling your intentions.

- One short blast—I intend to change course to starboard.
- Two short blasts—I intend to change course to port and will leave you to my starboard side.

Most often these are whistles or horns (airhorns) that can be purchased at any boating supply store. Boats over 12 meters (39.4 feet) in length must also carry a bell. The rules of the road, or in this case—water—both inland and internationally, specify that boats give sound signals to communicate intentions in heavy traffic, and to alert other skippers of your presence in fog, in heavy rain, or at other times of restricted visibility.

Meeting Situations

Vessels indicate their intention to maneuver by using sound signals.

When a sailor does not agree with or understand clearly what the other vessel's intentions are, he or she should sound the danger or doubt signal (5 short rapid blasts).

Each vessel should then slow or stop until signals for safe passing are sounded, understood, and agreed to.

The danger or doubt signal can also be used to tell another vessel that its action is dangerous. If a boat is backing up into an obstruction, you would sound the danger signal to warn the operator.

The first responsibility of a skipper is the safety of his ship and of his people.
—Charles F. Chapman

• • •

The sea never changes, and its works, for all the tales of men, are wrapped in mystery.
—Joseph Conrad

• • •

Yachting teaches humility to the mighty.

—Anonymous

In order to reduce confusion, we have quoted the rules as they are given by The Inter-Governmental Maritime Consultative Organization.

Definitions

- The term "short blast" means a blast of about one second's duration.
- The term "prolonged blast" means a blast of from four to six seconds' duration.

Equipment for sound signals

- A vessel of 12 meters or more in length shall be provided with a whistle and a bell and a vessel of 100 meters or more in length shall, in addition, be provided with a gong, the tone and sound of which cannot be confused with that of the bell. The bell or gong or both may be replaced by other equipment having the same respective sound characteristics, provided that manual sounding of the prescribed signals shall always be possible.
- A vessel of less than 12 meters in length shall not be obliged to carry the sound signaling appliances prescribed in paragraph (a) of this Rule but if she does not, she shall be provided with some other means of making an efficient sound signal.

Maneuvering and warning signals

When vessels are in sight of one another, a power-driven vessel underway, when maneuvering as authorized or required by these Rules, shall indicate that maneuver by the following signals on her whistle:

- One short blast to mean "I am altering my course to starboard"
- Two short blasts to mean "I am altering my course to port"
- Three short blasts to mean "I am operating astern propulsion"

A vessel intending to overtake another shall indicate her intention by the following signals on her whistle/horn:

- Two prolonged blasts followed by one short blast to mean "I intend to overtake you on your starboard side"
- Two prolonged blasts followed by two short blasts to mean "I intend to overtake you on your port side"

   The vessel about to be overtaken shall indicate her agreement by the following signal on her whistle/horn:

- One prolonged, one short, one prolonged and one short blast, in that order.

When vessels in sight of one another are approaching each other and from any cause either vessel fails to understand the intentions or actions of the other, or is in doubt whether sufficient action is being taken by the other to avoid collision, the vessel in doubt shall immediately indicate such doubt by giving at least five short and rapid blasts on the whistle. Such signal may be supplemented by a light signal of at least five short and rapid flashes.

- A vessel nearing a bend or an area of a channel or fairway where other vessels may be obscured by an intervening obstruction shall sound one prolonged blast. Such signal shall be answered with a prolonged blast by any approaching vessel that may be within hearing around the bend or behind the intervening obstruction.
- If whistles are fitted on a vessel at a distance apart of more than 100 meters, one whistle only shall be used for giving maneuvering and warning signals.

Sound signals in restricted visibility

In or near an area of restricted visibility, whether by day or night, the signals prescribed in this Rule shall be used as follows:

- A power-driven vessel making way through the water shall sound at intervals of not more than 2 minutes one prolonged blast.

- A power-driven vessel underway but stopped and making no way through the water shall sound at intervals of not more than 2 minutes two prolonged blasts in succession with an interval of about 2 seconds between them.
- A vessel not under command, a vessel restricted in her ability to maneuver, a vessel constrained by her draught, a sailing vessel, a vessel engaged in fishing and a vessel engaged in towing or pushing another vessel shall, instead of the signals prescribed in paragraphs (a) or (b) of this Rule, sound at intervals of not more than 2 minutes three blasts in succession, namely one prolonged followed by two short blasts.
- A vessel engaged in fishing, when at anchor, and a vessel restricted in her ability to maneuver when carrying out her work at anchor, shall instead of the signals prescribed in paragraph (g) of this Rule sound the signal prescribed in paragraph (c) of this Rule.
- A vessel towed or if more than one vessel is towed the last vessel of the tow, if manned, shall at intervals of not more than 2 minutes sound four blasts in succession, namely one prolonged followed by three short blasts. When practicable, this signal shall be made immediately after the signal made by the towing vessel.
- When a pushing vessel and a vessel being pushed ahead are rigidly connected in a composite unit they shall be regarded as a power-driven vessel and shall give the signals prescribed in paragraphs (a) and (b) of this Rule.
- A vessel at anchor shall at intervals of not more than one minute ring the bell rapidly for about 5 seconds. In a vessel of 100 meters or more in length the bell shall be sounded in the forepart of the vessel and immediately after the ringing of the bell the gong shall be sounded rapidly for about 5 seconds in the after part of the vessel. A vessel at anchor may in addition sound three blasts in succession, namely one short, one prolonged and one short blast, to give warning of her position and of the possibility of collision to an approaching vessel.

Women Pirates

Anne Bonny (Irish-born pirate, active 1720s)

Anne joined Captain Calico Jack Rackham while posing as a man. There she met Mary Read.

In 1720 her ship was attacked by a British Navy sloop off of Jamaica. She fought like the rest of the pirates, but was captured as was her fellow pirate Read. Bonny also escaped trial due to pregnancy, but there is no trace of her fate after her capture.

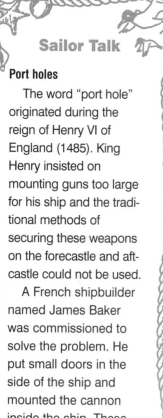

Sailor Talk

Port holes

The word "port hole" originated during the reign of Henry VI of England (1485). King Henry insisted on mounting guns too large for his ship and the traditional methods of securing these weapons on the forecastle and aftcastle could not be used.

A French shipbuilder named James Baker was commissioned to solve the problem. He put small doors in the side of the ship and mounted the cannon inside the ship. These doors protected the cannon from weather and were opened when the cannon were to be used. The French word for "door" is "porte" which was later Anglicized to "port" and later went on to mean any opening in the ship's side, whether for cannon or not.

- A vessel aground shall give the bell signal and if required the gong signal prescribed in paragraph (g) of this Rule and shall, in addition, give three separate and distinct strokes on the bell immediately before and after the rapid ringing of the bell. A vessel aground may in addition sound an appropriate whistle signal.
- A vessel of less than 12 meters in length shall not be obliged to give the above-mentioned signals but, if she does not, shall make some other efficient sound signal at intervals of not more than 2 minutes.
- A pilot vessel when engaged on pilotage duty may in addition to the signals prescribed in paragraphs (a), (b) or (g) of this Rule sound an identity signal consisting of four short blasts.

Distress signals

The following signals, used or exhibited either together or separately, indicate distress and need of assistance:

- A gun or other explosive signal fired at intervals of about a minute;
- A continuous sounding with any fog-signaling apparatus;
- Rockets or shells, throwing red stars fired one at a time at short intervals;
- A signal made by radiotelegraphy or by any other signaling method consisting of the group . . . - - - . . . (SOS) in the Morse Code;
- A signal sent by radiotelephony consisting of the spoken word "Mayday";
- A signal consisting of a square flag having above or below it a ball or anything resembling a ball;
- Flames on the vessel (as from a burning tar barrel, oil barrel, etc.);
- A rocket parachute flare or a hand-flare showing a red light;
- A smoke signal giving off orange-colored smoke;
- Slowly and repeatedly raising and lowering arms outstretched to each side;
- The radiotelegraph alarm signal;

- The radiotelephone alarm signal;
- Signals transmitted by emergency positioning-indicating radio beacons;
- Approved signals transmitted by radio communication systems, including survival craft radar transponders.

The use or exhibition of any of the foregoing signals except for the purpose of indicating distress and need of assistance and the use of other signals which may be confused with any of the above signals is prohibited.

Attention is drawn to the relevant sections of the International Code of Signals, the Merchant Ship Search and Rescue Manual and the following signals:

- a piece of orange-coloured canvas with either a black square and circle or other appropriate symbol (for identification from the air);
- a dye marker.

Sailing Craft

Sailing craft and boats propelled by oars or paddles have the right-of-way over power-driven vessels. An exception to this is if the sailing craft or self-propelled vessel is passing a power-driven vessel. In an overtaking situation, the overtaking vessel is the give-way vessel, even if it is not propelled by an engine.

Commercial Vessel Situations

If at all possible stay out of areas where there is commercial vessel traffic such as shipping lanes or traffic separation zones. Large ships and barges have special problems in maneuvering and cannot and will not get out of your way.

If you must operate around commercial vessels take heed of the following:

- Avoid ship channels. If you must cross, do so at right angles and as quickly as possible.
- Be alert. Watch for traffic.

- Be seen, especially at night.
- Know the sound signals, especially the danger or doubt signal.
- Keep your VHF radio tuned to channel 16 and listen carefully.
- Order all aboard to wear PFDs (lifejackets).
- Be familiar with the area and have current navigation charts.
- Don't be a non survivor of a collision with a large ship.

Restricted Visibility

When operating at night, or at other times of restricted visibility, the required navigation lights as set forth in the required equipment section are mandatory to be displayed. The lights themselves will let each vessel know which is the stand-on or give-way vessel and each vessel should react accordingly.

During night time operations vision can be tricky at best, so a proper lookout and safe speed need constant attention.

During times of restricted visibility such as smoke or fog, additional sound signals are required. Both inland and international rules require that any vessel under way in or near a restricted visibility area sound a warning signal every two minutes.

Motorboats must sound one prolonged blast every two minutes. Sailing vessels must sound one prolonged blast plus two short blasts every two minutes. When a power-driven vessel is stopped (under way but making no way) she shall sound two prolonged blasts every two minutes. Vessels at anchor shall sound rapid strokes on the bell for 5 seconds at intervals not less than one minute (however, if your vessel is less than 65 feet and you are anchored in a designated "special anchorage" you do not need to sound these signals). Vessels aground shall sound three distinct strokes on the bell ("I Am Aground"), followed by five seconds rapid ringing of the bell, followed by three distinct strokes on the bell ("I Am Aground").

Here again, the rules stipulate a precise procedure for signaling your intentions.

- *One short blast*—I intend to change course to starboard.
- *Two short blasts*—I intend to change course to port and will leave you to my starboard side.

- *One long blast*—I'm getting under way; used when leaving dock.
- *Three short blasts*—I'm backing up under power.
- *One long blast followed by one short blast*—Please open the drawbridge.
- *Five or more short and rapid blasts*—Danger or doubt signal; I don't understand your intent—then hold your station or take appropriate evasive action if necessary.

Note: Inland rules use sound signals to indicate intent to maneuver. In international rules, the signals are given when the maneuver is being executed.

The other vessel should repeat what he or she heard to confirm. If the other vessel does not repeat, he or she either didn't hear or doesn't understand horn signaling at all.

If you hear five short blasts, it means danger or that he or she didn't understand your intentions. In either case, halt and review the situation before proceeding.

Maneuvering

Because there are different-sized vessels traveling on every compass heading possible, each powered by a wide variety of vastly different methods with its own intrinsic capacity for handling, it's necessary to stipulate how each must act when it encounters the other.

Study the list that follows, because it forms the very basis of good seamanship.

Signaling intentions

We've looked at the mechanics of signaling with sound, now let's consider the interpretation as it applies to all parties.

So, you're sailing along and another vessel sounds a signal that you either do not understand or disagree with. Respond immediately by sounding your doubt or danger signal—five rapid, short blasts. Every vessel in the vicinity should now slow and stop until the signal for safe passage is sounded, understood, and agreed with.

Famous Sailors

Captian Joshua Slocum, *"America's best-known sailor"*

Departing Boston and arriving in Newport, Rhode Island, at the age of 51, between April 24, 1895, and June 27, 1898, Captain Joshua Slocum became the first man to achieve solo circumnavigation. His book, *Sailing Alone Around the World,* became an instant best seller and made Joshua the patron saint of small-boat voyagers and adventurers.

The epic tale has been translated into several languages and remains in print today. His vessel *Spray*, which he rebuilt himself from a derelict hull, has been copied by hundreds of boat builders worldwide.

You can also use the danger signal like a car's horn—to communicate to another vessel that they're in danger, as would be the case if they were to back up and were likely to strike an obstruction.

A vessel intending to overtake another shall indicate her intention by the following signals on her whistle/horn:

- Two prolonged blasts followed by one short blast to mean "I intend to overtake you on your starboard side"
- Two prolonged blasts followed by two short blasts to mean "I intend to overtake you on your port side"
    The vessel about to be overtaken shall indicate her agreement by the following signal on her whistle/horn:
- One prolonged, one short, one prolonged and one short blast, in that order.

When it's established and communicated who the give-way vessel is, the stand-on vessel should maintain its course and speed while the give-way vessel takes evasive action by staying well clear. In the event that the actions taken by the give-way vessel are either not sufficient or dangerous, the stand-on vessel must take whatever safe actions it can in order to avoid collision.

Head-On Meetings

When vessels approach on a head-on or near head-on course, either vessel shall indicate its intent to the other vessel, and the reply must be prompt. In a meeting situation neither vessel is the stand-on vessel.

The rule of the sea is that vessels always give way to starboard. In the head-on scenario, this means that the vessels should try to pass port to port, that is, keep right as you would if the water were a highway.

Okay. But how far to starboard does this rule extend? To be absolutely specific, the rules read that a boat 112.5 degrees or less off the starboard bow has the right of way. In addition, beyond the law it's common courtesy for large boats to slow down when passing small sailboats and rowboats to avoid swamping them with their wake.

Overtaking

When a vessel approaches from astern and wishes to pass, it must signal. The overtaking vessel is then the give-way vessel and must keep clear of the vessel it's passing. The vessel being overtaken is the stand-on vessel and must therefore maintain its speed and course. If the stand-on vessel assesses that the course intended by the give-way vessel is not safe, it must sound the danger or doubt signal.

If you're the overtaking vessel, understand that you're the give-way vessel until you're well past and safely clear of the stand-on vessel. Do not cut in front, impede, or endanger any other vessel anywhere in the vicinity.

Crossing

When two vessels driven by power are approaching at right angles, or nearly so, and there's a risk of collision, then the vessel to starboard is the stand-on vessel and must hold its course and speed. The other vessel is the give-way vessel and must take appropriate action that will keep it clear of the stand-on vessel, only proceeding when the stand-on vessel has passed, cutting its wake. If necessary, slow, or halt, until the stand-on vessel is entirely clear.

Sailing Craft

Remember the rule that power gives way to sail? Well, this is it. Sailing craft and boats propelled by oars or paddles have the right-of-way over power-driven vessels. An exception to this is if the sailing craft or self-propelled vessel is passing a power-driven vessel. In such an overtaking situation, the overtaking vessel is the give-way vessel, *even if it's not propelled by an engine*.

Commercial Vessel Situations

Wherever possible, stay away from well-trafficked areas where you'd anticipate commercial boating activity. These include: shipping lanes, commercial harbors and environs, and navigable rivers and estuaries. Ships and large barges are very difficult to maneuver and cannot be expected to get out of your way. And, if you're unlucky enough to meet by accident, guess who's going to win?

Examples of Horn Communication

Inland Rules

- "I intend to pass you on your port side"—two short blasts (one second)
- "Agreement"—two short blasts (one second)

International Rules

- "I intend to pass you on your port side"—two prolonged blasts/two short.

Inland Rules

- "I intend to pass you on your starboard side"—one short blast (one second)
- "Agreement"—one short blast (one second)
- "I intend to pass you on your starboard side"—two prolonged blasts/one short.

If you've got no option but to venture into the path of commercial activity, be very aware of the following points. In a nutshell, treat shipping channels the way you'd treat railway lines:

- Ensure you're familiar with the current navigational charts for the area.
- If you must cross them, do so perpendicularly and with haste.
- Know your sound signals intimately, especially the doubt or danger signal.
- Ensure you're highly visible, especially at night.
- Crank the volume up on your VHF radio and tune it to channel 16.
- Be extremely alert and keep a constant watch for traffic.
- Everyone aboard must don their PFDs.

Restricted Visibility

An inability to see your surroundings and be seen is one of the most hazardous predicaments any sailor can experience. In order to be safe as possible in these situations, standard operating procedure has developed a system of signals that can compensate to some degree for a skipper and crew's inability to assess visual clues.

Under these circumstances it's mandatory that the appropriate signals be executed.

Night operation

Night operation is the first and most obvious area to cover. When anyone operates a vessel at night there are standard navigational stipulations that govern how and where lights must be displayed and what color they should be.

The color and configuration of lights communicate which vessels are stand-on and which

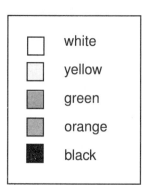

	white
	yellow
	green
	orange
	black

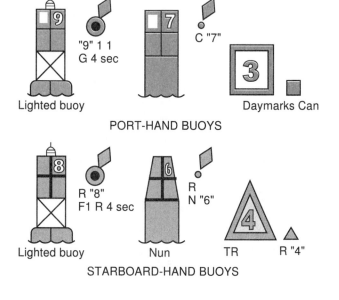

Lighted buoy

PORT-HAND BUOYS

Daymarks Can

Lighted buoy   Nun   TR

STARBOARD-HAND BUOYS

are give-way vessels, and, consequently, how each should act.

Because lights in and of themselves don't provide the same visual clues as to vessel speeds and precise heading, each skipper and crew needs to closely monitor their own speed and safe passage with even greater diligence.

Fog and smoke

By definition, although lights are mandatory under fog, smoke, and other visually restrictive conditions, their effectiveness is drastically reduced. To compensate, international rules for both sea and inland sailing dictate that a warning horn needs to be sounded every two minutes. No confusion should arise with communications horns since, within context, when fog and mist are present, sailors will be attuned and listening for the "prolonged" horn—the signals given for communication are short and occasionally long, but not "prolonged."

To differentiate power from sail vessels, motorboats sound a single prolonged blast, while sailing craft follow one prolonged blast with two short blasts.

A halted and drifting powerboat must sound two prolonged blasts every two minutes.

Anchored vessels must sound five seconds of rapid bell strokes with intervals of not less than one minute.

Vessels that are aground must sound three distinct strokes on the bell—communicating I Am Aground—followed by five seconds of rapid ringing. This pattern must be constantly repeated in that order.

Vessels sixty-five feet or less that are anchored in designated special anchorage areas do not need to sound these signals.

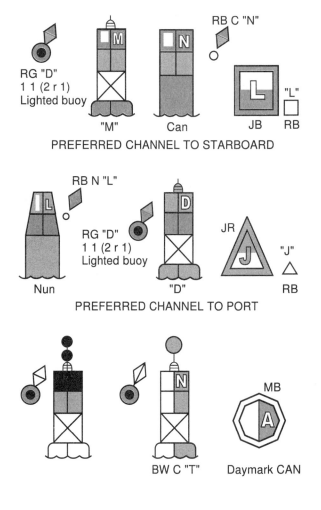

RG "D"
1 1 (2 r 1)
Lighted buoy

"M"   Can   JB   RB

RB C "N"

"L"

PREFERRED CHANNEL TO STARBOARD

RB N "L"

RG "D"
1 1 (2 r 1)
Lighted buoy

JR

"J"

Nun   "D"   RB

PREFERRED CHANNEL TO PORT

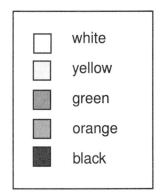

MB

BW C "T"   Daymark CAN

□	white
□	yellow
▨	green
▨	orange
■	black

Permanent and semi-permanent hazards

The sea is full of hidden surprises, and a lot of them can be very nasty and expensive. Chief culprits are rock pinnacles, reefs, and blinders where waves might suddenly break with no warning.

We're fortunate to live in a time when, through trial, error, and painstaking plodding, our forebears have charted most of these nasty fixtures that lie in wait for unsuspecting sailors. In U.S. waters the Coast Guard has spent decades plotting these onto charts and marking them with structures and anchored buoys. These are the warning signposts of the sea, and they are coded in order that you can make intelligent decisions as to how you should proceed in safety through that region.

Although not authorized to do so, private citizens are known to place their own markers. These might be as simple as a stick with a piece of bright fabric wrapped around it. Trouble is, how do you react to this nondescript snippet of information? As you can guess, these markers by well-meaning citizens cannot always be trusted for their accuracy, and it's best to proceed extra cautiously whenever you come across something that would resemble such an indicator.

Decoding the Rules

As stated, official markers speak a language of their own, one that must be learned if it's to be understood. As with traffic lights on our roads, red and green are marine colors also; On the sea, however, they do not mean stop and go.

The two systems for marking the waterways of the United States are:

- U.S. Aids to Navigation (USATONS) or the International System (IALA-B)
- The Uniform State Waterway Marking System (USWMS)

Color codes

The system used for sailing is called the lateral buoyage system, as it demarcates the safest channel. The basic rule when returning to shore is:

- Pass red markers on your starboard side and green markers on your port side.

- Proceeding inland you'll see that red markers are associated with even numbers, while green markers are associated with odd numbers. The easiest way to commit this to memory is with a silly alliteration: *Red, Right—Returning, Even* or *RRRE. Green, Port—Odd, Entering* or *GPOE.*

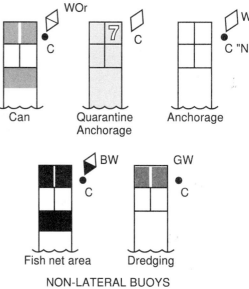

Can

Quarantine Anchorage

Anchorage

Even more confusing you might wish to use; *RRR2, GP12.* In English this translates loosely to—red begins with the numeral 2 and green begins with numeral 1.

Not all markers necessarily have red or green lights for night navigation. As you'd expect, ICWs or Intracoastal Waterways usually are quite well lighted, whereas local harbors sometimes only light their outermost markers, with one or two of the more dangerous paths en route illuminated. Unless you know the channel and have sailed it many times before under the cover of darkness, inch forward at slow speed, cautiously picking out the upcoming markers in the ambient light or with a spotlight before proceeding onward.

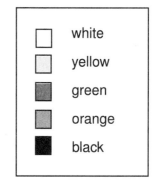

Fish net area

Dredging

NON-LATERAL BUOYS

These navigational features are marked on current charts of any navigable area. If they're unlighted, they're termed *beacons*; if lighted, they're *lights*; they're *buoys* if floating.

☐	white
☐	yellow
◪	green
◪	orange
■	black

Interpreting a chart

Entering from sea, the first marker you see is the open, or safe water, marker. The RW "G" means that it's a red and white striped marker with the letter G on it.

At night and during restricted visibility, a lighted marker flashes. The next marker you'll encounter as you proceed into the waterway is the G "1" Fl G 4 sec. This communicates that it's green, has the number 1 on it, and it flashes green once each 4 seconds.

R N "2" plus the red symbol indicates a red nun buoy with the even number 2 on it. Conversely G C "3," is a green can buoy with the odd number 3 on it.

When traveling from the sea you come across two channels, which separate into different directions. An RGN "C," or junction marker, codes the top color as the major or primary channel. This is represented by a red and green nun buoy, which in this case has a C on it. If your intention is to follow the primary channel, you then consider the uppermost color and shape as a stand-alone marker. In this instance, leave the red nun to the right.

Shape codes

When mist is down, you can often spot an outlined shape easier than a color. To assist you in safe passage, the shape of a marker can also communicate its function.

There's no guarantee that these shapes will be in use, but there are enough of them around to make it worth mentioning.

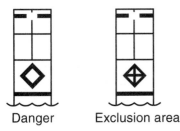

Danger   Exclusion area

UNLIGHTED BUOYS

- Green buoys are generally cylindrical like a can, and therefore loosely termed *can buoys*.
- Red buoys are generally conical, with the point uppermost like a nun's hat. This outline has earned them the term *nun buoys.*

Posts atop buoys mark GPOE with a square, while RRRE uses a triangle.

Offshore buoys

These are usually taller than can or nun buoys and sport bells, gongs, whistles, or lights. Their shape is not significant, but their color is. The mournful clang or groan these lonely castaways make when visibility is down to nothing can save all kinds of heartache by giving you a reference point and warning you of a hidden danger.

Of course, under hazardous conditions the markers can be dangers in themselves. When sailing blind and in their vicinity, slow to a crawl and put all hands on alert with all engines ready to back you up or race you out of trouble. Maintain as much quiet as you can, and let your ears be your early warning system.

Seaward headings

On your way down a river, or out to sea and away from land, the color, number, and shape system works in reverse. Now, of course, keep the even-numbered red markers on the port side, and odd-numbered green or black markers on the starboard beam.

Special situations

In situations where channels run parallel to the coast and confusion might arise regarding seaward versus landward travel, the authorities have designated which is which. Looking at the map of the U.S. coast and proceeding in a clockwise direction, the red marker is always on the landward side.

Inland buoys

The Uniform State Waterway Marking System (USWMS) has been adopted by all states. It's the same as the lateral system, however, black is substituted for green in the GPOE system. In addition, the shapes of buoys have no meaning and all are cans.

White cans are your directions. They have orange borders and symbols and use black lettering to communicate submerged hazards, speed, directions, or warn of swimmers.

Give Way to Starboard

As we learned earlier, as with driving, we keep right and pass other oncoming vessels with our port side to their port side. To do so you may have to alter your course slightly to starboard. Obviously you don't go out of your way and steam half a mile to starboard in order to follow this rule. Treat it as though it's a keep right rule in an open shopping mall parking lot. If you're within proximity, you adjust to starboard.

However, there are times that this becomes difficult or even impossible. Say there's a rock or marker to starboard, what now?

Bring your vessel to dead slow and signal danger by blowing five short bursts on your horn.

Too many boaters seem to fall into bad habits and use their horns like they do their car horns—they don't bother to signal the danger, instead they use it as chastisement in lieu of or in addition to a foul hand signal. This is neither correct nor a good idea.

Earlier in the text, when exploring sound signals, we reviewed the six basic horn signals. Now it's time to understand how boaters should react.

Seaquakes

Rarely ever discussed, the word *seaquake* was coined in the 1880s by Eberhart Rudolph, Professor of Geophysics at the University of Strassburg in Germany.

The unlucky sailor who ever encounters one of these anomalies would experience a sudden shuddering of the vessel, enormous spouts or bubbling columns of water, and seriously damaged hull and equipment below decks.

One sighting occurred on 12 January 1878 when observers saw " the sea thrown up to a great height, possibly 80 feet or more, in a column; this occurred 3 to 4 times, each upheaval lower than the one before…"

Thankfully, these mysteries are exceedingly rare and unlikely to ever be encountered.

Night Lights

As mentioned, all boats operating at night need to be lighted, and not arbitrarily so but to a set system of coding so that other vessels can understand their approximate type and heading with just one glance.

Small boats often have a single running light at the bow, with two lenses showing red to the port side and green to the starboard side. Larger vessels have more expensive separate lights showing red and green to port and starboard, respectively. These lights are adjusted so that they split their beams precisely on the heading and to 112.5 degrees angle back from dead ahead.

Powerboats of less than forty feet usually have a single white light over their stern that is visible from 360 degrees around. Larger vessels restrict their white stern light to an angle of 135 degrees around the stern.

Armed with this knowledge, if you see a white light at night, it's heading away from you and is not a danger. However, if you see either red or green, you can guess at its general direction to you. If you see the light periodically alternating from red to green, the boat is headed your way—just hope it's not a big one!

Vessels that are longer than forty feet are required to show a masthead light situated forward of the stern light. In addition, this light must be more than 8.2 feet above the gunwales and be limited in its visible arc to 225 degrees ahead of the bow. Sailboats can also display a green light below a red light on their mast.

When at anchor, all small boats are required to show a white light to the full 360 degrees. This can either be its stern light or its masthead light.

Navigation
Which Way Is Home?

On land we use landmarks as reference points. However, there are no such things as "seamarks," unless they're actually pieces of terra firma real estate—such as a rock pinnacle—visible at sea. With more than 70 percent of the globe's surface covered by water, there are huge areas of sea that have no form of land nearby so our

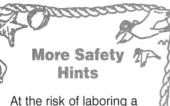

More Safety Hints

At the risk of laboring a necessary point: My late granddad, whose gritty and self-taught knowledge of the sea put food on the family table through the worst years of the great depression, always repeated one mantra: "Play *on* the water, never *with* the water."

- Never tow anything or anybody across the path of oncoming boats or ships.
- Big ships move a lot faster than you think—let me emphasize that—a *LOT* faster.
- Passing ships don't leave wakes, they leave WAVES! Stay out of their path at least 350 feet.
- Even miles away, ship waves are enough to send fast-moving boats airborne.

coastal waters are more like the oases of the oceans. Naturally, under some circumstances sailors don't intend to be out of sight of land; it just happens. Consider a sudden gale blowing up from the land, or the very common sea mist that reduces visibility and sun-referencing opportunity to nil. Without equipment to bolster your reduced perceptive senses, every direction you sail appears to be pretty much the same—whether there's a deadly reef only a quarter mile away or absolutely nothing for four thousand miles.

Today, thanks to improvements in sailing techniques, well-charted weather patterns and charts, and the safety net of a well-trained Coast Guard, it's unlikely you'll ever accidentally be out of sight of land. However, early explorers were not so fortunate, and countless of them paid in a very real sense with their lives for the equipment we can buy today.

Consider the navigation equipment we place aboard our boats like portable road signs and our own private landmarks. Understanding their use and application takes practice and requires experience. Because navigation is the basis of any safe journey, this is not a subject that you can learn haphazardly by trial-and-error. To be properly competent, you'll need to enroll in a school that teaches practical hands-on navigation. This section is only intended to offer you the most meager overview of the subject and should not be considered in any way to be definitive or comprehensive.

Aids to Navigation

Between satellites and computers, technology has delivered the art of navigation to just about anybody. For a relative pittance, you can buy a handheld GPS (global positioning system) that'll tell you where in the world you are to within a few feet. Having seen how quickly this revolution has occurred, and noting that there's no sign of the trend slowing anytime soon, we can only imagine what will be available within the next decade.

However, and we hate to be naysayers, but do note that we didn't say technology has delivered *safe* navigation. Don't get us wrong, we're not saying that the results these modern instruments

compass

deliver are in any way inaccurate or questionable. But, sailing is a watery pastime, and water and electronics are not the best of friends.

Besides, even in this sophisticated twenty-first century, we can be certain that we'll continue to have dead batteries, loose wiring, and blown fuses. So when the crisis of failing modern equipment strikes, it's suddenly back to basics. For this reason, let's take a few moments to consider the old tried-and-trusted systems for navigation and the skills you'll need if you're to implement them.

The compass

Most people should be fairly familiar with the compass and its attraction to point at the magnetic north pole. Thus far in history, and to the best of our knowledge and research, the magnetic North Pole's batteries have never quit and there have been absolutely no blown fuses. So the compass has and must always remain at the core of your navigational quest.

Because a compass relies entirely on the earth's relatively weak magnetic fields, and because our modern world is filled with magnetically strong sources—such as steel and electrical fields—a compass has to be properly and professionally mounted and accurately calibrated in order to compensate for interference.

A rule of thumb is that the larger the compass, the easier it is to get more accurate readings. Depending on the quality of the compass, expect to pay anywhere from $40 to over $1000.

The *compass card* is a free-pivoting card inside the compass that marks the geographic directions.

A *lubber line* is a line on the forward part of the compass housing or dome that is aligned with the keel and used for sighting. Thus, when the card aligns the 180 marking with the lubber line, your heading is due south.

Variable variation

There's one small problem with relying on an uncalibrated compass reading, but it's relatively easily compensated for. Year in and year out, charts are drawn with meridian lines that never alter and always form a grid around geographic north.

However, magnetic north is a little more fickle and likes to wander around, never staying at one fixed physical location. The further away you are from magnetic north, the less it affects you, but the closer you come to this wandering point, the more radical must be the compensation factor you apply. In California you'll find a deviation of around 10 degrees, while up near Maine the figure is closer to 20 degrees. Fortunately, charts make provision for this altering shift and print details of how much deviation you should allow.

The difference between the geographic and magnetic north is known as *variation*. On shorter voyages, variation is relatively insignificant, but the longer the journey, the more it becomes a factor that could throw your course off by hundreds of miles and, consequently, have you reading charts that don't show the true dangers, like reefs, that lie in your path.

When sailing on the East Coast, add the degree of error to your compass reading and plot it accordingly on a chart. On the West Coast, subtract the amount of error from your compass reading. A little rhyme we use is a corruption of another used for plotting, "On the East, compass least. On the West, compass best."

Deviation

Remember the note on calibration of the compass to compensate for magnetic interference? Well, what this interference does to the compass is called *deviation*. Though a professional can mount the compass with minimum deviation, there's no way to completely eliminate it.

The amount of deviation your compass experiences is not affected by your locations, but your boat's heading will affect it. In order to compensate, place the boat on a known heading, then take bearings on a distant marker and record the deviation the compass is experiencing. This is best conducted by someone who knows what they're doing and can show you in a hands-on scenario.

In addition, it won't help you to have your compass carefully calibrated and isolated and then lay a great big chunk of iron or an electricity-emitting object right next to it.

When steering your boat, you'll only know you're going off course when you've gone off course. In order to stay on course, put yourself on a compass heading and then pick a distant beacon

Sailing Trivia

- What country has the longest coastline? Canada wins, with 56,453 miles of coastline.
- Which is the deepest ocean? The greatest average depth is 4,282 meters and found in The Pacific Ocean.
- Where can you find the longest coral reef? The Great Barrier Reef, in Australia. It's about 1,243 miles long.

to steer toward. This could be a cloud, a buoy, or a land feature. Occasionally glance at the compass to ensure that your heading is true, but don't spend your entire time watching the compass and steering by its every swing, or you'll be weaving all over the ocean.

Electronic navigation

Provided there are no glitches, the modern wonders of electronic navigation will give you a second-by-second reference of where in the world you are. In addition, sophisticated autopilot features allow you to lock your current coordinates in and plot your destination's coordinates. The boat will then be delivered around all charted obstacles while maintaining a constant running monitor with radar for any unexpected hazards drifting ahead. But this little luxury comes at a hefty price.

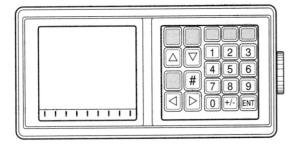

Loran

Loran

Although quickly being outdated, Loran, or long-range navigation systems, is still popularly in use—particularly with deep-sea anglers.

Loran systems memorize a location and can boast a proud tradition of returning your boat to a precise location time after time.

GPS

Because GPS, or global positioning system, is a cheaper option than Loran, the government is phasing Loran towers out, leaving the way open for GPS to become the primary system of the future.

For the technophobes out there, all of the buttons and complex-looking functions of both GPS and Loran can look rather intimidating. However, within about half an hour, most people can handle these machines with proficiency.

This ultimate navigator uses satellite triangulation to bring you within a few feet of your destination. As its name implies, a major benefit over Loran is the fact that you're not bound to being in range of a shore-based station. In addition, GPS is equally at home on a lake, river, mountain, or in the desert. All this for around $200.

Do-it-all chart plotters

For those who have flown on international flights in recent years, you'll be familiar with the aircraft's charted course repeated onscreen moment by moment. This inshore navigational tool works the same way and uses a built-in GPS, with a screen, to display your progress and plots navigational points you'll encounter.

Depth finders

The days are long since gone when you needed a sailor in the bow with a weighted line, repeatedly throwing and retrieving the weight, shouting out the "marks" or depth of the water.

Anglers use depth finders to find reefs and fish, but for the sailboat they're an invaluable "eye" that keeps track of the depth and saves you from grounding. The depth is simply repeated in numerals of fathoms, feet, or meters.

Cathode-ray tubes or CRTs

These sound like they're a weapon in a James Bond flick, but they're actually just depth finders that display the submarine topography like a television screen.

A futuristic-looking display panel makes this baby look somewhat intimidating, but it's really just a case of single-button functions that allow you various viewing options. Possibly more intimidating than their look is their price tag, but what these dollars will buy you is a color-coded impression of anything you sail over. For your common yachtsman, so what? But, if you're a diver or fisherman, what a boon to know that you're over sand, rock, bait, or a game fish shoal.

A handy extra—radio direction finders or RDFs

An excellent backup to a GPS, these movable antennae help you plot the direction of incoming radio signals. By picking up more than two signals from known coordinates, you'll be able to triangulate your position.

Radar shows it all

When the lights are down, radar still sees into the inky darkness or through the pea soup of mist. But, at upward of $1,500 for the unit, only larger boats are generally equipped with these. Radar's radio

---

Sailing Trivia

- How deep is the deepest point on the ocean floor? 35,802 feet.
- Where is it located and what is it called? In the Marianas Trench, off the coast of Guam, and it is called the Challenger Deep.
- Where is the deepest lake? Baykal Lake in the USSR, with a maximum depth of 5,315 feet.

beacon gives you a visual picture of all objects above the water, and allows you a visual of their bearing, distance, and movement.

Dead reckoning—not dead at all

The original mariners developed a system they called dead reckoning to plot their position by calculating their speed, time, and course. Today, the electronics are so simple that there is a tremendous resistance to the rigors of learning and applying this old art. But, when all of the modern wonders fail—as they periodically do—a knowledge of this time-honored art will still get you where you need to go.

Other Navigational Aids

Lighthouses

Since ancient times, land-based navigational aides in the form of light beacons and sounds have been used to warn vessels of dangers. Their tall towers are visible by day, their sweeping light is visible at night, and their groaning horn is audible whenever visibility is impaired. In addition, lights and sound can be coded so that a skipper can compare what he or she sees or hears to a chart to pick up a bearing.

Range markers

These use a very simple concept of two markers set one behind another so that the skipper who aligns them will automatically be following the safest passage. Of course, making the rear marker taller, with different features or colors, helps the skipper stay on course. When aligning markers that are lit at night, make sure one light is placed over the other.

The moment the two poles divide from your approaching perspective, you are moving out of the safest passage and need to correct your heading. Of course, these are only effective for a portion of an approach, so you need to get an idea of when to pick up the marker and when to abandon it and pick up another.

Water color

On your home turf, and with much experience, you'll be able to get a good idea of water depth just by looking at it. This is an art, not a science, and it's not something that can be easily taught.

The deeper the water, the darker it'll be. Shallow water ranges between pale blue and pale green. But area, specific average, clarity, and other factors will all cloud the inexperienced eye.

There's a catalog that records various features you can interpret just from looking at the water's color. Knowing and understanding these points can be interesting in the least, and very rewarding at best:

- Dark green spots that are surrounded by light green spots are generally patches of grass or rock on a sandy bottom.
- A broad, dark green to gray area in water that you know is fairly shallow is probably sea grass and therefore good fishing.
- Brownish spots might well be crustacean fields, such as oyster or mussels dangerously near the surface. Since these typically grow on rocks—beware!
- Dark blue or emerald grinning through an otherwise pale green is good news. This is probably a deep channel.

Communication or Comms

Hardware

When the chips are down and you need help in a hurry, there's nothing like radio.

Inland

On inland waterways and very close and populated coastal stretches, your cell phone is not an entirely bad bet. If you've got a waterproof container and remember to charge the batteries, so much the better.

VHF—the backbone of safe sailing

VHF, or very high frequency radio, is the most popular nautical radio system. Once set up, usage is free, and you don't need to

---

Do You Know...

- Why the oceans looks blue?
  Because it absorbs all of the reds, yellows, and greens, leaving only blue light to be reflected by the water molecules.
- Why it looks green in some areas?
  Because the blue water mixes with the yellow pigments present in floating plants.
- Why the Black Sea is so named?
  It contains little oxygen.
- Why the Red Sea is red?
  It contains seasonal blooms of algae that color the surface water red.
- About the Yellow Sea?
  It contains yellow mud carried into it by adjoining rivers.

Sailor Talk

Eight Bells

The practice of using bells stems from the days of the sailing ships. Sailors couldn't afford to have their own time pieces and relied on the ship's bells to tell time. The ship's boy kept time by using a half-hour glass. Each time the sand ran out, he would turn the glass over and ring the appropriate number of bells.

Aboard Navy ships, bells are struck to designate the hours of being on watch. Each watch is four hours in length. One bell is struck after the first half-hour has passed, two bells after one hour has passed, three bells after an hour and a half, four bells after two hours, and so forth up to eight bells are struck at the completion of the four hours. Completing a watch with no incidents to report was "Eight bells and all is well."

know any telephone numbers to stay in touch with nearby vessels and land bases. Depending on your rig, you'll be limited to a twenty-five-mile radius on open water.

Priced between $150 and $700, select an antenna of six to nine feet to have decent performance.

If you ever get a punctured hull or have a similar emergency, channel 16 is set aside just for you. It's the 911 of the sea and should always be treated with the utmost respect in terms of receiving or broadcasting.

Since most boats monitor this channel, you'll virtually be guaranteed to find somebody listening. Place your request in a succinct message, then maintain silence and wait for a reply. Once you've found who you want, don't chitchat or you'll have your ear severely chewed by others monitoring the channel. Move on to the other designated working channels between 68 and 72 if you want to talk.

NEVER, ever send hoax distress messages on any channel, but especially on channel 16. The authorities will not be very impressed with you, and you won't be very impressed with their lack of humor—not if—but *when* they catch you. The Coast Guard monitors this channel around the clock, and they can triangulate your signal from their various listening posts. If you broadcast the international distress signal MAYDAY to the world, they'll be scrambling their search and rescue crews within moments.

Handheld VHF

I had one of these when I was a kid and bugged the heck out of the fishermen by climbing a local mountain and constantly inquiring how they were doing. These days they're down in size a bit, and you can get some that aren't much bigger than a cell phone. They're an excellent option for small boats and great to carry if you split your party while at anchor. This piece of equipment will cost between $120 and $700.

Protocol, Services, and Other Equipment

Lingo

My mother always said, "You can sing together, but you can't talk together." If there ever was a place that this was true, then it's with VHF. Unlike a telephone, you've got to press the "talk" button in order to broadcast, and the moment you do so the radio ceases to receive. The effect is that incoming messages will not be heard as long as you keep the talk button pressed.

In order to compensate, there's a system for telling listeners when you're going to say something, abbreviating what you need to say, then telling them what kind of response you expect, and letting them know you're done. In short, the lingo of the airwaves is a codified pattern that is very succinct.

Phonetic alphabet

In order to eliminate confusion and convey absolute accuracy when speaking on radio, the alphabet can be phonetically spelled out as follows:

A—Alpha	N—November
B—Bravo	O—Oscar
C—Charlie	P—Papa
D—Delta	Q—Quebec
E—Echo	R—Romeo
F—Foxtrot	S—Sierra
G—Golf	T—Tango
H—Hotel	U—Uniform
I—India	V—Victor
J—Juliet	W—Whisky
K—Kilo	X—X-Ray
L—Lima	Y—Yankee
M—Mike	Z—Zulu

In practice, if you wanted to spell out the name of your boat, *scuttlebutt*, you'd say: sierra, charlie, uniform, tango, tango, lima, echo, bravo, uniform, tango, tango.

Phonetic numbers

Similarly, numbers are spelled out with pointed articulation:

1—ah-one-ah	6—ah-six-ah
2—ah-two-ah	7—ah-seven-ah
3—ah-three-ah	8—ah-eight-ah
4—ah-four-ah	9—ah-nine-ah
5—ah-five-ah	0—ah-Zer-ro

Double-digit numbers are spelled out too. In other words, for thirteen, you'd say: ah-one-ah—ah-three-ah.

Weather

Because weather is so very important to folks at sea, VHF broadcasts the National Weather Service forecasts around the clock. To listen to the report for your neck of the woods, just press the "WX" button.

Calling Home

If you need to call someone on the telephone, you can get patched in by calling a marine operator. On channels 24-28 and 84-88, a marine operator is available to connect you to a land-based line.

That's No 10-4 Good Buddy

Leave your CB radio at home. At sea, nobody's dialed to the channels you'd be talking on.

Single Sideband Radio (SSB)

By contrast, if you're willing to fork out $1,500 or more, and don't mind at least twenty feet of antenna perched on your vessel, SSB can give you an incredibly wide area of service.

DOCK 8

Sailing Etiquette and General Advice

S ailing is generally a team sport. And, more than this, sailing also has a very long history. As such, it is almost an international culture unto itself.

Sailors operate within a code of unspoken ethics and rules. Whether we personally agree with them or not, there is little we can do to change them and, if we want to enter the world of sailing and remain respectable members of the community, we need to know, understand, and apply the rules of etiquette in every given situation. For your information the Boating Safety Hotline is (800) 368-5647.

Rules by Another Name

Although etiquette applies to the interpersonal niceties onboard and relative respect shown to and between skippers, crews, and accomplished individuals, this section is really an extension of sailing rules. Etiquette is comprised of the little nuances that are voluntarily extended, which make sailing that much safer and that much more enjoyable.

Sailing etiquette is really just a collection of the conformities and norms that will make you a nice individual to be around and your boat and crew a welcome addition to the waterways. When we as a community cease volunteering to offer etiquette, much of it will probably have to be forced on us by legislation.

In the best Hollywood tradition, here's the tough-guy speech. For best effect, please read it with a John Wayne-style swagger: "There are two ways of doing this, the easy way or the difficult way; the choice is yours to make."

In Practice

Experience shows that the sailors who typically display the best etiquette are those who've been involved in the sport for many years. On the other end of the scale are newcomers. Perhaps it's just that nobody's explained the easy and difficult way of doing this, or perhaps the big outlay on equipment they've just made clouds their perception of how important and invincible they are within the greater scheme, but invariably they're not doing anyone any favors.

They want to test the limits of their new craft, and too bad for those around them. What do you think? Do you let them get away with it? People buy fancy new cars all the time, which they doubtless want to blast, but the highway patrol is so finicky about giving them a break. Will the Coast Guard be any less so once they've legislated against it?

Decades ago, the sailing community was so small that there was virtually no need for even a single rule and no need to have Big Brother breathing down your neck ensuring that you comply. Today, the very freedoms we turn to sailing for are slowly being eroded. And this situation is likely to worsen as the boating zones clog with ever more upstarts who don't respect the traditions of the ages.

Enough said.

Other Contentions

Power Always Gives Way

Under the bows of a super tanker, you'll certainly suspend this rule, but that's not etiquette, that's survival. The question is, if you can easily give way while the powered vessel would be compromised in some way, what do you do?

Personally, we think you should give way and tip your hat. The gesture will be appreciated and duplicated down the line—until the time comes that you receive the same fine gesture.

Perhaps this is one area that you can't see ever being legislated; on the other hand, if people were more courteous then the local lake down the road from us wouldn't have to be segregated with sailors here, skiers there, and paddlers somewhere else. In short, we'd all have a wider range to enjoy.

Clothing at the Club

Besides reserving a little modesty while on deck and among other craft, the issue of club dress isn't to force everyone into bow ties and jackets, although these might lend a touch of elegance to the occasional event. The point can be much more practically made.

> He that will not sail till all dangers are over must never put to sea.
> —Thoman Fuller, M.D.

> • • •

> The freedom of the seas is the sine qua non of peace, equality and cooperation.
> —Woodrow Wilson

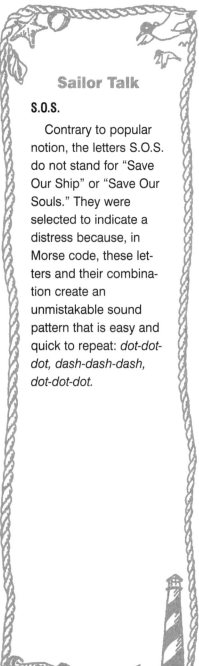

Don't traipse through the club while dripping wet or sit on chairs with a less than dry rump. It's not fair for those who follow you.

It's not particularly kind to other members for you to break from swabbing the bilge and then sit down to Sunday lunch in all your aromatic finery.

It's not fair to bring your scantily clad and ill-behaved hordes into the club for a drink when you know retired corps is holding its annual convention.

Idiosyncrasies

The skipper sets the tone. Whether you agree or not, while on the water, the big boss holds sway, even on rudimentary issues that others might believe are silly.

The rule here is that all others should ask if they are in doubt. This goes for what equipment can be used or handled, and when; where and how goods should be stowed; if, where, and when smoking is allowed; whether glass is allowed aboard; or even if the helmsman can be spoken to at different times.

Some of the skipper's rules might seem petty, and if so, nobody is obliged to sail under that skipper ever again. The point is that it comes down to different strokes for different folks—providing the skipper agrees.

Circumstances

Pre-Embarkation

As host

We've already covered the fact that if guests are to be used as crew, the skipper owes it to them to explain in detail every aspect of the duties that they'll be required to perform. Don't trivialize jobs that might be difficult, dangerous, or unpleasant. Lay it on the line and give them the option to step ashore.

Boats are a great place to party, and captains must take their job of keeping rowdy or dangerous practices within reasonable limits. Passengers need to know this before departure.

The Ten Commandments

Since we're writing these unwritten rules down, let's just stop beating about the bush and call them what they are—RULES. Okay. Repeat after us until you can say them in your sleep. Thank you.

Though shalt:
- Never disobey posted rules—even though you may not be observed and could get away with it.
- No pranks, practical jokes, or otherwise foolish behavior such as rough-housing.
- Never make waves for other vessels, especially in harbors and places of rest.
- Not anchor in a trafficked place or in a channel or trafficked area, or with so much rode that the boat might drift into such an area.
- Never release thy trash or other foreign matter overboard.
- Not maketh a nasty din.
- Not speak in an improper manner to other boaters or on the radio.
- Never allow thine upper decks and hull to look like a den of iniquity or other place of ill-repute—allowing paint to chip; algae, garbage, or clutter to build up.
- Not misunderstand or fail to respond to flag or other signals.
- Never hang out thy dirty laundry—in literal, visible, or audio terms.
- Not be a boor, twit, or other unsociable animal in any other ways.

Oops, that was eleven, but who's counting?

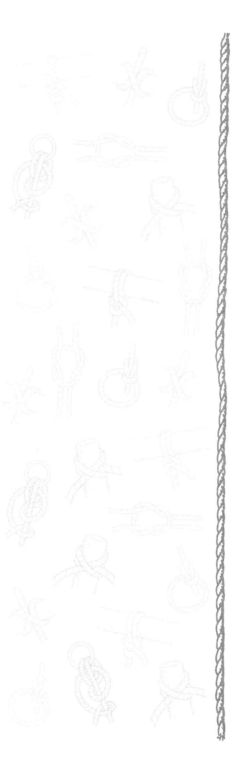

Above all else, the skipper needs to put the safety of crew and other boaters first on the agenda. Let everyone understand safety procedures and be familiar with safety equipment.

As visitor

Although tradition dictates that visitors offer to bring a gift or to pay for fuel, the Coast Guard has already ruled that this transaction fits the parameters of "carrying passengers for hire." Because, by the purest definitions, the skipper would then be required to have the appropriate licensing requirements in order to operate a chartered fee business, it's a sensitive issue that the individuals need to discuss among themselves.

Guests need to understand that sailing is fraught with chores, and they need to be prepared to give reasonable assistance.

Although the boat might have sufficient safety equipment and foul weather gear for the regular complement and some guests, wherever they reasonably can, guests should be prepared to bring their own personal equipment.

In addition, when they have special needs such as foods or medication, the guest is certainly expected to provide these.

The guests' attitude should certainly be open to learning the elementary aspects of sailing, courtesy, and safety. Beyond this, food preparation and general cleanup will probably be on the roster, and guests need to be prepared to lend a hand.

Either way, be prompt

Everybody—skipper, crew, and guest alike—have a fiduciary responsibility to be at the departure point, on time, every time.

Facing the Elements

Sun protection

As already stated, sailing offers notoriously ferocious sunburns. All aboard should cover for one another by providing whatever sun protection they can. These may be hats, creams, clothing, or sunglasses.

Dress

To have a pleasant sailing experience, it's vital to dress appropriately to the conditions. Light colors do the best job of reflecting and keeping the individual cool. On the other hand, dark colors and rainproof gear do the best job keeping the cold, wet, and wind out. Modern fabrics such as Gore-Tex are a godsend to the sailor.

Wrap the noodle, too

Heat loss through the skull can be extremely high at sea. Ensure that everyone has headwear for both sun and cold. Also, don't forget gloves if there's any chance of cold. The wind-chill factor out at sea can be surprisingly severe.

What you pay for

What you get is precisely what you pay for. Apparel at sea needs to be more than a fashion statement; it needs to be practical. Ensure that you've got good quality foul weather gear.

The Sperry or Docker rip-offs you picked up on sale for $9.99 may look pretty close to the cutting edge of chic, but will you be landing on your posterior with the first step you take on a damp deck?

Other Advice to Sustain You

All creatures great and small

Don't let the wildlife spoil your day. Bring appropriate repellents or other chemical agents commonly used in mankind's quest to maintain indoor peace while in the great outdoors.

Food and drink

There's nothing like the wind and water to build up an appetite. Petite birdlike creatures can unexpectedly transform into calorie-guzzling gannets within a few hours.

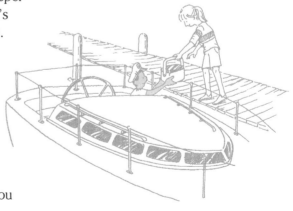

More correctly called victuals in the nautical world, whatever you're planning to bring along as grub, just make sure that there's plenty of it. There aren't a lot of places you can pick up a quick snack if you run out.

Some larger boats are outfitted with wonderful galleys, but it's generally best to bring ready-prepared meals that can easily be warmed or tossed together in no time.

Barbecues

The larger boats might also have barbecues out over the stern. When you do fire up the barbecue, ensure that you're on a single bow anchor so that the smoke and embers can blow away to sea and not into the sails. On a note of etiquette, make sure that you're not upwind of other vessels whose day your enjoyment will destroy. Precooked chicken will take a lot less time to grill on the coals. Use the self-starting type of charcoal since it's clean, fast, safe, and easy to use. Line the bottom of the grill with foil to stop grease from dripping onto any part of the boat. This way you can simply discard the foil after use, leaving the grill easy to clean.

H_2O—the potable kind

Make no mistake, while exercising in the wind, you'll need to drink an awful lot, so bring far more water than you need.

H_2O—the flushable kind

On cruises longer than a day or two, the time will come when most civilized beings will begin to think about scraping the salt from their bodies. Sea water isn't always the water people want to wash in, so storage tanks need to be provided for this purpose. On the other hand, water weighs quite a bit and takes up valuable stowage space; therefore, it's not an endless resource for trippers. Sound conservation methods and rationing systems should be observed and everyone aboard needs to be keenly aware not to use more than their allotment.

Once Afloat

The Helping Hands

It's the skipper's responsibility to educate his or her crew as to a particular vessel's special needs and his or her idiosyncrasies in terms of a docking procedure and where and how lines need to

Victual Stowage

Sailors of yore suffered from a nasty affliction called scurvy. Even if you've never heard the symptoms before, it is one of those diseases that you know you never want to get.

Scurvy is a disease human beings experience as a result of a prolonged dietary deficiency of vitamin C. It causes progressive bodily weakness, spongy and inflamed gums, loose teeth, swollen and tender joints, and a tendency toward absorption by the tissues of blood from ruptured blood vessels. Anemia often results from such hemorrhaging.

Scurvy became common when sailors began spending months at sea without fresh vegetables. In 1795 lime juice was issued to all British naval vessels, and scurvy soon disappeared among British sailors–hence, the British are still referred to in disparaging terms as "Limeys."

Though it is technically still possible for sailors to suffer from scurvy, modern diets and the availability of foods and refrigeration make it unheard of these days.

We're not suggesting that your Sunday afternoon jaunt will deliver you to work Monday morning looking like you've been living in Manhattan's underground sewers for six months, but it's a bit of useless trivia we thought you might want to know.

The reason our unfortunate sailing ancestors suffered from scurvy was because storing foods—particularly fresh and unsealed foodstuffs near the sea—attracts an awful lot of musty mold. It also takes up a lot of room.

It's caused by a deficiency of vitamin C and characterized by spongy and bleeding gums, bleeding under the skin, and extreme weakness.

Dangers of improper food storage at sea are similar to those on land. Meat, vegetables, or fruits will spoil in a similar way, though possibly somewhat more quickly than on land as a result of the higher levels of humidity associated with life on the water.

Many of our modern mini-galleons have refrigerators and cupboard space for cans, but space is generally very limited, so only stock essentials and bring the luxuries as tastes dictate and space allows. Then, periodically conduct regular clear-outs when you destroy and discard damaged or rusted cans.

be secured. Therefore, any botched efforts that are not pure negligence or apathy on the crew's part can only be ignorance, in which the skipper is solely to blame for not communicating the requirements thoroughly enough.

Congestion

Politeness over din

When waterways become very congested, some understandings beyond basic rules of navigation need to be established if a continuous barrage of radio, horn, and whistle cacophony is to be avoided.

This comes down to a few simple gestures, skipper to skipper.

Greetings

When sailing in close confines, all vessels should be at absolute slow pace and keep a lookout for possible hazardous situations. Experienced skippers graciously wave one another by.

Altering course

Of course, the finest gesture any captain can make under these conditions is to see a situation developing and avoid it altogether by a timely and slight alteration in course.

Handling the sails

Sails are designed to capture hundreds and perhaps even thousands of pounds of wind pressure. If a sail is flapping wildly, stay on the windward side of it or you'll receive a smack you won't forget in a hurry. Try to fold and collapse it onto itself to make it lose power quickly.

Beware, synthetic sails can be slippery, so standing on them could be a potentially hazardous mistake.

At Anchor

Wherever there's a favorable or charming spot to anchor, you can be pretty sure that neighboring vessels will not be far away.

The first to an anchorage has the seniority, and, provided their anchor does not drag, the vessel that anchors second is obliged to reset its anchor in the event there's any interference between vessels.

It's clear then that whichever boats drag anchor should have the good grace to admit to this fact and not embroil themselves in arguments with their fellows. Of course there's the element of ego and power play at stake, but this human peculiarity aside, resetting an anchor is really not so tough a task.

The amount of rode that you have out (scope) when at anchor is generally dependent upon water depth and weather conditions.

The deeper the water and the more severe the weather, the more rode will be required. For recreational sailing you should have out a minimum of five to eight times (5 to 1 scope for day anchoring and 6 to 8 to 1 for overnight) the depth of the water, plus the distance from the water to where the anchor will attach to the bow. For example, if your measure of water depth shows four feet and it is three feet from the top of the water to your bow cleat, you would multiply seven feet by six to eight to get the amount of rode to put out.

If other boats are anchored in the area you select, ask the skipper in the boat adjacent to the spot you select what scope he or she has out so that you can anchor in such a manner that you will not bump into the neighboring vessel. Anchor with the same method used by nearby boats. If they are anchored bow and stern, you should too. If they are anchored with a single anchor from the bow, do not anchor bow and stern.

At Sea

Coming about

Keep in mind that your sails will create a blind spot behind which obstructions and victims might be masked. Therefore, never make a turn that is not well planned and properly communicated to all parties who could be affected.

Radio manners

- Use channel 16 for distress and hailing only.
- Keep communications on channel 16 as short as possible.
- Avoid interfering with other broadcasts already in progress, listen before transmitting.
- Use minimum transmission power whenever possible.

Famous Privateers

Gráinne O'Malley (Anglicized as Grace O'Malley, Grany Malley)

Grace was an Irish noblewoman who, between 1576 and 1593, led a band of 200 sea-raiders from the coast of Galway, determined to salvage some part of her family's inheritance.

Grace was widowed twice and imprisoned twice. In 1593, she was finally captured and condemned for piracy. A tenacious survivor, Grace gained an audience with Queen Elizabeth I in London and secured a pardon for herself and restitution from the crown. She became one of the few sea-raiders ever to retire from the sea and die in her own bed.

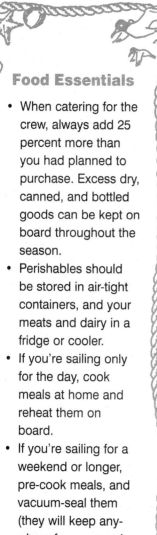

Food Essentials

- When catering for the crew, always add 25 percent more than you had planned to purchase. Excess dry, canned, and bottled goods can be kept on board throughout the season.
- Perishables should be stored in air-tight containers, and your meats and dairy in a fridge or cooler.
- If you're sailing only for the day, cook meals at home and reheat them on board.
- If you're sailing for a weekend or longer, pre-cook meals, and vacuum-seal them (they will keep anywhere from a couple of weeks to a couple of months).

(continued)

Vigilance at all times

Use every instrument and sense you have to maintain a constant shield around your boat and party. Be aware of what is in, and what will shortly be in, your path. Watch your crew, other vessels, and the weather with a fanatical vigilance. Choose prevention rather than cure.

Foul weather

Double safety standards, reduce speed, and post lookouts.

At the Dock

The approach

As previously pointed out *ad nauseam*, your wake is your responsibility. To keep it to a minimum, reduce speed and trim your boat to raise the stern.

Finding a mooring

Just as you wouldn't appreciate someone parking in your driveway, respect others' private property and reserved moorings. When approaching a marina or wharf where you'd like to tie for a time, contact the appropriate authority—either the club secretary or harbormaster—to reserve a spot. If you're on a planned overnight voyage, call ahead by telephone. Alternatively, when in VHF range, hail them and set up the docking details then.

Rates

Docking rates are a little like hotel rates in that they alter by season and by day of week. It's not a good idea to try discussing rates over the open airwaves.

Offensive fenders

As you approach, by all means have the fenders secured and ready, but keep them on the inside of your guardrail and only toss them overboard during your final approach.

Generators

Whether alongside or at anchor, respect other boaters by not using your generator early in the morning or late at night. Sound can travel an awful long way over the water, so this really is a no-no.

Keeping Everything Shipshape

The way a boat looks in just one glance is generally the way it is. In other words, if it looks grubby, unkempt, and generally shoddy, it's probably not the type of vessel you'd want to go to sea on.

With this in mind, that's precisely how passengers, crew, and the wider community in general view vessels and their owners. Keeping a tidy boat is a very important element of sailing and indicates what kind of sailor you are.

To assist you, select a vessel constructed from low-maintenance material (such as fiberglass), and your job will be much easier.

Since the innate structure of this material is so stable and resistant to all kinds of attrition—from prolonged exposure to the elements to organic infestation—fiberglass boats don't take a lot of care, hence its popularity in pleasure craft. By contrast, wood is beautiful, but it's a constant battle against the elements and microscopic fauna and flora who would make your plaything their home and grub.

Eco-sensitivity

Even in relatively small doses, detergents and cleaners can devastate a local marine ecosystem. Wherever possible, try to conduct the following chores with your boat on land. In addition, try to select cleaning materials that are eco-sensitive and biodegradable.

Scrubdown

Hardy materials aside, your boat is a major investment, one that offers you a wonderful return if only in personal value of sport and entertainment. To keep everything functioning well and to avoid

Food Essentials

- Keep flasks of hot soup handy in cold sailing conditions.
- Keep high energy/high protein food (chocolate, dried fruit, nuts, cake, nutrition bars) in sealed containers for emergencies.
- Make sure to have enough drinking water available.
- Keep canned beans or vegetables in a safe area away from sunlight and damage.

becoming an eyesore for guests and onlookers, regularly washing the vessel down with fresh water and occasionally scrubbing with mild detergents is a must.

A sponge and bucket will be all you'll need for smooth surfaces, but for non-slip decking and crevices, rivets, and screws, you'll need a hard bristle brush.

Wash metals well; even chrome and stainless steel will eventually feel the effects of their salt-brine home.

Tough grime

Algae loves to build up around the waterline, and there are anti-algae solutions available to take care of this situation. In addition, in particularly polluted harbors an oily scum buildup might also be present that will call for appropriate treatment. If you're battling, cruise the marina and seek out a vessel of similar era and construction to yours, then ask the owner how he or she keeps everything shipshape. They'll certainly appreciate your compliments and most likely be overjoyed to help.

Fishy fouling

Live fish aren't too relaxed when brought aboard. Even if released, scales will cover everything and eventually make your boat look and smell like a trawler.

A mild solution of bleach will normally remove the worst with little effort. Common kitchen cleanser spray bottles that contain bleach are very handy for spot cleaning. Be sure to label the container clearly and keep it away from children.

No abrasives, if you please

When cleaning fiberglass avoid using abrasive powders, as even the dullest surfaces don't like them. Use a micro-abrasive or cleaner like Soft-Scrub, which can be used with gentle pressure.

Rigging

Because of the intricacy in design, and lots of nooks and crannies for salt to do its corrosive job, your rigging calls for special attention. Neglect will ultimately lead to weakened structure and the possibility of disaster when under the most pressure in the most hostile of circumstances.

Weekly fresh water hosing and periodic scrubs with soap and brush will be a good preventive measure.

The extra mile

About once or twice per year, purchase a purpose-designed wax and apply it after washing and drying the boat. Make sure you don't use a slick wax on deck areas; if you have doubts as to whether the wax will turn slippery when wet, test it on an out-of-the-way but representative surface. Once satisfied, try it on another limited area of low traffic, wet it down, and test your footing with various footwear and bare skin.

Below decks

Mildew can be a curse. Whenever possible, bring upholstery, life jackets, and any other susceptible fabrics into the sun to allow the UV rays to kill off the pesky microscopic critters.

Try to dehumidify the below decks in whatever ways you safely can.

Hang dehumidifying bags, available at sailing supply stores, in lockers, cabinets, bilge compartments, or anywhere you want to minimize mildew.

The best way to prevent mold-related illnesses is to stop mold at its source of growth, which means stopping moisture. Keep the boat dry, especially in predictably damp areas, such as heads, galley's, anchor, wet gear, and line storage. If an area of your boat starts smelling of mildew, it has already taken hold and you will need to get the mildew under control.

Thoroughly bleaching the moldy area is the first step. However, mold is resilient and can grow back even after the area is cleaned, so it is a good idea to dehumidify damp areas.

Ironically, the boat becomes most heavily exposed to mold particles during the cleaning process. The cleaning stirs settled particles and the air movement causes them to become airborne again.

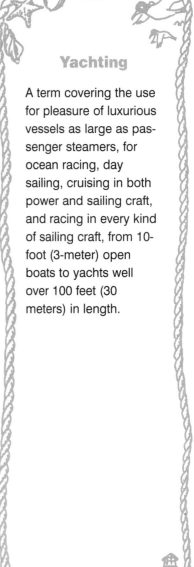

Yachting

A term covering the use for pleasure of luxurious vessels as large as passenger steamers, for ocean racing, day sailing, cruising in both power and sailing craft, and racing in every kind of sailing craft, from 10-foot (3-meter) open boats to yachts well over 100 feet (30 meters) in length.

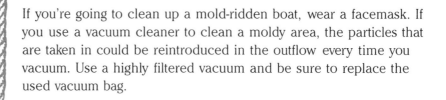

If you're going to clean up a mold-ridden boat, wear a facemask. If you use a vacuum cleaner to clean a moldy area, the particles that are taken in could be reintroduced in the outflow every time you vacuum. Use a highly filtered vacuum and be sure to replace the used vacuum bag.

Clutter

Back on deck, beyond having a clean profile, the deck should also be clear. In addition to its being unsightly to have clutter and rope lying around, it's a very real safety hazard. Be meticulous about not letting clutter build up.

Awnings and covers

Draw all awnings and covers taut and as close to horizontal as possible. In addition to being more attractive, it'll stop them from flapping and making a noise while rubbing to threadbare destruction.

Noise

Besides loud and raucous guests and blaring radios, the clinking and clanking sounds of halyards against masts can be a major source of irritation to other boaters. Whenever possible, secure these away from the mast or give them a wrap around it.

Laundry

Don't turn your schooner into a clothesline. If you must dry garments on deck, try to keep them as low as possible.

Garbage

Take only memories and leave only your wake—nothing more needs be said.

Sanitation

Since the environment can be extremely sensitive to human sanitation or ablutions such as sewerage and detergents, follow the prescribed procedures for your vessel's design. Make sure that you use bio-degradable detergents and ensure that your waste tanks have no leaks and are emptied in accordance with prescribed club or local rules.

Below the Line

Everything you've done to this point has been easy. Now comes the hard work.

The waterline is that point at which air and water surface meet. Keeping the lower half clean is more important than you may first realize.

From the point of view of a crustacean or other aquatic creature, the underside of your hull is a reef. In fact, it's a wonderful reef that delivers a regular variety of tasty delicacies that they can filter out of the passing water whenever you're on the move.

If you're feeling benevolent, you might be inclined to allow them this prime piece of submarine real estate, but it's only fair of us to warn you that—apart from being unsightly and ultimately damaging to the value of your vessel—their lumpy and bumpy profile does nothing for the performance of your sailing. In short, you'll need to regularly eliminate these critters.

Barnacles

Algae and seaweed are problems, but when you graduate to a hardy barnacle invasion, you're dealing with a much tougher customer. And don't think that these little devils are only a scourge in oceans. Their prevalence in fresh waterways is increasing all the time.

In some areas, within just a week of launching, you'll already feel the sandpapery grittiness of their telltale calcium deposit beginning to build on your highly polished hull. The longer you allow them their reign, the more extensive will become their hold. By the time they're dime-sized, they'll require power sanding and concerted scraping—a messy, difficult, and expensive undertaking.

Again, ask other skippers whose boats don't seem to suffer such hardships and you'll be told about a regional solution that works.

Sailor Talk

Fathom

The term "fathom" was originally a land-measuring term derived from the Anglo-Saxon word "faetm" meaning to embrace. In ancient times, most measurements were based on average size of parts of the body, such as the hand or the foot. A fathom is the average distance from fingertip to fingertip of the outstretched arms of a man—about six feet. Since a man stretches out his arms to embrace his sweetheart, Britain's Parliament declared that distance be called a "fathom" and it be a unit of measure. A fathom remains six feet. The word was also used to describe taking the measure or "to fathom" something. Today, of course, when one is trying to figure something out, they are trying to "fathom" it.

Anti-fouling paints

The trick is to make your hull inhospitable from the outset. These paints contain elements that are toxic to marine organisms and are available at marine supply stores. Before you point out our earlier caution about being kind to the environment, do know that the toxin is not DDT. The main active ingredient is copper, which evidently makes for a bad neighborhood as far as barnacles and their like are concerned but is gentle on the aquatic ecosystem.

Beyond fiberglass

When you buy a boat, make sure it's constructed out of a low-maintenance material. However, if the beauty of wood is completely irresistible, be forewarned that your investment in effort to keep it beautiful will be big.

Ask around within the sailing community about the different materials and their maintenance requirements and cost.

Repairs
Holes in the Hull

Besides cleaning considerations, another vital criterion for material selection of the hull is repair. Fiberglass is probably the simplest, cheapest, and most effective base to repair. It's a simple case of preparing the surrounding surface and then applying successive layers of fresh fiberglass and sanding flush. Other materials become a little more tricky, costly, and less stable post-patching.

The Tools You Need

There is no getting away from the fact that your boat will need periodic attention—both scheduled maintenance alongside or onshore and emergency fixes while at sea. With the right tools and a little practice, the type of work is not rocket science and anyone with a couple of fingers and enough brains to open a can of beans can get by. If you feel you'd rather have professionals handle the scheduled work, great, but there's no way on earth that you should leave the wharf without some basic equipment aboard. Even if you're not interested in using it under normal conditions, you'll see how interested you become when an emergency strikes. At the very least, you can hail another vessel and hopefully they'll have someone capable aboard.

Elementary Equipment

This includes hammers, screwdrivers, pliers, socket spanners, wrenches, and any other tools that would be more specific to the equipment you've got aboard.

Odds and ends

Some spare parts are likely to be universally useful on almost any boat and in almost any situation.

- Stainless steel screw clams in several sizes to fit everything from bilge pump connections to fuel hoses are an absolute must.
- Assorted stainless steel bolts, nuts, washers, and screws can be like manna from heaven out in the blue. Keep them sorted by size and type in waterproof containers. Most marine stores generally stock complete kits that will take the effort out of developing and storing your own.
- Wire in two or three gauges—and put a wire cutter in your tool chest.
- Nylon string or rope and a couple of stretchable bungee cords will never go to waste.
- Nylon tie-wraps are excellent as quick fixes that can temporarily mend radio antennae or secure fishing reels to rods.
- Adjustable tools of the one-size-fits-all variety.
- Locking pliers in nine- and five-inch versions.
- Crescent wrenches in twelve-, eight-, and six-inch variety.
- If you've still got something in your budget, get a ten-inch slip-joint plier. This will allow you to grab pipes or larger nuts.

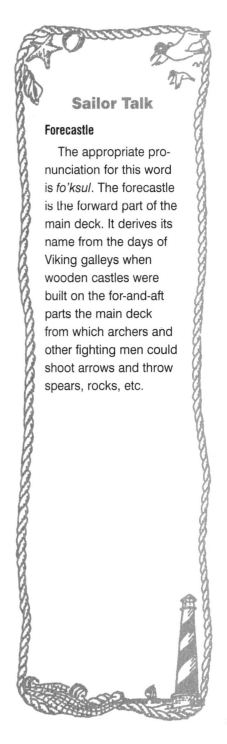

Sailor Talk

Forecastle

The appropriate pronunciation for this word is *fo'ksul*. The forecastle is the forward part of the main deck. It derives its name from the days of Viking galleys when wooden castles were built on the for-and-aft parts the main deck from which archers and other fighting men could shoot arrows and throw spears, rocks, etc.

Sticky stuff

There are some things on a boat that come loose or fly around that all the line, screws, and ties in the world won't fix. Often the best solution here is in the sticky department, so it's well worth investing a small amount into some additional odds and ends.

- Duct tape—this one almost needs no explanation. With enough of it aboard they could probably have saved the *Titanic.*
- Epoxy resin-based body filler will certainly also find a thousand uses aboard.
- Hot glue in stick form can be melted with any open flame and dripped into areas that need a quick fix.
- 3M makes an excellent marine sealer coded as 5200 Sealer. Alternatively, any similar competitor product will be useful as a tough, stick-anything-to-anything patch or adhesive.

Slippery Characters

Sometimes you want things to stick, but other times you desperately need to have them slippery. A grease gun and a can of WD-40 will find no end of uses—from squeaky hinges to stubborn trailer rollers.

Electrical Surprises

It should not come as a shock that circuits and the nautical life are not happy bedfellows, so the only surprise here would be if the electrical system didn't have occasional problems.

- Ensure you're stocked with several fuses to cover all of your circuitry needs.
- Insulating tape will get you out of many binds.
- Insulated wire of various sizes will also be a great savior.

Tools in Every Variety

- If you become all thumbs when you pick up tools, you'll want all the help you can get retrieving parts and screws lost down cracks and into the bilge. Do yourself a favor and buy a magnetic wand. It'll save you hours of stress, some knuckle skin, and possibly even the damage you'll cause trying to retrieve the illusive item with cutlery from the galley.

- Large and small versions of both Phillips-head and flat screwdrivers with long and short shanks will be very useful.
- A set of hex keys can be pretty handy. Hex keys are hexagonal or six-sided bare-metal shafts bent 90 degrees at one end, which you'll need to loosen set screws with a corresponding head. They're available at any hardware store or sailing supplier. Typically, you won't often need them, but without them you will not be able to insert or remove screws that require this variety of tool.
- Claw hammers can be used in a bunch of creative ways.
- Electrical pliers, wire strippers, and other electrical equipment will eventually come in handy too.
- Bolt and screw cutters are not a bad idea either.
- A torque wrench is not an absolute must, but it's something that's worth having.
- A spare battery is not really a tool, but it's worth mentioning here because it really can be a lifesaver. Ensure that it's charged at all times—if it's dead, it's a little tough to get out and push while at sea.

Swiss Army or Leatherman knife

These are compact and handy little gizmos that slip into your pocket and can really solve a lot of scratching for that perfect but missing tool.

Other Illuminating Ideas

Do ensure that there are several good quality and preferably waterproof flashlights of different sizes and charged with operational batteries aboard. The more robust the better.

In this age when smokers are becoming as scarce as hen's teeth, having a way to make an open flame is not always a "you got a light" question. Ensure that you have a supply of matches and cheap disposable lighters—just in case that barbecue refuses to ignite.

Tool Storage

Buy top-quality, stainless-steel tools, then oil them regularly and store them in a moisture-proof container with a dehumidifying agent. Keep the tools neat and tidy inside the box and store the box in the same accessible spot every time.

DOCK 9

General Regulations

T hese days, all boating is regulated to one degree or another. Before you put your boat in the water, find out what governing authorities potentially could have jurisdiction over you, your boat, and your actions. To do so, contact your local Coast Guard or any other marine authority or interested party. Details of Coast Guard jurisdiction follow in this chapter. Even local fishing retailers would be able to point you in the right direction.

But let's have a look at some of the organizations that might impact your day.

Port Authorities

In order to obtain an updated list of regulations and information, contact the American Association of Port Authorities at the following address:

> The American Association of Port Authorities
> 1010 Duke Street
> Alexandria, Virginia 22314–3589
> Tel: (703) 684-5700
> Fax: (703) 684-6321
> email: info@aapa-ports.org

This is the major port authority in the United States, Canada, Latin America, and the Caribbean. In addition, it also represents a host of associate members, firms, and individuals who govern coastal waters and ports.

National and International Regulations

Contact the following organizations to get a current list of their area of authority, regulations, and other recommendations.

FMC

The Federal Maritime Commission was established in 1961 as an independent government agency, responsible for regulating shipping in the foreign trades of the United States. The Commission's five members are appointed by the President with the advice and consent of the Senate.

FMC Headquarters
800 North Capitol Street, N.W.
Washington, D.C. 20573

Skipper Licenses

To qualify for a skipper's license, contact any of the following organizations in order to establish precisely what tuition you'll require, where you can get it, and how to enlist for the appropriate examination:

- Local sailing and yacht clubs
- The American Red Cross
- Community groups
- Sailing and racing organizations and associations
- U.S. Navy bases
- Sailboat rental and charter companies
- Sailing schools

All of these organizations should be easy to find through any local, state, or national chapter, or in the phone book.

Staying out of Trouble

Insurance

We'll put it quite simply: If you can't afford the insurance on your vessel, seriously consider selling it and buying a vessel you can afford to insure.

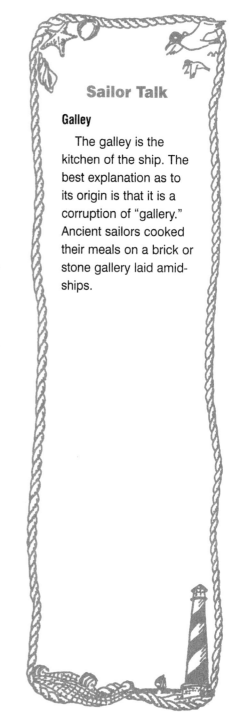

Sailor Talk

Galley

The galley is the kitchen of the ship. The best explanation as to its origin is that it is a corruption of "gallery." Ancient sailors cooked their meals on a brick or stone gallery laid amidships.

The water is unpredictable, and damage to vessels really does occur. Insurance assessors will take into account the condition of your boat, your general age and experience, the waters you sail, and any specific coverage that you request.

If you are not going to have coverage of your vessel, at the very least take out third-party coverage. That way you're protected in cases of injury or death.

Common Sense

Avoidance of problems is the best advice we can give you. Although this may be easier said than done in some instances, there's still a lot you can do to handle any unexpected problems that do crop up.

A Float Plan

Tell someone where you are going. Better yet, write out a float plan—a written log that records your intentions for those ashore. Include your intended destination and schedule. In addition, include the following information:

- Skipper's name and phone number. This way, in case there's a mix-up and you end up at home while the rest of the world is out looking for you, potential rescuers can make a simple call and short-circuit the whole song-and-dance routine.
- Describe your boat: its color, design, size, and registration numbers.
- Emergency contacts, including next of kin.
- Other emergency numbers, such as the Coast Guard, sheriff's office, lifeguards, and marine patrol.
- It's best to lodge this information with harbor authorities, but if this is impossible or impractical, at least leave it with a responsible adult ashore. Then, don't forget to contact that person once you return so that they don't call out the cavalry on a false alarm.

U.S. Coast Guard

We all know they're there, but do we really know what they do, who they govern, and how they can help us? For further information and reading, check out these Web sites or call these toll-free numbers:

- http://www.cglalb.com/license.htm
- http://www.uscg.mil/
- Coast Guard Infoline.
  1-(800) 368-5647
- Marine Environmental Protection
  1-(800) 424-8802

The Coast Guard has a broad distribution of authority and responsibility. The following list includes their most important responsibilities:

Recreational boating safety
- Search and rescue
- Aids to navigation
- Navigation information
- Coast Guard auxiliary

Other regulatory jurisdictions
- Commercial vessel safety
- Vessel traffic services
- Commercial vessel safety services
- Commercial vessel stability approvals
- Bridge administration services
- Icebreaking services
- Domestic ice operations

Storm Warnings

The instant you *suspect* there's a storm on the way, head for a safe port. If you're far from your ultimate destination and the storm is imminent, any port or shelter will do. This advice goes just as well for sea mist.

The National Weather Service defines mist as "visible aggregates of minute particles suspended in the atmosphere that reduce visibility to less than 7 miles." Unlike drizzle, it does not fall to the ground. In other words, "sea mist" is common fog.

Drizzle is defined as "fine drops (less than 0.02") that are very close together." Drizzle appears to float, but it fails to the ground.

If your boat's on land, get it under cover.

Get to know your sailing area and find areas that give shelter during hurricanes. As an absolute last resort, if you're stuck in a hurricane and trapped in a bay where you believe that your boat is certain to be wrecked, it's better to purposefully sink it on your own terms. Naturally, your first priority would be the safety of lives, but once you've got everyone to safety, scuttle the boat in water that is neither so shallow that waves are breaking nor is so deep that it'll make recovery too difficult. If possible, get all electronics onto shore.

Boats Are Replaceable—Lives Are Not

No boat in the world is worth your life. When you've done all you can, get out of the ocean and onto terra firma.

Loading and overloading

Next to alcohol abuse, one of the most foolish things a skipper can do is to overload his or her vessel. Many authorities place upper limits on a boat's carrying capacity. Find out if any apply to your boat in the areas you intend to sail.

Regulations and live bodies aside, any cargo aboard—including fuel, equipment, shipped- or rain-water in the holds—adds to the boat's displacement or load. Besides reducing freeboard, or distance from the gunwales to the water's surface, it can change a boat's center of gravity and cause innumerable problems when the boat moves in any direction or on the roll of swell.

Speed Thrills but It also Kills

Of course, in sailing terms this would apply mainly to tenders. Nevertheless, it's necessary to point out once more just how hard the water becomes at full speed.

Running Out of Gas

Fuel gauges are notoriously inaccurate, and the safest course is to top off the fuel tank every morning before you head out. Let's face it, out in the blue yonder it takes a very special kind of person to jog to the nearest gas station.

Experience

There's no substitute for experience. There's no textbook and no sailing course that'll prepare you fully for all of the joys and dangers you might well encounter.

Put in your time as a crew member and then as a junior "officer" under every sailing condition you can before you try to pull it off and fly by the seat of your pants.

It's dangerous out there—enjoy but be safe.

Sailing and Fitness

The type of sailing you plan to participate in will dictate your minimum level of fitness. For competitive racers, maintaining a high level of physical fitness will be every bit as important as developing optimum sailing technique.

Besides making good common sense, by maintaining your weight, strength, and stamina, you will get much more enjoyment out of every sailing trip.

Remaining fit ensures that fatigue and pain will take longer to appear during long trips. This will, in turn, allow you to keep your mind clear and ready for those moments when decisions are the most important.

For small craft sailors, better physical conditioning means safer sailing, getting more fun out of it, and recovering faster after a long and intense effort and after races. In addition, reduced fatigue and pain can help you keep your concentration on the race and on your tactics.

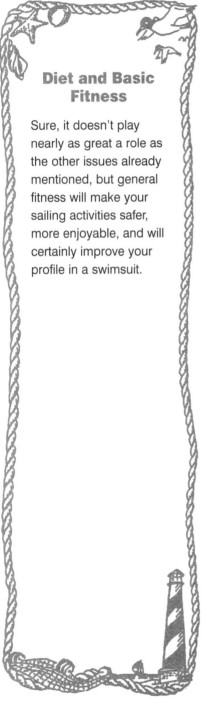

Diet and Basic Fitness

Sure, it doesn't play nearly as great a role as the other issues already mentioned, but general fitness will make your sailing activities safer, more enjoyable, and will certainly improve your profile in a swimsuit.

Even keelboat crews can improve their teamwork and their reaction time. Working the deck or just trimming the jib as fast as possible requires a physically fit crew. All around, the more fit you remain, the less fatigue you will experience and the better and faster your work will be.

To improve at sailing requires you to sail often. Your conditioning program should therefore include exercises that are similar to the routines you'll undertake on board.

Your training program should begin with a general shape-up period when you develop overall fitness. Once your fitness level is reasonably good, begin to include exercises that simulate specific sailing routines.

If you're somewhat out of shape, a well-founded training program will take at least six weeks to build you up to a minimum level. That means that if you intend to sail in March, start preparing your fitness levels by mid-January. Also, it will be a good idea to continue training during the sailing season—and maintaining the regimen even after the season has ended.

Listen to your body, eat a well-balanced diet, sleep well, and train smart. If you're not comfortable designing your own fitness or diet routine, have a professional at your local gym do it for you.

Stretch to stay flexible. This will help avoid injuries and improve your joints' range of movement—and thus, your mobility.

DOCK 10

Health and
Safety

Seasickness

If you've ever suffered this illness, the mere mention of the word will probably raise a gooseflesh up your spine. Even writing this section, I'm tormented by serious Pavlovian memories of being ten years old and lying sprawled on deck, praying to die while everyone around seemed oblivious.

Health and safety at sea fall into two categories—transient temporary or permanent.

Ailments such as seasickness or hypothermia fall into the first group and are temporary. However, because they disorient their victim, and impair judgment and balance, by not taking proper precautions, they can lead to permanent injuries or safety issues such as falling overboard or becoming snagged by equipment. Therefore, even the temporary and relatively minor—though extremely uncomfortable—ailments that life on a wet, windy, and rocking boat can cause, need to be explored, understood, and dealt with.

It Will Affect You

Regardless of whether you're ever afflicted, you're certain to be affected. Whether you're sailing lakes or the open ocean, the fact that you're on the water when there is wind chop practically guarantees that you'll have to deal with seasickness at some point in your career. Even if you're fortunate enough not to be directly afflicted, at some time or other you'll have crew or passengers who are, and you'll need to be involved by at least preparing them for it or assisting them through it.

Causes—a Very Nonmedical Viewpoint

As with any motion sickness, seasickness starts as a disagreement between the information from the eyes and the balance mechanism in the inner ear. The eyes say, "The world is not moving relative to me," and the balance mechanism says, "Oh yes it is!" The brain tries for a while to reconcile the two, and then the stomach gets involved and threatens to jettison its contents if the other two won't agree.

With three organs now in dispute, the brain becomes awfully tired and sets up a yawning routine while trying to close the eyes—presumably to distract the other organs from beginning a trend. Just as everything seems to be finding an equilibrium, the stomach makes good on its promise and the rest of the body begins to shiver and shake.

All onlookers see and smell the victim, and, like yawning, their organs then get in on the act.

Symptoms

Symptoms vary from mild nausea to outright debilitation. On the severe side of the scale, victims will display all the joys of someone with a raging hangover: nausea, dizziness, gastrointestinal afflictions such as vomiting and slick bowel movements—the works.

These symptoms can all be very nasty and can even be dangerous for the sufferer if the dehydration of fluids through the body's elimination is allowed to continue for prolonged periods.

The good news is that this would be rare since the trip will probably be over before any lasting damage can be done, and the sufferer generally rallies within minutes of coming ashore. On the other hand, if the trip is a little longer, the body will generally adapt to the motion and the sickness will disappear. When returning to land, some sufferers claim to experience landsickness because the ground is no longer moving and their balance mechanism thinks it ought to be.

Scared Sick

We've got a theory that when an individual has been seasick once, he or she is hypnotized that it's likely to happen again. At the mere mention of putting to sea, the stomach appears to have the best memory of all the organs since it will immediately begin doing the twist without needing any disagreement between sight and balance. By the time the latter two do begin, the stomach is so ready that it's positively gleeful to be sick.

On the bright side, with perseverance the body does eventually become immune to the rocking and rolling of nautical life.

History of Yachts, I

- The first American yacht is considered to have been an 83-foot (25-meter) brigantine, *Cleopatra's Barge,* built in 1816 for George Crowninshield. However, records do show that Americans kept boats for pleasure as far back as the early 1700s.
- Yacht and boat clubs were organized in the United States as early as 1811, when the Knickerbocker Boat Club of New York was founded, but none lasted long until the formation of the New York Yacht Club in 1844.
- Yachting has become popular in many other countries such as South Africa, Australia, New Zealand, Cuba, Brazil, Argentina, Italy, Spain, Portugal, France, Belgium, Netherlands, all the Scandinavian countries, Canada, and Great Britain.

Prevention

There are several techniques and medications to allay the worst of seasickness. By watching the horizon and keeping one's eyes out of the boat, sight is brought a little more in sync with balance, but this is not a panacea by any means.

Because the stomach is one of the primary problems, sufferers should try to avoid odors of any kind and keep the freshness of the breeze in their face. Often, cold water splashed on the face and neck, and, if possible, a swim are immeasurable helps.

Some swear by certain food combinations the night before and during the event. Others absolutely shun alcohol intake for dozens of hours before putting to sea, while a few crazies reckon—very unwisely and without foundation—that a shot of whiskey can settle the stomach. This is unfounded and to be dissuaded at all costs.

Certainly, producers of pills and wristbands claim that their products work. However, our personal experiences and observations do not bear this out.

A technique that does seem to work is to get good sleep prior to embarkation, and avoiding alcohol, spicy or fatty foods, and coffee before and during the voyage.

Motion sickness pills have a tendency to create drowsiness, while these authors have had little success with wrist patches.

By contrast, ear patches, according to our experience, are the most successful preventative measure. They're placed behind the ears several hours before setting off, and evidently work by tranquilizing one of the major culprits that sets up disagreement—the inner ear balance mechanism. Manufacturers claim that they continue to work for up to three days.

Dramamine? Other seasickness remedies?

The most widely used remedy is *Transderm-Scop*. This four-layer patch is worn behind the ear. Its principal ingredient, scopolamine, is painlessly time-released through the skin into the bloodstream and prevents motion-induced nausea.

Dramamine, once dispensed by prescription but now available over the counter, is one of the earliest seasickness remedies. It was originally formulated to relieve allergies in pregnant women, but was found to soothe nausea. It is actually a sedative.

Sea-Band, a bracelet that uses principles of acupressure to reduce nausea, has a small button that applies pressure to the wrist. It can be worn indefinitely, but only needs to be applied when you feel nauseated. A similar product, called *QueasyAide*, is distributed by a company aptly named *Mayday Inc.*

For some reason, most sufferers resist the idea that the best antidote for seasickness is to go up on deck where one can breathe fresh air and see the horizon (the only thing that isn't moving). The worst thing you can do is stay in your cabin.

Here are some other tips for warding off seasickness:

- Wear loose-fitting clothes. You'll be more comfortable.
- Avoid liquids, which will slosh around in your stomach.
- Forget the dining room. The smell of food is the last thing you'll want to face.
- Stay amidships, where the center of gravity is reduced, i.e., where there is the least motion.

When Disaster Strikes

Try as we might, and plan as we might, life and sailing are simply arenas where trouble will strike from time to time.

Listed below are just some of the issues you could quite conceivably encounter during your sailing career.

Facing a Wave

If you're unfortunate enough to ever face an unexpected wave about to break and don't have time to run away from it—if you've seen the wave it's usually too late—make absolutely sure that you're not broadside to its movement or it will roll or capsize you. Being stern-on to such a wave is not the ideal angle either.

To prove this, sit and watch people playing along the seashore where waves are crashing. Those who pay no attention to oncoming waves get flattened into the sand. Those who spot a wave about to curl over them and try to run away get nailed almost as hard. However, those with experience face the wave and shove through it with power and the sharpest part of their body—their head.

Seasickness Prevention Tips

- Eat and drink moderately the night before a voyage, and have normal sleep.
- Eat a light breakfast, such as cereal and fruit. Don't eat anything greasy.
- Stay outdoors.
- Keep as close to the boat's center of gravity as possible. Try to reach the closest point to the pivot around which the boat is moving, without going below deck.
- Stay as close to the water level and amidships as possible.
- Drink carbonated soda and eat dry crackers.
- Avoid oily and aromatic foods.
- Know that no matter how bad it might get you will feel better back on solid ground.

Power and Steering

What you've got to try to do is keep the sharpest part of your boat, namely your bow, up into the oncoming rush and get your weight back to lift the bow—but not so far back that it can easily roll you over backward. Then, the moment before you're hit, apply forward thrust and simultaneously throw as much weight as you can muster toward the bow as you strike the rushing water.

Restrain from the Bow

In a worst-case scenario, as in a prolonged storm where the waves are likely to keep rolling at you for many minutes or hours and you can't afford to take even one on the broadside, you'll need to take some additional precautions. In a similar way that an arrow is just a stick if it doesn't have feathered flights, without a thrust from behind your boat, and a steady hand on the tiller, your boat is no more than a cork in a river rapid. In this scenario, even the most experienced skipper would be hard-pressed to keep his or her vessel head-up into driving surf for more than a few minutes without making a mistake.

You'll desperately need to get something over the bow that will act like the flights of an arrow—only in reverse. The idea is not to weight the bow down, but to offer the surf the most resistance at the bow and allow the stern to trail toward the line of least resistance. Parachute-like devices are ideal.

Aground

If you've run aground, you need to get into deep water as soon as possible. Scan quickly to see how you can achieve this with minimal damage to the hull. The usual course will be full astern—or the direction from which you've just come—but this is not always the case.

If you can, reduce the load at the point that is grounded and distribute it to the region on the boat that's still in deep water. Outboard tilt can often help pull the stern deeper—if this would be a benefit—but be careful of striking submerged obstructions with the props.

Under Tow

It's obviously best to tow a boat from its bow. Reduce speed and attach the line as close to the bow as possible, as this will cause the towed vessel to follow more closely in the wake of the boat providing the tow.

F... Fi... Fi... Fire aboard!

Oh, no, this is not a good one. Fortunately, it's not a particularly common problem either, but it does happen. Fight the fire all you can, but if it becomes overpowering, get into the water and just hope the gutted hull remains afloat.

In the event of a fire, observe the following procedure:

- Crew closest to fire deploy extinguisher
- Helmsperson cut engine
- Turn off propane gas
- Radio for assistance (if necessary, or at least radio a distress call and ask boats in the vicinity to stand by for assistance)
- Orient the boat so that any flames are blown away from the boat and the sails
- Deploy flares (if necessary, or at least prepare flares for deployment)
- Conduct a quick headcount and account for all hands
- All hands to don lifejackets
- If fire is below decks, close all hatches, portholes, and doors
- Stand by to abandon ship

Abandon Ship Procedure
- All hands don lifejackets
- Call mayday on radio
- Deploy life raft
- One crew member boards life raft
- Load provisions onto raft (if time allows)
- Remaining crew board raft
- Skipper board raft
- Deploy flares
- Stand by on handheld VHF

First Aid Afloat

Every boat needs a basic first aid kit, and every skipper should undertake, and encourage his or her crew to undertake, a basic first aid course.

As a minimum, the first aid kit should contain the following items:

- ☐ A basic first aid manual
- ☐ Antiseptic ointment
- ☐ Rubbing alcohol
- ☐ An assortment of bandages, gauze pads, and tape
- ☐ Tweezers
- ☐ Sunburn lotion
- ☐ Aspirin and other over-the-counter pain medications
- ☐ Pepto-Bismol or other diarrhea treatments
- ☐ Eye drops such as Visine
- ☐ Plastic gloves and antiseptic soap

Fire Extinguishers

It is highly recommended that you carry a fire extinguisher capable of meeting any eventuality your craft might encounter. There are numerous types and sizes of extinguishers. Ensure that the one you select/have is U.S. Coast Guard approved.

Fire extinguishers are classified by letters and numbers according to the class and size fire they can put out. The letter A, B, C, or D indicates the class of fire. The number is a measure of the capacity of the extinguisher—the larger the number the greater the capacity to put out a fire.

- "A" is for combustible solids like wood.
- "B" is for flammable liquids such as gasoline.
- "C" is for electrical fires.
- "D" is for combustible metals like magnesium

Although some boat fires involve burning wood and paper (Class A), these fires can be put out with water. Do not use water on gasoline, oil, or electrical fires. Water causes gasoline and oil fires to spread and electrical current is conducted through the water.

Make sure to inspect your fire extinguishers monthly to make sure they are properly stored, and charged and that they are undamaged. Portable extinguishers should be mounted where they are accessible. Check the gauge to make sure the extinguisher is still charged. Check the seals to make sure they have not been tampered with. Replace cracked or broken hoses and keep nozzles free from obstruction. You should also weigh them to assure that they meet the minimum weight stated on the label.

Class of Fire vs. Type of Extinguisher
- Carbon Dioxide (CO_2) A, B, C
- Halon (until year 2000) A, B, C
- Dry Chemical B, C
- Foam B

Fire Precaution

Once you use a fire extinguisher, you should either have it recharged, if it is rechargeable, or replaced if it is a disposable type. In any event, always make sure that your extinguisher label indicates that it is a U.S. Coast Guard approved marine-type device.

An onboard fire is a serious event. If the fire cannot be controlled where do you go except in the water? The fire triangle consists of fuel, oxygen, and heat. All three must be present to start a fire and the removal of any single one can extinguish a fire.

Fuels, such as gasoline and propane, can be very dangerous if precautions are not taken. The fumes of these fuels are heavier than air and tend to collect in the cabin, bilge, and other lower areas of the boat. Because they naturally are surrounded by oxygen all that is necessary to start a fire is heat. This could come from something as simple as a spark from an ignition component. All you did was turn the key to start the engine, and BOOM...

You should read and understand the instructions on your fire extinguisher(s). If a fire starts you should be prepared and not hesitate. Grab the fire extinguisher, activate it, and direct it at the base of the flames using short bursts and sweeping it from side to side.

Distress

The call MAYDAY...MAYDAY...MAYDAY... is only for life-threatening emergencies and is used as a last resort.

For this reason, ensure that all emergency equipment—bilge pumps, fire extinguishers, and leak-stopping and shoring equipment tools and materials—is maintained in proper working order

Also, ensure that any sailing course you enroll in has some emergency procedure as part of the curriculum.

Person Overboard

The traditional cry might well be "man overboard," and in the heat of the moment it won't really matter what you do shout, but to welcome all women into the sailing fraternity, we've de-masculinized the term but not detracted from its potential for severity.

Preventing Man Overboard

An ounce of prevention is worth ten tons of cure. Institute strict rules, such as below, and enforce them unyieldingly.

- No standing or riding on gunwales or bow.
- No horseplay whatsoever—ever.
- Restrict deck movement to a minimum.
- Crew and passengers should remain low and hold on whenever they move—they must be touching some part of the vessel with at least three limbs at any one time.
- When weather deteriorates or any other bad circumstances occur, all aboard should don life vests.
- When heavy weather rolls in, all on deck should be secured to safety lines.

This list could continue *ad infinitum*; suffice it to say, practice common-sense safety regulations.

It's always serious

Depending on the circumstances and waters you are sailing, losing someone overboard can seem anything from hilariously funny to life-threateningly dire. As a rule, though, this is not a subject that should *ever* be treated lightly. Even if you're sailing at midday through the balmy shallows of some safe tropical haven, and cousin Joe—who is a great swimmer—has just made a total twit of himself by tripping over his own feet and landing in the drink, hold back the laughter till you've got the clown safely aboard.

It would be impossible to explore all of the potentially bad scenarios that poor Joe could experience—that you just couldn't see—as he took the plunge. Perhaps he's taken a knock to the head or suffers a cardiac arrest from the sheer embarrassment of the event; either way, he'll be in deep trouble while you and your crew are creased over with delight and not coming to his assistance. You'll be shocked just how long it takes to get your boat back to the spot—if indeed you find the spot—if Joe slips below the waves.

You get the point? Get Joe aboard—then you can laugh all you want, and for as long as you want.

Recovery Procedure

In the unfortunate event of losing a member overboard, *immediately* take the following steps. If you're in a trafficked area or racing, sound and display the appropriate alarm signals.

- The first person who sees someone going overboard (spotter) must shout "crew overboard" or some reasonable variant of this. They should also yell whether to starboard or port and point to the spot or person in the water.
- For the duration of the recovery procedure, the spotter must continue to point to the person and never relax this directional signal.
- All crew not otherwise engaged in bringing the boat about should take up the cry and be prepared to take over pointing duties if they see the victim in case the spotter loses sight of the victim.

- In order to push the stern and propeller away from the person in the water, the helmsman must immediately swing the boat in the direction that the person fell and shift the engine to neutral and stop the boat. If Joe fell over the port side, swing hard to port.
- Immediately throw a lifesaving device to the victim.
- Unless absolutely necessary, nobody else should enter the water, and then only wearing a PFD.
- The helmsman must keep the victim in view as he or she carefully brings the boat about.
- Approaching into the wind or current, carefully navigate back to the victim.
- Cut the engine as you draw up to the victim.
- Attach a line to the victim with all haste and ensure that he or she gets a PFD on before attempting to re-board.
- If a small vessel, ensure that weight is evenly distributed as the victim comes aboard.

Surviving the Water

When overboard, there are several techniques a victim can implement while waiting to be picked up. At this point it would be really great if you have on some form of PFD or other buoyant material. But, whatever you do, *do not panic*. This is easier said than done, but it's also vital, as panicked thrashing in water is counterproductive.

When clothing becomes wet, it sinks. However, it also provides a degree of insulation against cold and offers something for rescuers to grab hold of and pull you aboard. Therefore, keep your clothes on.

With a PFD

Roll to your back, cross your arms over your chest to conserve heat and energy, and lay as motionless as you can, keeping your head and face out of the water if possible. If the water is rough, extend your arms and hold them in a crucifix position. Allow your legs to rise as high as possible.

**Proper Position to Float
with a PFD**

Alternatively, to raise your head and chest higher out of the water, allow your legs and torso to sink to the vertical orientation.

Floating without flotation assistance

Unless you're a good swimmer or have practiced survival floating, you could be in deep trouble.

To employ survival floating, hang vertically, feet down, extend your arms, and let your head drop backward so that your face is toward the sky. Push down on the water with your arms and you should rise enough to take a deep breath. Relax your limbs. As long as you hold the air in your lungs you won't sink more than an inch or two. When you need another breath, push down once more and you should rise once again to repeat the exercise.

Treading water

Treading water is a lot more energy-sapping than simply floating, but it'll allow you more access to the air and it'll be much more effective in heavy conditions.

The procedure requires two movements:

- Your legs need to kick with a scissors motion, as in the leg movement for a breaststroke kick.
- Meanwhile, your arms need to rotate on the horizontal plane, with the palms of your hands held downward and tilting to form a planing surface that pushes you upward with each stroke.

Hypothermia

In layman's terms this condition might vary from being darned cold to icy and dead. Medically, it's defined by the U.S. Department of Health and Human Services as: "A decrease in the core body temperature to a level at which normal muscular and cerebral functions are impaired."

It therefore ranges from unpleasant to downright dangerous.

Conditions Leading to Hypothermia

To avoid hypothermia, you need to understand what factors contribute to the condition:

- Cold temperatures
- Improper clothing and equipment
- Wetness
- Fatigue, exhaustion
- Dehydration
- Poor food intake
- No knowledge of hypothermia
- Alcohol intake, which causes vasodilation leading to increased heat loss

"Hypothermic" Temperatures

Hypothermia is a condition in which body temperature falls drastically because of exposure to cold. In hypothermia, the body shuts off blood flow to the body's surface. We can talk glibly about being cold, but what are common parameters for a hypothermic condition?

- Near or below freezing temperatures
- 40 degrees Fahrenheit with wind and rain
- 60 degrees Fahrenheit with hurricane-force winds
- Strictly, any body temperature less than 98.6 degrees can be linked to hypothermia. Certainly, the sick and the elderly have a lower tolerance to temperatures and would experience the condition long before a healthy young person

The condition is associated with poor peripheral circulation, trench foot, and frostbite

Symptoms and Stages of Hypothermia

Watch for the "umbles"—*stumbles, mumbles, fumbles,* and *grumbles.* These strongly indicate a change in motor coordination and levels of consciousness

Proper Position to Float for Heat Conservation

Group
Huddle together for warmth

Alone
Pull knees up
and hold yourself in fetal position

Mild Hypothermia

- Body temperature of 98.6–96 degrees Fahrenheit
- Shivering—not under voluntary control
- Can't do complex motor functions, such as tie knots, furl or unfurl sails, but can still walk and talk

Moderate Hypothermia

- Body temperature 95 to 93 degrees Fahrenheit
- Dazed consciousness
- Loss of fine motor coordination—particularly in hands—can't zip up parka due to restricted peripheral blood flow
- Slurred speech
- Violent shivering
- Irrational behavior such as Paradoxical Undressing in which person starts to take off clothing, unaware s/he is cold
- "I don't care" attitude. Apathetic and having a lack of interest or concern, especially regarding matters of general importance or appeal, an indifference toward or lack of emotion or feeling for circumstance and others.

Severe Hypothermia

- Body temperature 92 to 86 degrees Fahrenheit and below (immediately life threatening)
- Shivering occurs in waves—violent then pause—pauses get longer until shivering finally ceases; because the heat output from burning glycogen in the muscles is not sufficient to counteract the continually dropping core temperature, the body shuts down on shivering to conserve glucose
- Person falls to the ground, can't walk, curls up into a fetal position to conserve heat
- Muscle rigidity develops—because peripheral blood flow is reduced and due to lactic acid and CO_2 buildup in the muscles
- Skin is pale
- Pupils are dilated
- Pulse rate decreases

Quick Checklist Before Launching to Sea

- ☐ Do a general cleaning (windows, hatches, canvas, bimini, dodger, bilges) and make sure drains and scuppers are clear
- ☐ Put on a good coat of wax and polish metal if necessary
- ☐ Clean and polish metal
- ☐ Check all spare parts and tools
- ☐ Make sure registration is current and onboard
- ☐ Check for any hull abrasions and blisters
- ☐ Check and replace zincs
- ☐ Check rub rails and ladder
- ☐ Inspect and test trim tabs
- ☐ Check shaft, cutlass bearing, strut, prop, rudder, and all fittings
- ☐ Check stanchion, pulpits, lifelines, ground tackle, lines, fenders, chainplates, and cleats
- ☐ Check hull/deck joint, deck, windows, and port lights for leaks
- ☐ Inspect anchor, blocks, pad eyes, windlass, winches and lubricate
- ☐ Check seacocks and lubricate if necessary, as well as condition of hoses and clamps
- ☐ Make sure below waterline hoses are double clamped
- ☐ Check bilges pumps for automatic and manual operation as well as for oil
- ☐ Check limber holes and make sure they are clear
- ☐ Check battery terminals for corrosion, check water level
- ☐ Check bonding system and inspect all wiring for wear and chafe
- ☐ Test all gauges and electronic equipment for operability
- ☐ Check shore power and charger and make sure you have spare fuses onboard
- ☐ Check navigation lights, antennas, distress signals, PFDs, fire extinguishers, compass, charts, radar reflector, bailer, and hand pump
- ☐ Check water system and pump for leaks and proper operation
- ☐ Check refrigerator, clean stove, check that all burners and oven are working
- ☐ Check general condition of sails and inspect bolt rope
- ☐ Inspect: mast and spreaders; spreader boots and shrouds; rivets and screw connections; reefing points and reefing gear; sail track; rigging, turnbuckles and clevis pins; stays; forestay and backstay connections; masthead fitting and pulleys; roller furling; halyards; tape turnbuckles, cotter pins, and spreader

- At 90 degrees the body tries to move into hibernation, shutting down all peripheral blood flow and reducing breathing rate and heart rate
- At 86 degrees the body is in a state of metabolic icebox—the person looks dead but is still alive

Death from Hypothermia

- Breathing becomes erratic and very shallow
- Semiconscious
- Cardiac arrhythmias develop; any sudden shock may set off ventricular fibrillation; heart stops, death

Treating Hypothermia

The basic principles of rewarming a hypothermic victim is to conserve the heat they still have and to replace all the body fuel they are burning up to generate that heat. If a person is shivering, they have the ability to rewarm themselves painfully and slowly.

Treating Mild to Moderate Hypothermia

General

- Reduce heat loss
- Add additional layers of clothing
- Change to dry clothing
- Increase physical activity
- Seek shelter

Add fuel and fluids

- It's essential to keep a hypothermic person adequately hydrated and fueled.

Food types

- Carbohydrates are quickly released into the bloodstream for a sudden brief heat surge. These are the best foods to use for quick energy intake, especially for mild cases of hypothermia.

- Proteins are slowly released and give off heat over a longer period
- Fats are slowly released but are good because they release heat over a long period; however, it takes more energy to break fats down into glucose. It also takes more water to break down fats leading to increased fluid loss.

Food intake
- Hot liquids provide calories plus heat source.
- Sugars (kindling).
- GORP has both carbohydrates (sticks) and proteins/fats (logs).

Things to avoid
- Alcohol—increases peripheral heat loss.
- Caffeine—causes water loss increasing dehydration.
- Tobacco/nicotine—increases risk of frostbite.

Add heat
- Fire or other external heat source
- Body-to-body contact

Treating Severe Hypothermia
General
Reduce heat loss with a hypothermia wrap. The idea is to provide a shell of total insulation. No matter how cold, patients can still rewarm themselves internally much more efficiently than any external rewarming. Make sure the patient is dry and has a polypropylene layer to minimize sweating on the skin. The person must be protected from any moisture in the environment. Use multiple sleeping bags, wool blankets, wool clothing, and *Ensolite* pads to create a minimum of four inches of insulation all the way around the patient, especially between the patient and the ground. Include an aluminum "space" blanket to help prevent radiant heat loss, and wrap the entire ensemble in plastic to protect it from wind and water. If someone is truly hypothermic, don't put him/her naked in a sleeping bag with another person.

Add fuel and fluids

- Warm sugar water. For people in severe hypothermia, the stomach has shut down and will not digest solid food, but it can absorb water and sugars. Give a diluted mixture of warm water with sugar every fifteen minutes. Diluted Jello works best since it's part sugar and part protein. This will be absorbed directly into the bloodstream providing the necessary calories to allow the person to rewarm him-or herself. Do not give full-strength Jello even in liquid form; it's too concentrated and will not be absorbed.
- Urination. People will have to urinate from cold diuresis. Vasoconstriction creates greater volume pressure in the bloodstream. The kidneys pull off excess fluid to reduce the pressure. A full bladder is a place for additional heat loss so urinating will help conserve heat.

Add heat

- Heat can be applied to transfer heat to major arteries: at the neck for the carotid, at the armpits for the brachial, at the groin for the femoral, at the palms of the hands for the arterial arch.
- Chemical heat packs such as the Heat Wave provides 110 degrees F for 6–10 hours.
- Hot water bottles, warm rocks, towels, compresses.
- For a severely hypothermic person, rescue breathing can increase oxygen and provide internal heat.

Semi-Annual Boat Safety Checklist

Personal Flotation Devices (PFDs)

- ☐ Check for wear or abrasion, weak or torn seams, secure straps and buckles.
- ☐ If your PFDs are equipped with inflation devices, check to be sure cartridges are secure and charged.

Fire Extinguishers

- ☐ Do you have the required amount and types?
- ☐ Are they easily accessible?
- ☐ Is there one accessible from the helm or cockpit?
- ☐ Does everyone on board know how to use them?
- ☐ Have you checked them within the past 12 months?
- ☐ Are serviceable units tagged by a licensed facility?

Fuel System

- ☐ Is the system properly grounded at the filter, tank, deck, pump?
- ☐ Is the fuel tank free from rust or contamination?
- ☐ Are there any leaks from tank, hose or fittings?
- ☐ Is fuel tank secured?
- ☐ Is there a fuel shut-off valve on tank and at engine.
- ☐ Is the engine compartment and engine clean and free of oily rags or flammable materials?
- ☐ Is there a blower switch at a remote location?
- ☐ Is your fuel system protected from siphoning?

Safety Equipment

- ☐ Are the rails or lifelines in good condition?
- ☐ Make sure the stanchions or pulpit are securely mounted.
- ☐ Ensure that all hardware is tight and sealed at deck.
- ☐ Are grab rails secure and free of corrosion or snags?
- ☐ Are the non-skid surfaces free from accumulated dirt or excess wear?

Ground Tackle

- ☐ Do you have at least two anchors on board?
- ☐ Is your anchor and rope adequate for your boat and bottom conditions?
- ☐ Is the tackle properly secured?
- ☐ Length of chain at anchor.
- ☐ Thimble on rope and safety wired shackles.
- ☐ Chafing gear for extended stays or storm conditions.
- ☐ Anchor stowed for quick accessibility.

Courtesy

Everyone who uses or enjoys the waterways, whether boating, walking along the shore-line, or actually living on the water's edge, has equal rights to enjoy the resource.

- Never disturb private property owners by docking on their land.
- Always be aware of your wake, its size, and who it might affect.
- Control your speed and obey speed limit signs.
- Because sound carries farther over water than land, keep voices, music, and other noises to a minimum.
- Control your waste. Pollution laws prohibit throwing refuse into the water.
- Carry bags aboard and dispose of waste and garbage properly.

Stoves

☐ Labeled and designated for marine use.
☐ Properly ventilated to remove carbon monoxide from cabin.
☐ Retainers or rails for pots and pans while underway.
☐ If built-in, properly insulated and free from combustible materials, CNG and LPG (propane).
☐ Stored in separate compartment from vessel's interior and engine room.
☐ Tightly secured shut-off valve at tank.
☐ Proper labeling and cautions in place at tank location.
☐ Hoses, lines and fittings of approved and inspected type.
☐ Compartment is ventilated overboard and below level of tank base.

Electrical System

☐ Wiring approved for marine applications.
☐ Is system neatly bundled and secured?
☐ Protected against chafing and strain.
☐ Adequate flex between bulkhead and engine connections.
☐ Clear of exhaust system and bilge?
☐ Is system protected by circuit breakers or fuses?
☐ Are grounds to Zincs if required?
☐ Are wire terminals and connections sealed to prevent corrosion?

Bilge Pumps

☐ Will pump(s) adequately remove water in emergency?
☐ Do you have a manual backup?
☐ Are bilges clean and free to circulate (clear limber holes)?
☐ Do you check bilges frequently and not rely on automatic pumps?

Corrosion Prevention

☐ Through-hulls, props, shafts, bearings, rudder fittings, and exposed fastenings free of non-destructive corrosion.
☐ Zincs are adequate to provide protection.
☐ Through-hulls are properly bonded.

☐ Inspect the steering cables, engine control linkage and cables, engine mounts and gear case for corrosion.

☐ These items are properly lubricated or painted to prevent undue corrosion.

Through-hulls

☐ Strainers, intakes and exhaust or discharge fittings are free from restrictions such as barnacles, marine growth or debris.

☐ Inspect sea valves for smooth operation.

☐ Handles are attached to valves for quick closure.

☐ Hoses are in good condition and free from cracking.

☐ Double hose-clamps below the waterline.

☐ Anti-siphon valve fitted to marine toilet.

☐ Through-hull plugs are near fittings or attached to hose in case of emergency.

Batteries

☐ Stored in non-corrosive, liquid tight, ventilated containers.

☐ Non-conductive covers are fitted over posts.

☐ Batteries are well secured.

Sailor Talk

Took the wind out of his sails

Often we use "took the wind out of his sails" to describe getting the best of an opponent in an argument. Originally it described a battle maneuver of sailing ships. One ship would pass close to its adversary on its windward side. The ship and sails would block the wind from the second vessel, causing it to lose headway. Losing motion meant losing maneuverability and the ability to carry on a fight.

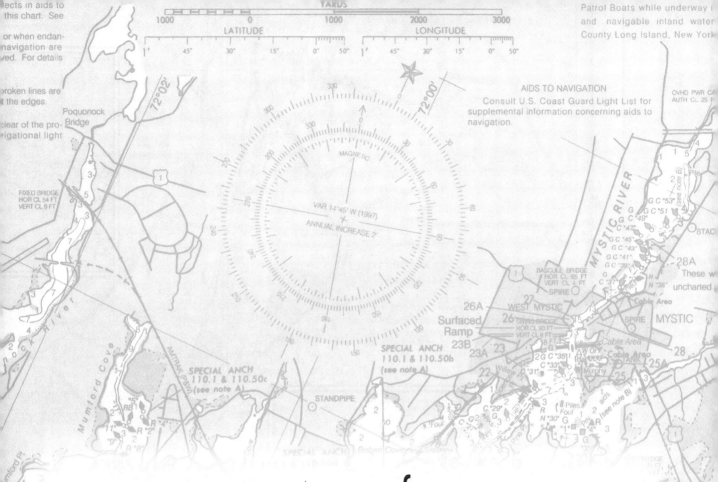

p a r t   f o u r

RACING AND INTERNATIONAL SAILING

DOCK 11

Competing in Races

Introduction

Although this section is written with organized racing in mind, the principles that apply would nonetheless be equally applicable to any area of competition—even if that competition is only against your own best abilities to sail to a destination in the shortest time and display the greatest technique.

Even if no competitive criteria apply to you, and you don't have the slightest inclination to care about logging good performance, this section is still worth reading if only to have some point to add when other yachties are discussing their competitive technique back at the club. Besides, by reading on you may wind up feeling the prickle for challenge beginning to rise from within.

Once you have mastered all the fundamental elements of sailing, it is time to move on to more complex and exciting things.

Competition brings out the highest level of performance in all of us. When we compete we have a chance to compare our skills and equipment against those of others and, humans being what we are, we will generally increase our efforts and skills to meet the challenge.

What Is Covered?

Whether your craft of choice is a catboat, a sailboard, or an ocean-crossing cruiser, the issues covered will be applicable. We've tried to keep them as generic as possible.

On the other hand, competitive sailing is an entire subject in itself, and it's beyond the scope of this book to explore every possible angle as it may apply to the type of boat or type of races that you might be interested in. Beyond what can reasonably be covered in this section are excellent books that specialize in the exhaustive details of technique, tactics, and discipline-specific analysis.

What follows is an exploration of the priorities you need to understand about competition.

How Do We Define Competition?

Perhaps the greatest competition you could ever have is simply with nature. Milking the wind for every ounce of push, while remaining on the living side of safety, is what the sport of sailing is all about. Any attitude less than this is simply drifting.

Maybe we should alter your frame of reference here and suggest that you're not so much competing against yourself, others, or time as you're competing against Mother Nature.

Under this definition, there's not a sailor afloat who can afford to skip this section.

Get Good Instruction

Beginners at Different Levels

Whether a beginner in sailing as a whole, or racing as a sport, as soon as possible is the very best time to receive some professional instruction. It's tempting, particularly for the intermediate participant, to believe that we're no longer beginners and cannot benefit from what others have to teach us. But Olympic athletes and other achievers who constantly explore the limits of human ability wouldn't employ the world's most expensive trainers and tutors if there weren't any value in being taught.

Get good instruction—don't try to reinvent the wheel.

How to Find a Good Sailing Instructor

To claim instructor status, it's absolutely necessary that an individual or organization can show some kind of formal certification. To check out what sort of standing the instructor's affiliate has, simply ask around within the sailing community and you'll soon get the scoop.

A good instructor would typically be able to show a resume that includes certification from the U.S. Sailing Association, American Sailing Association (ASA), or some nationally or internationally recognized authoritative body.

What Kind of Certification Will You Attain?

Of course, the aim of certification is to ensure that, at the very least, you attain a minimum standard of knowledge and ability. In

Resources

The American Sailing
   Association
13922 Marquesas Way
Marina del Rey, CA 90292
Tel: (310) 822-7171
Fax: (310) 822-4741
E-mail:
   ouch9@cinenet.net
www.asa.com

United States Sailing
   Association
Toll free Fax-On-Demand:
   1-888 US SAIL-6
PO Box 1260
15 Maritime Drive
Portsmouth, RI 02871-
   0907
Tel: (401) 683-0800
Fax: (401) 683-0840
E-mail: ussailing@
   compuserve.com
www.olyc.com/ussailing/

addition, it should also entitle you meet the specifications of regulating bodies such as sailing clubs, state and federal government, or other authorities that will be important to your particular ambitions.

Sailing Clubs

Once you've graduated from a sailing school, joining a sailing club and competing against others of similar skill level is the next step toward honing your skills. Sailing clubs are supported by the communities they serve, and in the same way some tennis clubs consistently produce top-class league teams and individuals, so too do sailing clubs.

To help you with the selection of what is likely to suit you, consider the following pointers, which might not be vital elements of the competitive environment but do indicate various levels of member involvement and a strong core that will likely prosper and grow for many years:

- Does the club organize social events such as barbecues, dinners, dances, and regular races?
- Some clubs set up group trips to classic sailing destinations. Does this club undertake such events? It'll mean a lot of reduced-rate travel and the chance to check out new venues at a fraction of the cost.
- Does the club ever offer seminars by experts? It's a real boon to have visiting celebrities and equipment manufacturers on-site to discuss technique and problems.
- Are there any eligibility restrictions? Some clubs are more or less community-based and not very hospitable to outsiders. Others require that you're introduced by a member and have you jump through a bunch of screening-selecting hoops before a board will accept or reject your application. This is great once you're in, although it does mean that your loutish buddies might not make the cut!
- Are there any reciprocal membership affiliations whereby you can receive benefits at other organizations if you are a member at a particular club?

Other Issues to Consider

You might want to get an idea of the following in order to see if the lessons will benefit and suit you:

- What type/size of boat will be used in the program? Make sure the boat suits the type of sailing you intend to do.
- Does the school provide textbooks, instructional videos, and classroom training? It's important that a school include theory as part of its curriculum.
- How many students per class? More than four students per instructor will minimize your crucial personal attention.
- How long has the school been operating? Also, ensure that the school is both accredited and insured.
- Will the school provide graduate references? Chatting with recent graduates is the best way to gain an unbiased view of the program and what it delivers.
- How much can you learn, and how far can you go with this school? Are there advanced courses, and will the school help you to become part of the sailing community by recommending a club?

It's quite important to do your homework before simply joining a particular club. To receive a comprehensive list of clubs and schools, contact the ASA.

Vital Tips

Attitude

As with any other human endeavor, the paramount component of a winning formula is the attitude—of the crew and skipper. It's the one ingredient that'll ultimately make for a champion. It's the element that keeps you reinvesting equipment and technique and keeps you focused on the long-term goal to be the best—regardless of short-term defeats.

Mistakes

There isn't a champion who hasn't made major blunders in his or her career and who doesn't make lesser errors during every event he or she participates in. The difference is that champions never quit. Although they might agonize over the mishap for months, out on the course they forget about what happened and concentrate their energies on what is going to happen.

There is certainly enough information and theory available that, if applied, would ensure that no skipper or crew would ever make a mistake. At the risk of laboring a point, that's the entire reason for racing: *we race in order to establish who will make the least mistakes.* The person or crew who makes the least errors is called a winner, but they're only a winner until the next event. Every time an event comes up, the "losers" get to prove that they've learned from their mistakes.

Concentration

At the start of any event all you know is all you know, and all the equipment you have is all the equipment you have. That

---

Yacht Clubs and Sailing Clubs

Check out http://sailing.org/iyru/yachtclubs.html for a complete list of club Web sites.

might seem like a bit of an obvious statement, but read it again—s-l-o-w-l-y. The currency you pay for your victories in is *concentration*.

It's no great leap of faith to see that, good fortune aside, the only difference you can make to the outcome of an event—but more particularly to attaining the limits of your own ability—is by spending the currency of your concentration wisely. And, like all currency, those who invest wisely receive handsome returns.

Therefore, spending your valuable concentration thinking about situations that have occurred up to any particular point in a race will yield you no dividends. What matters is what is currently happening around you and how you can influence that moment's circumstance to alter what will happen.

All the cussing in the world does little but unsettle the crew. During the course of a career, every sailor will face even doses of bad circumstances and equipment failures, but in a crisis it's necessary to understand that you're just putting another of the hassles behind you. Remaining proactive under stressful conditions is the difference between champions and regular folk.

Choose to be proactive

Aggressively learn from your mistakes. The more senses you can involve in this learning process the better. Immediately after an event, record the mistakes, explore what led up to them, how this lead-up could have been avoided, and how your reaction could have rectified or improved the situation. By writing it down, you have involved additional senses that just thinking about the situation wouldn't have. By seeing it on paper you'll become your own best and most constructive critic, rather than simply being mad at yourself or someone else.

Event after event, as you build your dossier of errors, you'll begin to see a trend. Perhaps you're having trouble on a particular tack or lose ground coming about. Besides putting in more time practicing these maneuvers, as you find yourself leading up to a similar circumstance in other races you'll know to lift your level of concentration to new heights.

Practice
How to practice
Because sailing is both a science and an art, practice is the most vital element of improvement. As hinted, what you need to do is focus on your weakest areas. Remember, over the long term, the winner is the person who makes the least mistakes.

Without a coach to look over your shoulder, it's also important that you have a written list of areas you need to improve. Prioritize these to ensure that you don't become sidetracked practicing what is fun when it's practicing that which is frustrating that will make the only difference to your results.

Priority list
What follows is a sample list of priorities that might serve as an example.

- *Tacks*—Practice the ideal approach and concentrate on powering through the transition.
- *Beating*—Learn to feel the wind and the effects that steering through the sail rather than with the rudder has on overall performance.
- *Close quarter sailing*—Practice with a buddy. Alternate position and practice techniques for sailing through one another's blanket and backwinds.
- *Clean starts*—Learn to bring your boat up to a precise predetermined position and heading at an allotted moment in time. To do so, learn to stall your boat as well as pour on a sudden boost.
- *Mark roundings*—Pick a spot or object—preferably a buoy—and bring yourself in on an imaginary course. Practice tacking through varying degrees of severity of angle.

As mentioned, conduct these maneuvers out of the way of traffic and beyond the limits of physical confines. Whenever possible, try to practice with other boats as a competitive gauge.

The only record I would cherish would be for the longest circumnavigation, the most dilly-dallying on the way.
—Gwenda Cornell, *Pacific Odyssey*

• • •

Your Yachtsman would lose much of his enjoyment if he were obliged to do for pay what he is doing for the love of the thing itself.
—Louis D. Brandeis

Being a Great Student

There is no growth in praise. We only learn when we are corrected. Therefore, the quicker you learn will depend on how well you learn to savor criticism—not just bear with it.

Constructive vs. Destructive Criticism

Learn to discern the difference between constructive and destructive criticism. Destructive criticism is a comment aimed only to strip you of your confidence and has no merit or advice attached to it. By contrast, constructive criticism usually comes from well-meaning individuals who have noted some aspect of your conduct that could be improved.

Acting vs. Reacting

When faced with criticism, choose to act rather than react. One of the toughest things to do when someone points out your shortcoming is to say Thank you and really mean it. Sure, there are an awful lot of people in this world who only wish you were taller so that their criticism of you could raise their self-esteem higher, but by reacting negatively to their undermining comments, you'll only serve to deliver them a victory.

Off in privacy you can try out their remarks, or research them a little further to test them for validity. And, who knows, perhaps they're inadvertently delivering you a pearl of wisdom with which you can defeat them next time you're out on the water. Success is, after all, the best revenge.

Mentoring

Choose one or more mentors, people who consistently achieve better results than you, and sit in their wake mimicking everything they do. Try to understand why they're doing what they do. If you just can't figure it out, bring it up in conversation. It's a little like that birds-and-the-bees talk with your kids. Once you're advanced enough to have figured out what they're doing, most sailors will tell you why they're doing it.

Great Sailing Re-Enactments

There can be little question that great sailing feats took place in ancient times with very rudimentary equipment. Because we have no accurate records of the actual events, modern explorers have attempted to prove to a skeptical public both the possibility and probability that these voyages were fact and not fiction.

The name Thor Heyerdahl is synonymous with taking theory out onto the waves and proving by example what could or couldn't be achieved with very elementary equipment and a lot of tenacity.

A multimedia mogul before the term "multimedia" existed, Thor was part scientist, part adventurer, and part showman. This Norwegian explorer's dedication has proved countless "experts" wrong when they swore that his sailing contraptions would sink long before he reached the horizon.

All of the following voyages belong to this great modern-day, retro-explorer:

Kon-Tiki Expedition

Constructed of nine balsa wood logs, *Kon-Tiki* was a raft built along the lines of a prehistoric South American vessel. In 1947, a crew of six took 101 days to sail from Callao in Peru to the island of Raroia in Polynesia. This successful voyage of 4300 miles proved that the islands in Polynesia were within the range of such a vessel. A documentary of the voyage won an Oscar in 1952, and a book about the expedition has been translated into no fewer than 66 languages.

Easter Island

In 1955 Thor undertook an archaeological expedition to Easter Island and Polynesia. Although self-financed, the expedition had patronage from King Olav V of Norway. Thor´s archaeologists found that the famous *moai* stone heads showed evidence of a large papyrus boat with mast and sail carved into them.

The expedition also discovered a previously unknown type of statue normally associated with South America. The members of the expedition also visited secret family tombs where they found skeletal remains and small stone sculptures.

Based on this evidence, Heyerdahl concluded that epic yet unrecorded voyages had taken place in ancient times.

The *Ra I* and *Ra II* Expeditions

In 1969, with the aid of members of the Burundi tribe from Chad in Central Africa, Thor built a 45-foot-long copy of an ancient Egyptian papyrus vessel at the foot of the Pyramids. In honor of the ancients, the vessel was named after the sun god Ra.

Ra was later transported to Safi in Morocco, from where it set sail westward for Barbados. After 3000 miles, problems with the construction of the stern forced abandonment of the trip just short of their destination.

Ten months later, four Aymara Indians from Bolivia who were master of the traditional art of building reed boats, built Ra II.

Ra II made a successful transatlantic crossing by covering the 4000 miles in just 57 days.

Practice Sessions

Don't attempt to crowd every practice session with the entire repertoire of areas you need to improve. Pick just two or three of your worst shortcomings that would fit neatly into a complementary routine and concentrate on those till the end of session. Unless you're going for Olympic gold, if you've got a two-hour session to work with, set aside the last half-hour for playing and doing all the things you and your crew really enjoy. If you devote the entire session to a grinding routine of just polishing the negatives, you'll begin finding reasons why you shouldn't repeat the experience, or your crew will mutiny.

Know Your Course

Regardless of the size of boat and length of course, one factor remains an obvious constant: All events are conducted over a predetermined course that is laid out and published. The best advantage that any competitor could therefore gain would be to thoroughly know the course before the race is staged.

If the race is being held in your backyard, so to speak, then this is no problem and you'd know all the tricks and characteristics of the particular area. However, if it's in some far-flung region, somewhere that it would be impossible to scout out in advance, then at least familiarize yourself with charts and literature on the area. Try to come to grips with typical weather and wind patterns for that season and understand all the other issues that might play a factor, like safe havens or average boat traffic.

Beyond the Course

Often a championship is won not on a single course but on a competitor's performance over a series of races. To achieve victory in this situation would obviously require that you devote quite a bit of time to research. On this note, don't become complacent. All other factors being equal, there's little that can consistently beat the sailor with a homeground advantage—even if only an advantage because you're more familiar with the course than others in the same championship.

Waves

- Ripples
  When the wind is light, ripples appear on a smooth water. If the wind gains strength, ripples will grow into chop.
- Chop
  These are larger waves that occur with strong winds. Even if the wind abates, the chop will continue and may develop into swells.
- Swells
  Large wave motions of water that are not related to the local wind conditions; they are found beyond the area of their origin.

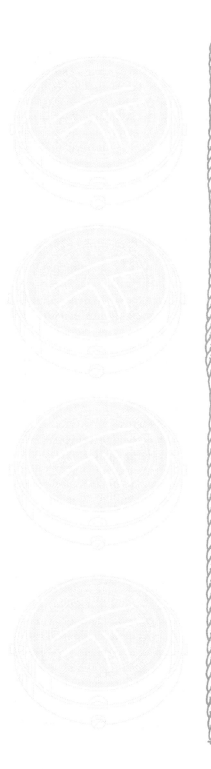

Before We Begin

Honesty

In this section you'll notice a lot of reference to relative progress. This can be taken two ways: Of course you're competing against the other competitors, but true champions plot their progress against their own potential within the circumstances. To do this you need to develop a cast-iron attitude of honesty. Whether your results are good or bad, always pass them through the sieve of truth and sincerity. This is very much an internal process and not for the benefit or common knowledge of anyone else.

Heads Up

Beyond what you're doing to win, the other issue is to constantly scan your surroundings, taking note of what everyone else is setting themselves up for.

Having said this, accept that you're probably not in contention to even place in the first few events that you participate in. Therefore, until you're at least acquainted with competition and sailing in a fleet, it's better to keep your focus on staying out of harm's way and simply concentrate on sailing to the best of your abilities. For a beginner, basics are far more important than tactics. Only once you're getting the most out of your equipment does the competitive environment become an issue.

The more you sail, the greater your skills will grow and the more concentration you'll then be able to devote to tactics.

When first exposed to a racing environment, spend 80 percent of your time focused on your speed and 20 percent focused on your position. Then, as sailing and competition become second nature, the bias will naturally shift until you feel the optimum edge of performance and can devote all your attention to strategy and tactics.

Handicap

Let's face it, when it comes to racing, not all boat designs are born equal. To open a race up and give every design class a chance of winning, a system of handicapping has been developed to place various classes on a level playing field.

Why penalize the specialist?

Perhaps this seems a little unfair to the purist who reasons that if an individual specializes in winning races by investing in superior design, why should a lesser vessel take honors?

Fortunately, this answer is simple: The specialized vessel and crew will still win on pure time and receive the accolades that go with victory. On the other hand, with equipment results removed from the equation, the also-rans are given a chance to test skill against skill.

All can be winners

In effect then, handicapping allows for two or more winners to emerge from one event. Besides taking honors for winning on time, there's nothing to stop a racing purist from sweeping to victory in several categories.

A sport of compromise

Sailing is like other sports in that dedicated equipment does not come cheap, and few individuals are fortunate enough to afford more than one craft at a time. It would therefore penalize the individual and the competition in general far more if racing were purely run on time alone.

Where will you find handicapping?

Besides long-haul racing, many clubs that don't have sufficient vessels in one class to create worthwhile competition will institute a handicap system.

How does the system work?

Various systems might be instituted. The most common is to review each boat and issue it a number that will serve as a factor or yardstick that will be multiplied against its time to arrive at an adjusted finishing position.

Another method is to allow for different start times.

Pre-Regatta Checklist

To keep you safe and competitive, go through the following checklist and ensure that all items are in good order and attachments are sound:

- Hiking strap ties
- Shackles
- Fitting connections
- Sail/battens
- Control lines
- Inspection ports
- Rudder, centerboard, tiller, and tiller extension
- Mast, mast rake, stays
- Halyard locking
- Boom
- Wind pennant
- Mainsheet
- Protest flag
- Spares (mast fittings, shackles, etc.)
- Sailing and safety gear

Beyond handicapping boats, individual skippers and crews might also have a handicap based on past performance.

On the Start Line

Getting a good start is no accident; it's the result of practice and planning.

The advice that follows is particularly tailored to racing in fleets where there's an armada of craft milling about, jostling for position and excitedly anticipating the start gun that will set them on their way.

The larger the fleet and the shorter the course you're starting, the more critical your start will be. Consider how much bad wind lies downwind of all those sails. You don't want to be anywhere near that zone, and you do want to have a clear run up to the first mark. At the start you want to be on the right tack approaching the line and have good speed. If you miss your mark you could find yourself way back with an awful lot of obstacles to overcome even before you can begin to maneuver.

Your best alternative is to formulate a plan and have every member of the crew keyed into it and aware of the role they must play to make it work.

Execute Your Plans

A dumb statement? Not at all. It's one thing to formulate a plan and quite another to stick to it in the heat of the final moment's excitement. This is especially vital if your crew is a new one and they are anticipating execution of the plan you'd strategized. Even if the gap you've seen appears to be a good one, invariably any gains you might make by taking it will be lost when the teamwork falls apart and the crew starts to doubt your promised word.

Timing

The elements of timing as they present themselves on the start line are being at a given position and traveling on the right heading at maximum speed at a precise moment in time. As a beginner, this task can almost be overwhelming. The steps that follow should help you keep a cool head.

Practice timing

Pick or drop a buoy in the water, then set yourself precise moments in time—say every five or ten minutes on the clock. Approaching the buoy from different angles and under differing wind conditions, try to place yourself exactly thirty seconds from the buoy at full speed, then cover that distance and pass the buoy—your imaginary start line—precisely on the allotted five or ten minute moment you've selected as your practice start time.

What you're seeking is how far back the thirty-second mark really is under various conditions of wind and approach. Once you've mastered the exercise, introduce more elements of realism. Link up with other boats that want to hone their skills. Synchronize your watches, drop two buoys in a similar configuration you'd expect to find on an actual race's start line, and hold a competition to see who's consistently the best judge of speed and distance.

On Race Day

Mill in the nearby vicinity just upwind of the location where you'd like to cross the line. With about ninety seconds to the start gun, try to put yourself on a course that will deliver you to your desired location when the gun fires. With thirty seconds to go, be absolutely sure that you won't prematurely cross the line. In most instances it's far better to err on the side of being fifteen seconds late to the line than one-and-a-half seconds early and overshooting it.

With ten seconds to go you should be under full power and moving at full speed.

Beginners

As a beginner, your primary objectives are to cross the line after the gun and to not hit anyone. Of course, the vast majority of competitors will have the same idea as you. If you're aiming for the optimum start position, you'll have stiff competition, so for your first few races, opt for a lesser position or hang a little further back and fall in behind the lead boats.

Racing boat

Having stressed that you should be on your approach run with just seconds to go, if you see other boats bearing down on you, it's much better to get out of the way—even if it means that you must come about and then tack back in behind them.

Make sure that you're not on a course to being trapped and squeezed between other participants and the committee boat.

Ideally—Late With Speed

It's indeed fine to be late, but only with speed. Hitting the line under full speed is more important than crossing the line at the moment the gun sounds. Far too many competitors concentrate on being right at the line for the start, forsaking speed in order to achieve this. Even if you hit the line a few seconds after them, they still won't be moving all that fast and you can shoot ahead.

Competition is like a game of chess. At first you must learn the rules and moves of each piece and how these affect the whole. Once you've grasped that concept you're ready to begin implementing set plays or game plans. Similarly, once you've amassed some experience handling the boat and have a couple of races under your belt, you can begin to consider more tactical starts.

Make the Wind Your Ally

Out on the water, get a feel for the wind and apply the knowledge that you have to get an idea of the ideal position to be in when the start gun fires. The elements that are important at this point are:

- Which side of the line should you be on?
- Which side of the course will offer you the best tactical advantage?
- What tack will place you on the ideal heading to place you on course?
- On this heading, under full power, how many boat lengths of speed are you making every fifteen seconds? This will give you an idea of the distance you need to be away from the line with thirty seconds to go.

These are decisions you can make some time before the final two-minute mark.

Leading into the final minutes, constantly reassess which boats appear to have a similar plan and consider which of them might be on an intersecting or collision course with your chosen bearing, then make the necessary adjustment to your tack.

Toe the Line

As soon as possible, bring your boat up onto the line and head to the wind. This will give you the opportunity to establish whether either the pin end or committee boat end is further ahead. This is particularly important on short courses. Of course, taking the wind and course into consideration, pick the closest end, at the least it will give you a head start.

Choose Your Tack

The rule you'll follow is to establish a tack that'll bring your boat to the mark on the straightest possible course. This rule is equally applicable on the other legs of the course. Naturally, the longer the race, the more variance in wind speed and direction you'll be subjected to. This is why your first races really need to be pretty short affairs. In terms of course and time on the water, it's exhausting.

While assessing your best tack, take into consideration that the port tack must give way to boats on a starboard tack. In other words, if you can, try to put yourself on the starboard side of all other vessels; they'll have to give way to you. Likewise, if boats appear on your starboard side, you'll have to give way to them.

Where the Wind Comes From

Sound like the lead into a fairy tale? In sailing, though, the side that the wind is coming from is the side of the course that you'll want to be on. This is a decision you can make about thirty minutes before the start. Simply look directly into the wind, and that's precisely where you want to place yourself.

Nautical Charts

A nautical chart is a graphic representation of the marine environment.

In addition to its basic elements, a chart is a working document used as a "road map" and worksheet. With navigational instruments, the chart allows you to plot precisely where on the water you are, what obstructions or hazards lie between you and your goal/safety, and the best course to set in order to arrive on schedule.

Charts might also indicate ocean depths and certain pertinent information such as restricted access, activity areas, or shipping lanes.

However, bear in mind that the wind direction and strength might alter and continue to vary right up to the start, so make a point of constantly reassessing the wind's direction relative to the start line.

It's one thing to see where you want to be, and quite another to maneuver your way to that spot through a fleet of milling craft. The best solution is to get to the course early and take care of all these preliminary decisions as soon as possible.

Start Skills

Slowing and Stalling

As boats converge on a start line, a lot of bad air is created and following craft run the real risk of collision with those ahead who have lost power in the doldrums. At this point you'll need to take evasive action to avoid disaster or a full tack to place you back on course.

Sailing is not all about power and speed at all costs. There are times, like the moments leading up to a start gun, when going slow is the name of the game. To do this on demand while retaining enough control to switch on the power at a moment's notice is a real skill that has to be practiced diligently.

What follows are several methods you can use. Some might be more appropriate for smaller craft, but they're worth noting if only for curiosity's sake. In order to turn these maneuvers into tactics you can implement on demand, you'll need to practice them often. During practice sessions, get a firm understanding of how much you can slow your boat and how quickly you can do so. In addition, get to know how quickly you can reverse the procedure and be under way again at a moment's notice.

- *Beam reach:* On a beam reach, head the boat into the wind and let the sail go as much as you need to. On smaller boats you can also shift your weight to stern and create more drag around the transom, which will provide even more braking effect.

- *Broad reach:* On a broad reach, where you can't effectively position yourself to luff the sails, overtrim them instead. It's not as effective a maneuver, but it'll certainly slow the boat down.
- *Close reach or close haul:* The trick for slowing on these two tacks would not be easy to perform in larger boats. The idea is to turn the sail into a brake by shoving it to leeward beyond the point that it naturally wants to reach.

You might consider practicing this technique with other boats. Take turns playing follow the leader, then keep a close watch on the boat ahead. When they begin to execute the maneuver, all down the line do the same.

- *Rudder drag:* Remember that the rudder can create enormous drag. On this occasion you can use it to your advantage, but beware of being overexuberant as you might encroach on other boat's lines and make yourself very unpopular.

  Make really big rudder movements and, beyond the significant drag you'll be creating below the waterline, you'll also effectively be putting more distance between yourself and the start line. Be sure to make these movements as expansively and as often as circumstances dictate.

Backward Sailing

Boats under sail don't like to go backward and perform horribly when they do, but it's something that can be done when necessary. In fact, you can have a lot of fun practicing this handy skill, and it'll be vital if you're about to overshoot the line or if you want a boat behind you to pass quickly. This is also a skill that might come in handy in a number of other situations other than competition.

Bring the boat into wind and wait for it to stop with the sail luffing. Shove the boom into the wind, countersteer on the rudder, and the boat should begin to move backward. Remember that the rudder will continue to act precisely opposite in reverse to the way it works in the forward direction.

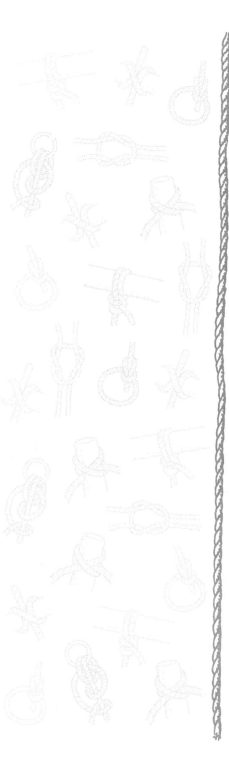

Halting

Halting is not somewhere between slowing down and reversing, it's a whole new skill in itself. The idea is to control your position, neither gaining nor losing ground—or water, in this instance. Maintaining absolute control over your boat is the name of the game, and you do this by fine-tuning your equipment against the force of the wind.

Bring your vessel almost to wind and maintain the position. You'll notice that the operative word is *almost*. If you bring the boat completely to wind, you'll certainly halt, but then the wind will begin to shove you in the direction of its travel and you'll again be moving, not stationary. Besides, you'll be in irons and have no capacity to steer.

On Course to Victory

Bunched Sailing

For the beginner, driving is not too difficult on flat and open terrain, but a move onto the highway lends an entirely new meaning to the word pressure. Similarly, the only way to become familiar with and successful while sailing in a pack is to practice sailing in a pack. You'll obviously have to get a bunch of friends together who'll cooperate, but it'll be an effort that can pay dividends.

In one exercise, each take a turn to be the lead boat with the other boats as tightly in tow as possible. The lead boat then goes through all of the maneuvers that they normally would in their buildup to the start, and the other boats try to maintain their relative tightly formed positions.

It takes a lot of skill and concentration to get this exercise right and keep it consistent. However, on race day you'll also have to add anticipation to this taxing mix of emotions and efforts, so it's well worth the effort of becoming familiar with whatever you can ahead of time and being a lot more prepared on the big day. Also, besides yourself, your crew will need all the practice they can get.

If you can't get anyone who'll practice with you, the next best thing is to practice where there's either a lot of flotsam, such as

Definitions

The following definitions can take the guess-work out of otherwise arguable situations:

- Abandon. A race that a race committee or protest committee abandons is void but may be re-sailed.
- Capsized. A sailboard is capsized when her sail or the competitor's body is in the water.
- Clear astern and clear ahead; overlap. One boat is clear astern of another when her hull and equipment in normal position are behind a line abeam from the after-most point of the other boat's hull and equipment in normal position. The other boat is clear ahead. They overlap when neither is clear astern or when a boat between them overlaps both. These terms do not apply to boats on opposite tacks; exceptions do apply.
- Finish. A boat finishes when any part of her hull, crew, or equipment in normal position crosses the finishing line in the direction of the course from the last mark either for the first time or if she takes a penalty.
- Interested party. A person who may gain or lose as a result of a protest committee's decision, or who has a close personal interest in the decision.
- Keep clear. One boat keeps clear of another if the other can sail her course with no need to take avoiding action and, when the boats are overlapped on the same tack, if the leeward boat could change course without immediately making contact with the windward boat.
- Leeward and windward. A boater's lee-ward side is the side that is, or, when she is head to wind, was away from the wind. However, when sailing by the lee or directly downwind, her leeward side is the side on which her mainsail lies. The other side is her windward side. When two boats on the same tack overlap, the one on the leeward side of the other is the leeward boat. The other is the windward boat.
- Mark. An object the sailing instructions require a boat to pass on a specified side, excluding its anchor line and objects attached temporarily or accidentally.

weeds, floating about, or in an area where there are other obstructions that would test your ability to tack, slow, jibe, and accelerate. So much the better if you can pick an area with a good flow of current.

Achieving the Right Air and Speed

On the start line it's often difficult to feel that you're in bad air (see the sections on bad air and backwinding earlier in this text). If you're unfortunate enough to land in this position right off the mark, you could be seriously hampered and will have little momentum to break through the doldrum pocket.

The idea is to be increasingly observant of the fleet building around you and position yourself so you can avoid such a situation. If necessary, move away from everyone else; then, with a few seconds to go, bear off a few degrees to build speed.

Match Racing

To this point, the advice given has been chiefly concerned with racing in fleets. However, racing can also take place as a one-on-one event, called match racing, and, as you'd have guessed, there's a slight variation you might want to employ in your technique.

Your objective in match racing is to gain the right-of-way advantage over your opponent's boat. To do so, fall into your opponent's wake and maneuver so that they cannot do anything but sail directly ahead.

- If they head up tack, you alter course and head up as well. You can both maintain this course for as long as you like, but they cannot tack with you in their lee; therefore, you are dictating their line.
- If they start to bear off and jibe, bear to their lee. With you in that position the rules dictate that they must stop and resume their heading.
- If they're cunning, they'll have a bunch of sneaky moves to cause you to break your hold. At this point, your well-drilled ability to slow your craft very quickly will be your most important skill.

Rounding Marks

Imagine a highway that makes a sharp curve, without painted lanes, and everybody in the bunch wants to be the first out to the far side of the corner and you've got a fair idea of what rounding marks can feel like. It's at this point that sections or entire events are won and lost. Sometimes there might be a dozen boats heading up to a rounding mark, all essentially in a tied position. By the far side of the mark, the distance between the first and last boat might well have been stretched to twenty-five or more boat lengths.

Laylines

A layline is the closest line you can take close-hauled and still make it around the mark. You'll certainly want to avoid laylines until the windward leg is over, and then aim not to reach them until you're about a dozen boat lengths away. If you don't observe this rule, the boats that tack in front of you will feed you bad air right up to the mark. Without tacking, you'll then be stuck. In addition, if boats are to your lee and you get a sudden lift, the leeward boats will get the good wind they're looking for and will make the mark before you, causing you to cover more distance than you needed to.

Windward Mark

With a small fleet, though exciting, rounding the windward mark is rarely eventful. What you're aiming to do is to power into the turn about a boat length above the layline, then bear off on your approach. As you round into the following leg, loosen the sails with in an even fashion and ensure the telltales flow and don't luff.

If you find yourself below the layline, tack once to bring you above it. If you've got enough momentum, you might want to risk momentarily running into the wind and hope you can coast around the mark, immediately bearing off into a smooth acceleration.

Sailors in History

Willem Barents (1550–1597)

Barents was a Dutch navigator who made three voyages from the Netherlands in search of a northeast passage to Asia. In 1594 he reached the northeastern extremity of Novaya Zemlya and returned. The following year, his second expedition of seven vessels was too late in the season, but on the third expedition in 1596 Barents discovered and named Spitsbergen (now Svalbard) and spent a miserable winter frozen in north of Novaya Zemlya. In 1597, the survivors set forth in two open boats, but Barents died shortly afterward. Some survivors reached the shores of Lapland and were later rescued. The Barents Sea, which he crossed in 1594, 1596, and 1597, and Barents Island in the Svalbard archipelago, are named in his honor.

Reach Mark

Another usually uneventful mark, what you're looking to do is avoid close competition in this area of the course. If you have other boats close to you, to ensure you get good air, it's sometimes a good idea to head up for a short period immediately after the mark. By doing so you'll also be in a good position to approach the leeward mark.

Leeward Mark

This is the big challenge where those with a deep understanding of racing rules and handling experience receive great dividends. It's a critical juncture where a lot of separation between vessels might occur when boats are bunched and aggressions run high.

Before the race, study the rules as they apply and you'll probably find that those on the outside are forced to allow extra room—a situation that could cost them dearly and deliver a distinct advantage to those on the inside.

Because this is such a critical section, try to practice it as often as you can and with as many willing skippers as you can muster. All you'll then need is a single buoy and you can play to your heart's delight. To add a bit of spice, see if you can wager for a "best of" series with the winner notching up the most number of first roundings.

Wide Approach

Try this method in different conditions and see if it works for you. With boats close behind, there's often the feeling that you need to keep a tight line to the mark in order to stop them squeezing through. However, this can often be a bad move on your part.

No boat that we know of can hug a mark without having to go wide at some point. Therefore, if you hold to the tightest line coming into the turn, you'll be pushed wide on the exit and not set up for an ideal line on to the next mark. On the other hand, if you run wide coming into the mark, the boats coming up will

Further Reading

Beyond what you've read here, you'll probably want to study certain aspects of racing in much more depth. The list that follows might well be a helpful referencing guide.

Rules
Understanding the Yacht Racing Rules through 1996 by Dave Perry.

Sail Theory
The Art and Science of Sails by Tom Whidden and Michael Levitt.

Sailing Software and CD-ROMs
Buying a boat
* *So Many Sailboats*. Ovation Digital Productions. 1996.

General Boating
* *Databoat International Ltd*. 1996.
* *Chapman Piloting: Hands-On Powerboating* on CD-ROM. 1996.
* *Get Your Captain's License* (CD-ROM). Charlie Wing. PB, 1997
* *Learn to Sail with Little Pines*. Little Pines. 1996
* *Power & Sail Collection Screen Saver*. Neil Rabinowitz. 1996.
* *Starpath NavRules for WinHelp*. David Burch. 1997.
* *Starpath Radar Trainer for Windows*. David Burch & Randel Washburne. 1997.
* *Starpath Weather Trainer*. David Burch. 1995.

More Definitions

- Obstruction. An object that a boat could not pass without changing course substantially, if she were sailing directly toward it and one of her hull lengths from it. An object that can be safely passed on only one side and an area so designated by the sailing instructions are also obstructions. However, a boat racing is not an obstruction to other boats unless they are required to keep clear of her or give her room.
- Party. A party to a hearing: a protester; a boat requesting redress; any other boat or a competitor liable to be penalized.
- Postpone. A postponed race is delayed before its scheduled start, but may be started or abandoned later.
- Proper course. A course a boat would sail to finish as soon as possible in the absence of the other boats referred to in the rule using the term. A boat has no proper course before her starting signal.
- Protest. An allegation by a boat, a race committee, or a protest committee that a boat has broken a rule.
- Racing. A boat is racing from her preparatory signal until she finishes and clears the finishing line and marks or retires, or until the race committee signals a general recall, postponement, or abandonment.
- Recovering. A sailboard is recovering from the time her sail or, when water starting, the competitor's body is out of the water until she has steerage way.
- Room. The space a boat needs in the existing conditions while maneuvering promptly in a seaman-like way.
- Rule.
  - (a) The prescriptions of a national authority, when they apply.
  - (b) The sailing instructions.
  - (c) Any other documents governing the event.
- Start. A boat starts when, after her starting signal, any part of her hull, crew, or equipment first crosses the starting line and she has complied with all the rules.
- Tack, starboard or port. A boat is on the tack, starboard or port, corresponding to her windward side.
- Two-length zone. The area around a mark, or obstruction, within a distance of two hull lengths of the boat nearer to it.

realize that if they try to squeeze in too early they run the risk of fouling you, and they'll probably resist the temptation.

Again, it's only practice that'll probably convince you this is true, and it's only practice that will polish your technique so that you don't foul it up under the heat of competition.

Try practicing as follows. Pick a mark and approach it along a port broad reach. Point your bow one boat width from the mark as you overlap the mark. At this point head up until you're on a close-haul course. Keep repeating this exercise until you find the optimum in efficiency.

Running and Reaching

Because on this leg the boats are pretty quick, positions will tend to be held with fewer changes in relative position than you'd expect in the beat legs. With this in mind, your aim here is to secure your position and set yourself up for rounding the leeward mark. Provided you don't make mistakes, although the boats giving chase may close the gap, it's unlikely they'll manage to pass. Even if you're overtaken, if you put yourself into the mark on the right course, you'll have a great opportunity to re-establish dominance.

Basic Concept

As always, try to ensure that no other competitor places you in a bad wind situation or forces you to make any significant course alterations since these might force you to sail additional distances and cost you time.

Jibing

Depending upon design, boats tend to be a little less stable on downwind runs; therefore, there is an associated risk of mistakes and mishaps. This is doubly true when executing a jibe, as the wind will suddenly change its orientation relative to the sail and the boat might react in several nasty ways such as pushing you way off course, run up into wind, capsize, or slam you into other boats.

When wind speed is moderate to heavy, it's important to ensure that the boat has plenty of speed. The closer you can get the

Protest Forms

Protest forms generally cover the following areas:

Event
Date
Organizing authority
Race number
Protesting boat
Boat name
Class
Sail number
Person in charge
Signature of member
Address
Telephone
NOTIFICATION: Did the protesting boat inform the protested boat of the protest? If so, how and when? Did the protesting boat display a protest flag? If so, when?
INCIDENT: When and where, witness(es)
Rules alleged to have been broken

boat's speed to match the wind's speed, the less apparent wind will be rushing by from behind, pouring additional power into your sail and making the entire maneuver so much more risky. If you've got reservations about committing to the jibe, get the boat going as fast as you can, then try to pick a time when the wind lulls for just a moment.

The other important trick here is to treat rudder movement with the utmost respect, and not make large or violent movements. Keep your course straight as the boom swings through the center of the boat. On smaller boats balance your weight evenly so that you can throw your weight appropriately if it becomes necessary.

Watching the Wind

On a run or reach, you'll certainly want to know if there are gusts coming up from behind. Look for more areas of gusts and try to steer into them whenever possible.

In The Homestretch

As far as finishing position goes, any part of the finish line is as good as any other; therefore, pick the side closest to your position. If it's a short race and your finish line was the same line you started from, you'll probably find that the ideal finish point is exactly opposite to the ideal start point.

Pick your point and hold your course. Often it's tempting to tack at this point, but that can cost precious seconds. Put yourself on a run that'll allow you to dash for the line at maximum speed and try not to use too much rudder on the way in to victory.

As you're coming in on your victory streak, if competitors are on your tail, try to keep them in your wake. On the other hand, if some dirty rotten scoundrel has managed to sneak by, don't just follow in their wake and give them an easy victory, make them work for it. Take a risk—at this point you've got nothing to lose.

Race Signals

Each racing discipline has its own variation of signaling that includes audio and visual uses of horns, whistles, and flags.

Sportsmanship and the Rules

Competitors are governed by rules that they're bound to follow. The fundamental principle of these rules is good sportsmanship, but in this day and age of loutish professionals in all sports assaulting opponents, spectators, and officials alike, what on earth is good sportsmanship?

Authorities reduce this nebulous concept to a simple enough formula: When a competitor has broken a rule, they're either penalized or must retire.

Racing Protest Forms and Rules
Introduction

Because sailboat racing is very technical and fraught with intricate rules that require interpretation, a system of lodging protests and counter-protests has been established. This section covers this system and simultaneously explores the major rules you'll need to know. However, it's by no means complete and should only be considered as a primary and generalized guideline for what to expect.

These rules are revised every four years by the International Sailing Federation (ISAF), the international governing body. The rules that follow are current at the time this book went to print.

Racing

A boat is considered to be racing from the moment of her preparatory signal until she clears the finish line and marks or retires, or until the race committee signals a general recall, postponement, abandonment, or disqualification.

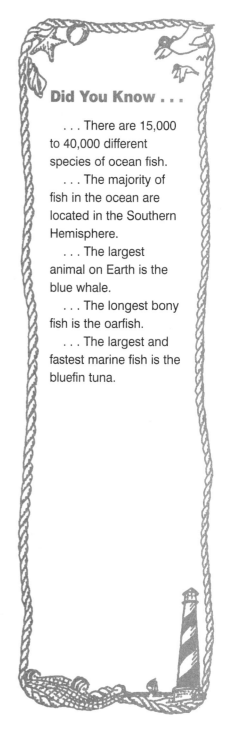

Did You Know . . .

. . . There are 15,000 to 40,000 different species of ocean fish.

. . . The majority of fish in the ocean are located in the Southern Hemisphere.

. . . The largest animal on Earth is the blue whale.

. . . The longest bony fish is the oarfish.

. . . The largest and fastest marine fish is the bluefin tuna.

Specific Racing Rules

The specific rules that govern racing will obviously alter from class to class and event to event. Suffice it to say that you need to familiarize yourself with the rules as they'd apply to you on any given racing occasion.

As an overview of rules that govern racing in general, what follows is a summarized overview.

Fundamental Rules

Safety

- Helping Those in Danger. A boat or competitor shall give all possible help to any person or vessel in danger.
- Lifesaving Equipment and Personal Buoyancy. A boat shall carry adequate lifesaving equipment for all persons on board, including one item ready for immediate use, unless her class rules make some other provision. Each competitor is individually responsible for wearing personal buoyancy adequate for the conditions.

Fair sailing

A boat and her owner shall compete in compliance with recognized principles of sportsmanship and fair play. A boat may be penalized under this rule only if it's clearly established that these principles have been violated.

Acceptance-of-the-rules

By participating in a race conducted under these racing rules, each competitor and boat owner agrees:

(a) To be governed by the rules.
(b) To accept the penalties imposed and other action taken under the rules, subject to the appeal and review procedures provided in them, as the final determination of any matter arising under the rules.
(c) With respect to such determination, not to resort to any court or other tribunal not provided by the rules.

Etceteras...

Since this book is designed as an overview of sailing, there's no need at this time to examine all of the warts of racing. We'll spare you the excruciating details and simply list some of the endless areas that racing rules govern, almost *ad nauseam*:

- When boats meet
- Right of way
- Avoiding contact
- Acquiring right of way
- Changing course
- Passing marks and obstructions
- Starting errors; penalty turns; moving astern
- Capsized, anchored, or aground; rescuing
- Interfering with another boat
- Conduct of a race
- Sailing instructions and signals
- Starting systems
- Race committee actions before the starting signal

- Starting recalls
- Starting penalties
- Touching a mark
- Shortening or abandoning after the start
- Changing the course after the start
- Mark missing
- Time limit
- Races to be re-started or re-sailed
- Personal buoyancy
- Outside help
- Propulsion
- Competitor clothing and equipment
- Penalties for breaking rules
- Hauling out; making fast; anchoring
- Person in charge
- Limitations on equipment and crew
- Fog signals and lights
- Crew position
- Setting and sheeting sails
- Moving ballast
- Manual power.

Decision-to-race

A skipper is solely responsible for deciding whether or not to start or to continue racing.

Drugs

A competitor shall neither take a substance nor use a banned method of performance enhancement.

Endnote

If you go into racing, you can then source the specific rules from rule-specific books or through one of the Internet addresses listed in this book.

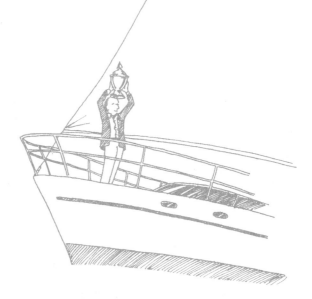

Dock 12

Regattas of the World

Global Events

The following lists will give you an idea of some international events that typically take place on a yearly basis.

EVENT	VENUE	DATES	ORGANIZER
Whitbread Round the World Race Leg 6	Sao Sebastio, Brazil—Fort Lauderdale, FL	March	Whitbread Round the World Race
International Rolex Cup Regatta	St. Thomas YC, U.S. Virgin Islands	April	St. Thomas Yacht Club
Whitbread Round the World Race Leg 7	Fort Lauderdale, FL—Baltimore,MD	April	Whitbread Round the World Race
Whitbread Round the World Race Leg 8	Annapolis, MD—La Rochelle, France	May	Whitbread Round the World Race
Whitbread Round the World Race Leg 9	La Rochelle, France—Southampton, UK	May	Whitbread Round the World Race
Spa Regatta	Medemblik, Netherlands	May	KNWV
Sony Industry Sailing Challenge	Solent, UK	June	Ocean Racing Agency
Mount Gay Barbados Regatta	Bridgetown, Barbados	May	Epic Ventures Ltd.
The Beaulieu Classic Boat Festival	Buckler's Hard, Hampshire, UK	May	Classic Boat
East Coast Classics	Walton, Suffolk, UK	May	Jon Wainwright
Kiel Week	Kiel, Germany	May	Kiel Yacht Club
Ford Cork Week	Ireland	July	Royal Cork Yacht Club
Sony Industry Sailing Challenge Final	Solent, UK	July	Ocean Racing Agency
Cutty Sark Tall Ships Race I	Falmouth, UK—Lisbon, Portugal	July	International Sail Training Association
Rolex Commodore's Cup	Cowes, UK	July	Royal Ocean Racing Club
Daily Telegraph Challenge	Solent, UK	July	Ocean Racing Agency
Skandia Life Cowes Week	Cowes, Isle of Wight, and Solent	August	Cowes Combined Clubs
Cutty Sark Tall Ships Cruise in Company	Lisbon, Portugal—Vigo, Spain	August	International Sail Training Association
Kenwood Cup	Honolulu, Hawaii	August	Royal Hawaiian Ocean Racing Club
Falmouth Classics	Falmouth, UK	August	Leo Philips
Cutty Sark Tall Ships Race 2	Vigo, Spain—Dublin, Ireland	August	International Sail Training Association
Austrian Lakes Week	Lake Neusiedl, Austria	September	Austrian Sailing Federation
Industry Sailing Masters	Solent, UK	September	Ocean Racing Agency

Long-Distance Races
International Events
- BOC
- BT Challenge
- BT Global Challenge Wellington Stopover
- Trophee Jules Verne
- Vendee Globe
- Challenge 2000
- Daytona Beach–Bermuda
- Grand Mistral
- Hong Kong Challenge
- West Marine Pacific Cup
- Round the Med
- Vic–Maui
- Around Alone
- The Race
- Darwin Ambon Race
- Bermuda Ocean Race
- Whitbread Round the World Race

Regattas
- America's Cup News
- America's Cup 2000 in New Zealand
- Ford Cork Week
- Sydney 2000–Sailing

North America
- Bayview–Macinac Island
- Boston–Halifax
- Chicago–Macinac Island
- Chicago–Macinac Island (another site)
- New England 100 multi-hull race
- Newport–Bermuda
- Newport–Bermuda (another site)
- Pacific Cup and Tahiti Cup
- Quebec–St. Malo, France
- Transpac
- San Diego to Mazatlan race
- Vic–Maui
- Worrell 1000 Distance Beach Catamaran Race
- Gulfport to Pensacola Race
- Pensacola to Panama City Race
- Around Long Island Race
- Marina del Rey–San Diego Race
- Marblehead–Halifax
- Round PEI Race
- Pensacola to Isla Mujeres Race
- Bermuda Race
- New York–San Francisco Race
- Trans Erie Yacht Race
- Dauphin Island Race

Europe
- Three Peaks Yacht race
- Europe 1 Singlehanded Race
- Figaro Solo
- King of the Derwent
- Round Gotland Race
- North Sea Race
- Race around Texel
- Shetland race
- Teachers Round Britain Challenge
- Round Texel
- Round Europe
- Le Figaro
- Fastnet
- La Transat des Alizes

Pacific
- Darwin to Ambon Yacht Race
- Melbourne–Osaka Doublehanded
- Sydney–Hobart

- Sydney to Mooloolaba
- Australia Cup

Elsewhere

- Cape Town to Rio
- Cape Town to Rio (official)

Regattas
North America

- CORK
- Farsight Cup
- Figawi regatta
- Hospice Cup
- ICYRA College Nationals
- Kenwood Cup
- Lake Ontario Solo Sailing series
- Miami OCR and SPORT
- Olympics
- Olympics—Unofficial Queen's Cup
- Youngstown Levels
- Leukemia Cup
- Whidbey Island Raceweek
- Cleveland Race Week
- LYRA
- Block Island Race Week
- Toshiba Unlimited Regatta
- Omnium Champlain
- Columbus Day Regatta
- Knickerbocker Cup
- Hispaniola Cup
- Fugawi

Europe

- Battle of Amsterdam
- Cowes Week
- Championnat de France de Voile Olympiques
- Tour de France a la Voile
- Kiel Week
- Queensland Nacra Champs
- SPA regatta
- Spi Dauphine
- United 4 Regatta
- Weymouth Speedsailing
- Kiel Race Week
- Moonsund Regatta, Estonia
- Saint-Tropez Rolex Cup
- Cowes Week
- Champagne Mumm Admiral's Cup
- North Aegean Cup
- Junior Mazda Swiss Open Championship
- Eurolymp Palamós—Spain

Pacific

- Shiseido Cup

Elsewhere

- Abaco Regatta
- Antigua Sailing Week
- Antigua and Barbuda Sailing Week
- BVI Spring Regatta
- St. Maarten Heineken Regatta
- Hispaniola Cup (Dom. Rep.)
- Philippine President's Cup Regatta
- Regatta Recife
- Rolex Cup, U.S. Virgin Islands
- Telkom International Sailing Week

Typical ISAF Match Race Calendar of Events

DATE	EVENT NAME	VENUE	LOCATION	CLASS
March	Summer Mid Week Match Racing Regatta	Perth	Australia	M-MR*
February	Australia Cup	Perth	Australia	M-MR
February	Steinlager Line 7 Match Race Grand Prix	Auckland	New Zealand	M-MR
February	Coca Cola Cup Int. Yacht Match Racing	Auckland	New Zealand	M-MR
March	Finlandia Sail Cup	Helsinki	Finland	M-MR
March	Panda Match Race	Malmo	Sweden	M-MR
March	IS Matchen	Sundsvall	Sweden	M-MR
March	PTHZ Spring Match Race	Malmo	Sweden	M-MR
April	Wihlborg Match Race	Malmo	Sweden	M-MR
April	Paskmallen	Sundsvall	Sweden	M-MR
April	Forars Cup	Jyllinge	Denmark	M-MR
April	Sundsvall Spring Cup 1	Sundsvall	Sweden	M-MR
April	Arthur Andersen Spring Match Race	Malmo	Sweden	M-MR
April	Swedish Spring Cup	Gothenburg	Sweden	M-MR
May	ACI Cup of Croatia	Split	Croatia	M-MR
May	Jyllinge Open	Jyllinge	Denmark	M-MR
May	XI Pedrini "Cento Cup"	Lake Garda	Italy	M-MR
May	Sundsvall Spring Cup 2	Sundsvall	Sweden	M-MR
May	KSSS Cup Qualifier	Saltsjobaden	Sweden	M-MR
May	Pedrini Cup	Korcula	Croatia	M-MR
May	Finnish Matchrace European Championship	Helsinki	Finland	M-MR
May	Helsinki Spring Championship	Helsinki	Finland	M-MR
May	Sundsvall Spring Cup Championship	Sundsvall	Sweden	M-MR
May	Qualifier Swedish Match Cup	Gothenburg	Sweden	M-MR
May	Cascadia Cup Match Racing Championship	Victoria	Canada	M-MR
May	Baggen Cup	Saltsjobaden	Sweden	M-MR
June	Hoya Royal Lymington Cup	Lymington	Great Britain	M-MR
June	ACI Women's Cup	Rovinj	Croatia	W-MR†
June	Helsinki Regatta Match Race	Helsinki	Finland	M-MR
June	Ullman Sails Cup 1999	Oslo	Norway	M-MR
June	Midnight Sun Ladies Match	Sundsvall	Sweden	. W-MR
June	Qualifier Sundsvall Open Match Race	Sundsvall	Sweden	M-MR
June	V Trofeo Challenge Roberto Trombini Selezione	Ravenna	Italy	M-MR
July	Swedish Match Cup	Marstrand	Sweden	M-MR
July	V Trofeo Challenge Roberto Trombini Match Race	Ravenna	Italy	M-MR
July	UK National Women's Match Race Championship	TBD	Great Britain	W-MR
July	Sundsvall Open Match Race	Sundsvall	Sweden	M-MR
July	Match Race Lake Constance	Lake Constance	Germany	M-MR

DATE	EVENT NAME	VENUE	LOCATION	CLASS
July	Wihlborgs Summer Match Race	Malmoe	Sweden	M-MR
July	KSSS Cup	Sandham	Sweden	M-MR
August	Stenungsund Match Race	Stenungsund	Sweden	M-MR
August	Alandia Match race	Marishamn	Finland	M-MR
August	Swedish Qualifier Match Race Nationals (South)	Malmo	Sweden	M-MR
August	Helsinki Match Race	Helsinki	Finland	M-MR
August	Sponsor Cup One and Two	Jyllinge	Denmark	M-MR
August	Swedish Qualifier Match Race Nationals East	Saltsjobaden	Sweden	M-MR
August	Swedish Qualifier Match Race Nationals West	Gothenburg	Sweden	M-MR
August	Swedish National Match Race Championship	Saltsjobaden	Sweden	M-MR
August	Finnish Women's Open Match Racing Championship	Helsinki	Finland	W-MR
August	UK National Youth Championship		Great Britain	M-MR
August	Norwegian Match Race Championship		Norway	M-MR
August	Women's Swedish National Match Race Championships	Gotenburg	Sweden	W-MR
September	Russia Open—Novoross Cup 99	Novorossyisk	Russia	M-MR
September	MT&T Polaris Block Trophy	Halifax,NS	Canada	M-MR
September	York Cup	Royal CanadianYacht Club	Canada	M-MR
September	KSSS Mastarmote	Saltsjobaden	Sweden	M-MR
September	The Richardson Trophy	Lake St. Clair	Canada	M-MR
September	Danish Club Championship	Jyllinge	Denmark	M-MR
October	Open Club Championship SSS	Sundsvall	Sweden	M-MR
October	Sportklubben Pokal	Helsinki	Finland	M-MR
October	Spring Mid Week Match Racing Regatta	Perth	Australia	M-MR
October	Portugal Match Race Championship	Lexoes	Portugal	M-MR
October	UK National Match Racing Championship		Great Britain	M-MR
October	Arthur Andersen Match Race	Malmo	Sweden	M-MR
October	Hostmatchen Qualifier	Saltsjobaden	Sweden	M-MR
October	VI Internationales de Espana de Match Racing	Bayona	Spain	M-MR
October	GKSS Klubbmasterskap	Gothenburg	Sweden	M-MR
October	Landrover Cup International Match Race	Leixoes	Portugal	M-MR
October	Hostmatchen	Saltsjobaden	Sweden	M-MR
October	Malmoe Autumn Match Race	Malmo	Sweden	M-MR
October	Sasongauslut—Express	Stockholm	Sweden	M-MR
November	SUPERCUP	Jyllinge	Denmark	M-MR
November	SSS Hostmatchen	Sundsvall	Sweden	M-MR
November	Nisse Cup	Jyllinge	Denmark	M-MR
December	Osprey Cup	Florida	USA	W-MR
December	Midwinter Championship	Sundsvall	Sweden	M-MR
December	Virgin Islands International Match Race	St. Thomas	Virgin Islands	M-MR

*M-MR= Men's Match Race
†W-MR= Women's Match Race

International Boat Shows

Every year there are hundreds of shows all around the world. The following table contains information about annual events. Call to find out the precise dates and plan your trips to these centers accordingly.

If you have a problem reaching the event organizers, contact the individual chambers of commerce in the various cities.

EVENT	VENUE	MONTH	ORGANIZER/CONTACT	TEL	FAX
Malta International Boat Show	Malta, Malta	March	Malta International Boat Show	+356 414445/6	+356 414439
Istanbul International Boat Show	Istanbul, Turkey	March	Interteks AS	+90 (9)212 225 0920	+90 (9)212 225 0933
Malaysia International Boat Show	Kuala Lumpur, Malaysia	March	Protemp Exhibitions Sdn Bhd	+60 3 717 2828	+60 3 717 2566
Norwegian International Boat Show— Sjøen for Alle	Oslo, Norway	March	Sjøen for Alle A/S	+47 22 43 04 20	+47 22 55 15 60
Budapest Boat Show	Budapest, Hungary	March	Hungexpo Co. Ltd.	+36 (0)1 263 6094	+36 (0)1 263 6104
POLYACHT Gdansk Fair of Water Sports	Gdansk, Poland	March	Gdansk International Fair Co.	+ 48 58 523600	+ 48 58 5522168
Boat Asia	Singapore, Singapore	April	IIR Exhibitions PTE Ltd.	+65 227 0688	+65 227 0913
China International Boat Show	Shanghai, China	April	Proshow	+44 (0)171 376 7777	+44 (0)171 352 0818
Pacific Sail Expo	Oakland, California	April	Sail America	401-841-0900	401-847-2044
Odessa Sports and Boat Show	Odessa, Ukraine	April	Marine Technologies Ltd.	+380 (0482) 24 60 18	+380 (0482) 25 09 66
Middle East International Boat Show	Dubai, United Arab Emirates	May	Dubai RAI	+971 4 319444	+971 4 319011
Internautica	Marina Portoroz, Slovenia	May	Marina Portoroz & Studio 37	+386 66 471 200	+386 66 471 510
Rio de Janeiro International Boat Show	Rio De Janeiro, Brazil	May	ACOBAR (Brazilian Marine Manufacturers Association)	+55 21 262 2483	+55 21 262 3720
National Boat Show & Fishing Expo	Melbourne, Australia	July	Emma Parkin	+61 (0)3 9328 4855	+61 (0)3 9328 4898
Asia Pacific International Marine Exhibition (APIME)	Hong Kong, China	July	Globex Ltd.	+44 (0)181 930 4457	+44 (0)181 930 4464
Sydney International Boat Show	Sydney, Australia	July	Boating Industry Association of New South Wales	+61 (0)2 9438 2077	+61 (0)2 9439 3983
IMTEC South Pacific (International Marine Trades Exhibition)	Auckland, New Zealand	August	IMTEC South Pacific	+64 (0)9 415 9230	+64 (0)9 415 8304
Brisbane Boat Show & Fishing Expo	Brisbane, Australia	August	Boating Industry Association of Queensland	+61 (0)7 3899 3333	+61 (0)7 3899 3051
Amsterdam Seaport Boat Show	Ijmuiden, Netherlands	September	Mrs. Cora Burger	+31 (0)20 549 1212	+31 (0)20 646 4469
Norwegian International In-Water Boat Show —Bater i Sjøen	Oslo, Norway	September	Sjøen for Alle A/S	+47 22 43 04 20	+47 22 55 15 60
Grand Pavois de la Rochelle	La Rochelle, France	September	Grand Pavois Association	+33 5 46 44 46 39	+33 5 46 45 32 24
Festival International de la Plaisance	Cannes, France	September	Société SEPA	+33 1 42 89 41 04	+33 1 45 61 12 00
Southampton International Boat Show	Southampton, UK	September	National Boat Shows Ltd.	+44 (0)1784 473377	+44 (0)1784 439678
Newport International Boat Show	Newport, Rhode Island	September	Newport Exhibition Group	401-846-1115 ext. 215	401-847-0560
Interboot—International Aquatic Sports Exhibition	Germany	September	Messe Friedrichshafen GmbH	+49 (0)7541 7080	+49 (0)7541 708110
Monaco Yacht Show	Monaco, Monaco	September	IIR Mediterranée	+377 93 10 41 70	+377 93 10 41 71
Norwalk International In-Water Boat Show	Norwalk, Connecticut	September	NMMA Boat Shows NY	212-922-1212	212-922-9607
International Marine Trades Exhibit and Convention (IMTEC)	Chicago, Illinois	October	NMMA Boat Shows	312-946-6262	312-946-0401
British Marine Trade Show	Windsor	October	National Boat Shows Ltd.	+44 (0)1784 473377	+44 (0)1784 439678
United States Sailboat Show	Annapolis, Maryland	October	Annapolis Boat Shows Inc.	410-268-8828	410-280-3903
Genoa International Boat Show	Genoa, Italy	October	UCINA (Unione Nazionale Cantieri Industrie Nautiche ed Affini)	+39 (0)10 576 9811	+39 (0)10 553 1104

Event	Venue	Month	Organizer/Contact	Tel	Fax
United States Powerboat Show	Annapolis, Maryland	October	Annapolis Boat Shows Inc.	410-268-8828	410-280-3903
Hanseboot International Boat Show	Hamburg, Germany	October	Hamburg Messe und Congress GmbH	+49 (0)40 35 69 21 40	+49 (0)40 35 69 21 49
Fort Lauderdale International Boat Show	Fort Lauderdale, Florida	October	Show Management	954-764-7642	954-462-4140
Athens Boat Show	Athens, Greece	November	Secaplas—PEEY	+30 (0)1 483 1846	+30 (0)1 483 1847
International Boat Show Berlin	Berlin, Germany	November	Messe Berlin GmbH	+49 (0)30 3038 2031	+49 (0)30 3038 2030
METS—Marine Equipment Trade Show	Amsterdam, Netherlands	November	Amsterdam RAI	+31 (0)20 549 1212	+31 (0)20 549 1889
Barcelona International Boat Show	Barcelona, Spain	November	Fira de Barcelona	+34 (9)3 233 23 62	+34 (9)3 233 23 69
Salon Nautique International—Paris Boat Show	Paris, France	November	Salon Nautique International	+33 1 41 90 47 10	+33 1 41 90 47 19
London International Boat Show	London, UK	January	National Boat Shows Ltd.	+44 (0)1784 473377	+44 (0)1784 439678

International and Domestic Sailing Associations and Clubs

Again, what follows is only a sample of the associations that might interest you. Consult your local directories or conduct some research to find those that would be more appropriate to your needs.

Argentina
- Yacht Club Argentino
  Viamonte y Rio de la playa
  Darsena Norte
  Buenos Aires, Argentina 1107
  E-mail: yca@yca.org.ar
  http://wwwyca.org.ar

Australia
- Hillary Yacht Club
- Goolwa Regatta Yacht Club

Canada
- Ashbridges Bay Yacht Club, Toronto
- Toronto Multihull Sailing Cruising Club

Ireland
- Skerries Sailing Club of Dublin

Germany
- Akademischer Yacht Club—AYC

Netherlands
- Boreas Sailing Association

New Zealand
- Otago University Yacht Club

Poland
- Krakowski Yacht Club AGH

Scotland
- Loch Ard SC

Switzerland
- CERN Yachting Club

United Kingdom
- Attenborough Sailing Club—Nottingham
- Queen Mary Sailing Club
- Royal Ocean Racing Club

Some of the Best International Venues

- St. Lucia
  (800) 456-3984
  Tel: (212) 867-2950
- Grenada
  (800) 927-9554
  Tel: (212) 687-9554
- Nevis
  (800) 582-6208.
  Tel: (212) 535-1234
- Dominica
  Tel: (212) 682-0435
- Bonaire
  (800) 826-6247
  Tel: (212) 832-0779
- The British Virgin Islands
  (800) 835-8530
  Tel: (212) 696-0400
- St. John
  (800) 878-4463
  Tel: (212) 332-2222
- Guadeloupe
  (888) 448-2335
- Jamaica
  (800) 233-4582
- Montserrat
  Tel: (516) 425-0900
- Trinidad and Tobago
  (888) 595-4TNT
- Fiji
  Tel: (310) 568-1616
  Fax: (310) 670-2318

Charter Companies

For a complete guide to charter sailing and motor yachts, check out the Yacht Charter Guide's Web site, http://www.guides.com/ycg/, or contact them at: Charter Guides
  104 Mt. Auburn St.
  Cambridge, MA 02138 USA
  E-mail: info@guides.com
  Tel: (617) 547-5811
  Fax: (617) 868-5335

- Barefoot Yacht Charters
  P.O. Box 39, Blue Lagoon
  St. Vincent and the Grenadines,
  West Indies
  Tel: (809) 456-9526/9334
  Fax: (809) 456-9238
  E-mail: barebum@caribsurf.com
- Cooper Boating Center
  1620 Duranleau Street
  Granville Island,Vancouver,
  British Columbia, Canada V6H 3S4
  Tel: (604) 687-4110
  Fax: (604) 687-3267
  E-mail: crew@cooper-boating.com
- Cosmos Yachting
  74 Kingston Hill
  Kingston-upon-Thames, Surrey KT2
  7NP, UK
  Tel: +44 (181) 547-3577
  Fax: +44 (181) 546-8887
  Toll Free: 1-(800) 376-9070
  E-mail: info@cosmos-yachting.co.uk
- Island Yachting Centre Inc.
  1035 Riverside Dr.
  Palmetto, FL 34221
  Tel: (941) 729-4511
  Fax: (941) 722-7677
  E-mail: IslandYC@aol.com
- J World Sailing School
  213 Eastern Avenue
  Annapolis, MD 21403
  Tel: (800) 966-2038, (410) 280-2040
  Fax: (410) 280-2079
- Sailboats Inc.
  250 Marina Drive
  Superior, WI 54880
- Southernmost Sailing, Inc.
  P.O. Box 369
  Key West, FL 33041
  Tel: (305) 293-1883
- Sunsail
  Annapolis Landing Marina
  980 Awald Drive
  Suite 302
  Annapolis, MD 21403
  Tel: (800) 327-2276
  E-mail: sunsailusa@sunsail.com

- USA Charters
  195 Concord Road
  Keene NH 03431
  Tel: (603) 357-4489
  Fax: (603) 357-4489
- Windjammer Charters
  764 Newcastle Avenue
  Parksville, British Columbia, Canada,
  V9P 1E8
  Tel: (250) 954-8954 (after 6:00 P.M.)
  E-mail: sail@island.net
- BVI Yacht Charters
  P.O. Box 11156
  St. Thomas, USVI 00801
  Tel: (888) 615-4006, (284) 494-4289
  Fax: (284) 494-6552
  E-mail: SailBVI@caribsurf.com
- Admiralty Yacht Vacations
  Admiral's Inn
  Villa Olga, Frenchtown, St. Thomas,
  VI 00802
  Tel: (800) 544-0493, (340) 774-2172
  Fax: (340) 774-8010
- Waterways
  P.O. Box 40455
  Washington, DC 20016
  Tel: (800) 340-2525, (202) 965-9352
  Fax: (202) 965-6919
  E-mail: sail@waterways.com
- Blue Cruise
  Tel: 90-(212) 243-1107
  Fax: 90-(212) 245-3673
  E-mail: travel@twarp.com
- Regal Yachting Ltd.
  P.O. Box 20020
  Wichita, KS 67208
  Tel/Fax: (316) 744-1529
  E-mail: meltemi@southwind.net

California Charter Companies

Paradise Bound Yacht Charters
4375 Admiralty Way
Marina del Rey, CA 90292
Tel: (800) 655-0850, (310) 578-7963
E-mail: captalex@gte.net

Charter on the Great Lakes

Charter Sailing, Unlimited
175 North Harbor Drive
Chicago IL 60601
Tel: (312) 856-1134
Fax: (312) 856-1084

Northeastern U.S. Charter Companies

- Schooner Appledore Iii
  9 Tuna Wharf
  P.O. Box 792
  Rockport, MA 01966
  Tel: (978) 546-3377
- Almeisan Charter
  P.O. Box 4180
  Norwalk, CT 06855
  Tel: (203) 852-8173
  Fax: (203) 857-4763
  E-mail: Almeisan@aol.com

Southeastern U.S. Charter Companies

- ASA Sailing School
  1290 Fifth Street
  Miami Beach, FL 33139
  Tel: (800) 537-0050, (305) 532-8600
  Fax: (305) 535-3179
- Quicksilver Charters, Key Largo
  MM100 Oceanside
  (Holiday Inn docks)
  Key Largo, FL 33037
  (800) 347-9972
  Tel: (305) 451-0105

Midwestern U.S. Charter Company

- Classic Yachts of Door County
  P.O. Box 519
  Sturgeon Bay, WI 54235
  Tel: (888) 868-0859, (920) 743-2478
  Fax: (920) 743-7280
  E-mail: gjones@classicyachts.com

Hawaii Charter Company

- PARAGON Sailing Charters Maui
  Slip 68, Maalaea Harbor
  RR 2, Box 43
  Kula, Maui, Hawaii 96790
  Tel: (800) 441-2087, (808) 244-2087
  Fax: (808) 878-3933
  E-mail: paragon@maui.net

Canadian West Coast Sailing Charter Companies

- Victoria B.C. Shopping
  101—65 Songhees Road
  Victoria BC V9A 6T3
  Tel/Fax: (250) 386-8015
- Adventure Charters & Sailing:
  Windjammer
  Howard Story
  764 Newcastle Ave
  Parksville BC, Canada, V9P 1E8
  Tel: (250) 954-8954
  E-mail: sail@island.net

- Seadog Sailing & Kayaking
  1345 Marina Way
  Nanoose Bay BC, V9P 9C1
  Tel: (250) 468-5778
  Fax: (250)468-5771
  E-mail: seadog@nanaimo.ark.com
- Cooper Boating Center
  1620 Duranleau Street
  Granville Island, Vancouver BC,
  Canada V6H 3S4
  Tel: (604) 687-4110
  Fax: (604) 687-3267
  E-mail: crew@cooper-boating.com
- Gulf Islands Cruising School Ltd.
  P.O. Box 2532I
  Sidney BC V8L 4B9
  2300 Canoe Cove Road
  Tel: (800) 665-2628, (250) 656-2628
  Fax: (250) 656-6433

Charter Companies in South America

- Brazilian Powerboat & Sailing Charters
  Av. Amaral Peixoto 455/311, 24.000
  Centro Niteroi, Rj, Brazil
  Tel: (021) 717-4259
  Fax: (021) 717-2797

Sailing on the World Wide Web

General Sailing Pages

Take a look at these, and you might find excellent links to all kinds of interesting stuff.

http://sailingsource.com/
http://kogs-www.informatik.uni-hamburg.de/~dreschle/sailing.html
http://www.navcen.uscg.mil/
http://www.nos.noaa.gov/
http://www.navcen.uscg.mil/gps/
http://www.uscgboating.org/index1.html

Pan-Pacific Links

- Satellite and SFC chart combo
  http://lumahai.soest.hawaii.edu/gifs/models/AVN/pac_AVNgoes.gif
- East Pacific satellite image
  http://wxp.atms.purdue.edu/maps/satellite/sat_ir_west.gif
- Current surface chart
  http://lumahai.soest.hawaii.edu/gifs/models/AVN/pac_AVNslp-000.gif
- Twenty-four-hour forecast surface chart
  http://lumahai.soest.hawaii.edu/gifs/models/AVN/pac_AVNslp-024.gif
- Forty-eight-hour forecast surface chart
  http://lumahai.soest.hawaii.edu/gifs/models/AVN/pac_AVNslp-048.gif
- Western Pacific satellite image
  http://lumahai.soest.hawaii.edu/gifs/gmsIRlast.gif
- US Navy FNMOC Weather Maps
  http://metoc-u1.fnmoc.navy.mil/wxmap/web/index.html

Tropical Weather

- Eastern North Pacific storm tracks
  http://www.hawaii.edu/News/localweather/nep.latest.gif
- Western North Pacific storm tracks
  http://www.hawaii.edu/News/localweather/nwp.latest.gif
- Worldwide Tropical Storms
  http://www.solar.ifa.hawaii.edu/Tropical/tropical.html
- Worldwide Tropical Weather (WeatherNet)
  http://cirrus.sprl.umich.edu/wxnet/tropical.html
- Pacific Climatology and El Nino
  http://naulu.soest.hawaii.edu/
- Sea Surface Temperature (U.S. Navy)
  http://www.fnoc.navy.mil/otis/otis_glbl_sst.gif

For West Coast Mariners

- West Coast and Hawaii tides
  http://www.opsd.nos.noaa.gov/westusa.html
- San Francisco Area Marine Weather
  http://www.nws.mbay.net/marine.html
- Oceanweather's California data chart
  http://www.oceanweather.com/data/cal.html
- Oceanweather's NE Pacific data chart
  http://www.oceanweather.com/data/uswest.html

Other Important Resources

- Oceanweather, Inc.
  http://www.oceanweather.com/
- Virtually Hawaii
  http://www.satlab.hawaii.edu/space/hawaii/
- Ocean Atlas of the Hawaiian Islands
  http://satftp.soest.hawaii.edu/atlas/
- USCG Marine Safety Office Honolulu
  http://www.aloha.net/~msohono/
- National Data Buoy Center
  http: //www.ndbc.noaa.gov/
- NOAA Weatherfax Data
  http://weather.noaa.gov/fax/ptreyes.shtml
  http://www.nws.fsu.edu/buoy/sw.html
- US Sailing's Review of Regatta Scoring Programs
  http://www.ussailing.org/race/main.html
- Art Engel's Guide to the new Racing Rules of Sailing
  http://www.lainet.com/~engel/guide/
- ISAF Standard Match Racing Sailing Instructions
  http://sailing.org/matchrace/newmrsailint.html
- ISAF Standard Match Racing Notice of Race
  http://sailing.org/iyru/mrnotice.html
- A Guide to Organizing A Small Regatta
  http://sailing.org/regattas/
- Basic Racing Manual
  http://www.uiowa.edu/~sail/skills/racing_basics/
- Race Management Tutorial
  http://www.voicenet.com/~drlaser/plfRORG_start.html
- Professional Coaching Services
  http://www.sailcoach.com/
- Measurement and Rating
  http://sailing.org/rating/
- International Sailing Federation
  http://sailing.org//
- Maritime and Admiralty Law
  http://members.aol.com/dangelaw/admir.html

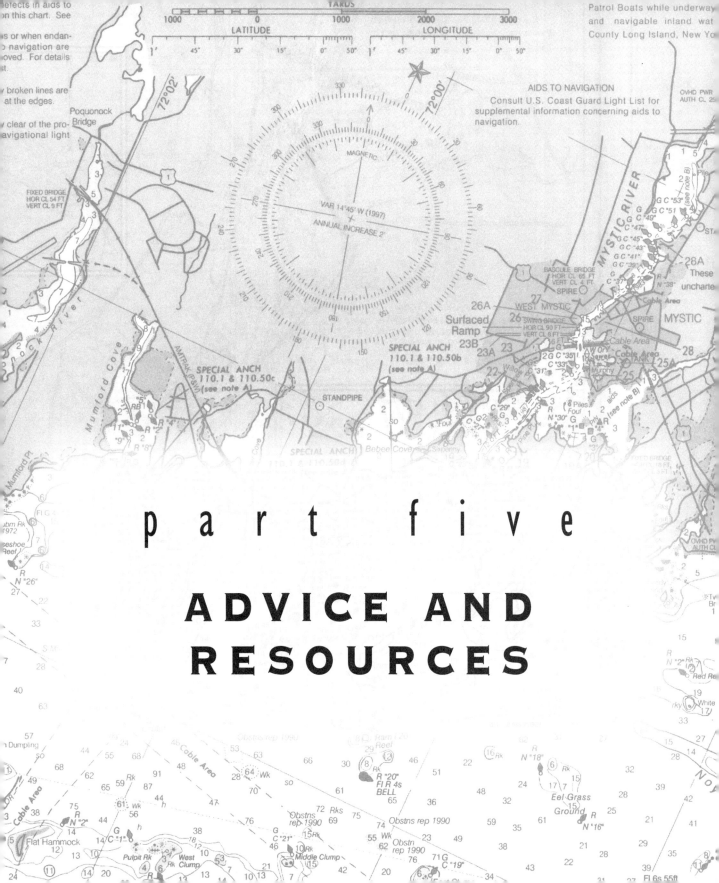

p a r t   f i v e

ADVICE AND
RESOURCES

DOCK 14

Buying Hardware Equipment

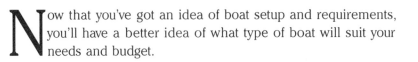

Now that you've got an idea of boat setup and requirements, you'll have a better idea of what type of boat will suit your needs and budget.

Deciding on a Boat

In sailing, the voyage is at least as important, if not more so, as the destination. No doubt, as your skills and needs change, you'll upgrade your vessel, but there's no need to invest in the wrong vessel this time because you plan to do it properly next time. Why not buy as close to the right vessel from the start? This section will help you through the task.

Choosing the boat that's appropriate for your needs is a multifaceted task that really takes a lot of time and planning if you're indeed to get it right the first time.

There are several issues to be covered here:

- First, what's your motivation: to cruise, to race, or to live aboard?
- Second, how big is your budget and how big a boat do you want?
- Third, will you build or buy? If you're buying, will it be used or new—from a private individual or through a broker?

The lists and questions that follow might seem endless, but so is the potential for making a hash of things, losing money, and becoming disillusioned. Our goal here is to keep you from experiencing problems long before you can set yourself up for them.

Choosing the Boat

In our experience, any boat on the water is some kind of compromise. You're either making do with less boat to suit your budget, forgoing space so that you can trail the boat behind your car, or trying to force your cruising vessel up to racing speeds because your lust to win is stronger than your cruising lifestyle. The list of compromises rolls on forever.

The point is that every purchase requires a list a mile long that balances items you really *want* against items you *need*. In addition, boats are not tennis racquets; you don't discard them, and you stand to make or lose significant money in any deal.

Fortunately, boats also last a long time and don't go out of fashion, so financing is reasonably easy to find. You should be able to negotiate a deal with up to a fifteen-year repayment schedule.

Acquiring the Boat and Equipment

There are several venues through which you can find a boat to acquire, with each offering inherent advantages over the other (e.g., better prices or more comprehensive after-sales service).

One of the best ways to get the inside track on the trade of boats is simply to ask anyone involved in the type of sailing you're interested in. We'd strongly advise that you spend a little time at a local club, race, or slip mingling with the crowd and putting feelers out.

Narrow the field

Before you rush out and buy, you'll want to narrow down your needs and create a short list of requirements—some vital, others flexible. Knowing why you want to sail is a good place to start.

- Is it for leisure or competition?
- Is this a racing animal or a booze-cruiser?
- How many people will you sail or cruise with?
- Must it have overnight capacity?
- How many bunks do you need?
- Is this a live-aboard vessel?
- What does your budget look like?
- How large a vessel do you need?
- How long do you plan to keep the boat?
- How big a cockpit do you want?
- What are draft limitations of your intended sailing area?
- Are you in a warm or icy climate?

Famous Pirates

Samuel Bellamy—Black Bellamy (English pirate, Early Eighteenth Century) In 1715 Bellamy, a young English sailor, persuaded a wealthy patron to finance a ship and crew which he used to search for sunken Spanish treasure off the coast of Florida. After failing in treasure hunting, his step into piracy was relatively small. Within a year Samuel became notorious; known as Black Bellamy, he went on to plunder more than 50 ships.

Black Bellamy's demise came in April 1717 when a stormy tempest's waves smashed his fleet to destruction off Cape Cod. Bellamy and most of his crew were lost to the waves, but two survivors gave a vivid account of the shipwreck, which was preserved in the oral tradition in Cape Cod folklore.

Wherever you go, collect boat brochures, which provide specifications that will help you to narrow the field. Don't forget to find out about fuel and water tank capacities and maximum sail area.

Listen and watch—this will give you a good idea of whether the boat that appeals to you will have a good resale market.

To Build?

Back when people had more time and many also had the tools and experience in craftsmanship, building boats was a hobby. These days it's a section that's almost not worth covering in any detail.

Suffice it to say that the economic realities of today more or less dictate that you'll probably get a much better deal if you shop around or buy a hull and fit it yourself.

If you're a hobbyist, we'll have little chance of dissuading you, but if you're anything like us, there's no way on god's green earth that you could be convinced to consider building.

Places to Look

Shows

Most major cities have regular boat shows where you'll find a wide variety of vessels on display. Spend some time visiting these shows and take along a note pad and carry bag so you can collect information to analyze and follow up on later.

Show time is prime time for gathering information that'll help you make a decision about whether and what to buy. Shows are the ideal place to check out what's really available. Check what's new, compare deals, and take a reality check of your own needs in light of what you find.

Shows are also a place where you might feel hustled into making rapid decisions: "and this special offer only lasts for today, sir/ma'am." In our experience, with such a high-priced item as a boat, take a rain check and you'll probably still be able to negotiate the discount deal a month later.

To Buy New or Used?

Most people prefer to buy rather than build. Below are some of the areas you'll want to look at.

Negotiation

Whether buying new or used, you'll want to negotiate at least a 10 percent discount. It's a straightforward knack for bargaining that'll earn you saving. It's like buying a car—you've just got to hang in there and stand your ground.

Of course, if the sale is for a used boat, and particularly if it's private, you'll expect to do a little better than 10 percent.

Here are some pointers that will briefly highlight the differences between the two options of new versus used.

If you buy new you:

- Can customize your purchase in terms of trim, interior finish, gear, rigging, engine, and electronics.
- Will probably be able to negotiate a bunch of additional package options to have extra equipment thrown in.
- Will receive the full benefits of warranty and be reasonably assured that you won't have upkeep and repair problems for some time.
- Will immediately take a resale knock off the price that you pay. The moment you take delivery you can expect to lose at least 10 percent on your investment, but chances are you'll lose 25 percent or more.

If you buy used you:

- Might save 50 percent if you're a sharp negotiator with a good eye for a bargain.
- Get a whole lot of extras such as safety, galley, and sporting equipment thrown in for free.
- Could possibly sell the boat the very next day for what you paid for it—or even more.
- Run the risk of buying a lemon with hidden faults that could cost you a bundle.

If you're planing to attend the show for more than one day or if you'll attend more than one show, use the first show day to form general impressions and collect literature. Also, only concentrate on boats that are apt to fit your needs.

Retailers

Besides the retailers you'll meet at the boat show, your local telephone directory will most likely have a listing for boating retailers. Naturally, anyone active in sailing will probably know of reputable stores.

Builders

Some boat builders will sell direct to the public. Again, check your local telephone directory or ask around where sailors meet.

Agents

Like real estate, boats are sold through agents who list them in various publications. Whether you're a buyer or seller, you'll find a list of agents in your local telephone directory or through other interested parties. The Internet is becoming a prime marketing environment for agents, and a simple search using any search engine of your choice will probably swamp you with more agents than you can check out.

Media advertisements

Most major newspapers list a column for boats offered. A better bet is to find a dedicated "for sale" publication that lists only boats or yachts. If you know what you're looking for, this is the place where you can really find bargains, but caveat emptor—let the buyer beware! Know what you're doing or have someone with you who does.

Auctions

What is true for media advertisements is equally valid for auctions. In fact, you'll be certain to find auctions listed in media advertisements.

Measuring Up Vessels

Whenever you face choices where there are multiple variables, each of which needs to be seen in terms of its impact on the whole, the more organized your search plan is the quicker and more fulfilling your results are likely to be.

The questions and issues given above are just a hint toward the kind of information that you'll probably want to collect. Get them down in written form as a checklist and then check candidate vessels off against them. In addition, you'll literally want to measure the vessel on sight and test sail it before coming anywhere near a decision to purchase. Use the following criteria and techniques to assist you through the process.

Notes on Boat Size Selection

Small Boats

Many people very wisely make their first vessel a small day sail boat. As mentioned before, the mix of wind and water is not for everyone. It's often a good idea to cut one's teeth on the sport side of sailing by investing a small amount on these more reasonably priced and cheaper-to-maintain vessels and not putting yourself through all the bother of securing sailing licenses and finding moorings.

On the other hand, the more Spartan and boisterous nature of smaller boats simply cannot offer the same luxury and reclusion that larger vessels can, so the choice to go small has to be tempered with this expectation.

Small vessel is a somewhat nebulous term that's more a personal label than a class. Small boats are a very broad category that encompasses a wide variety of design, rigging, and application. On the low end of the scale is the glorified rowing boat with a mast and sail. Then there's the purpose-built sportcat, right on up to daysailing vessels.

Race or leisure?

If your motivation is leisure, then the advice that follows will be applicable, but confining yourself to a particular class will be of no importance. On the other hand, if you're intending to race, chances

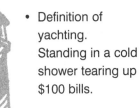

- Definition of a yacht. A floating box you throw your hard-earned cash into.

- Definition of yachting. Standing in a cold shower tearing up $100 bills.

Buyer's Kit

Put together a kit that contains items useful in quantifying a boat to your specs and in conducting a comparative study. Borrow or buy the following items:

• Notebook—to keep track of all measurements, conversations, and other incidental specifications, as well as to sketch details you might otherwise forget.
• Calculator—for quick conversions of numbers.
• Tape measure—to get a hands-on perspective of every nook and cranny.

(continued)

are you'll target a particular class that is both popular in your region and one that grabs your interest. Drop by local racing events to get an idea of how active the race scene is and what level local competition attains. Then it's simply a case of deciding whether the people you meet there and the entire atmosphere suits you.

Try not to talk to salespeople regarding the local conditions. Speak to the sailors and spectators.

Another important element to consider when selecting the type of racing you're aspiring to is the physical size of the racer. Small boat racing is a bit like horse racing in that the boats are greatly affected by the load and its distribution on board. Tall and lanky sailors with weight distributed toward their upper torso can, pound for pound, exert a much greater leverage out over the beam than a shorter squat sailor. The skill and age of the sailor will also be a factor when deciding whether to choose a mainsail rig only or one with a jib. A final factor to look at will be how easy the vessel is to trail, rig, and launch.

Racing boats

The Sabot and the Optimist are excellent choices for children who wish to either race or simply learn to sail. Both are very stable and easy to rig and have active one-design classes across the country. In addition, they're light and easy to transport atop your car.

Along the same lines you might also consider the Vanguard Pram and JY Club Trainer.

Generally, Optimist or Sabot sailors stay with the class for two to four years. This means that it's a very active used boat market, which makes buying and selling quite easy and risk free. After four years, most sailors have generally grown too large or have become more skilled and wish to move on to a more challenging class, which they find in the Laser or Club 420.

The Laser is unique in that the basic hull can be matched with one of three rigs—the 4.7, the Radial, or the standard Olympic-class rig. Many sailors begin with the 4.7 since it has the minimum of sail area, which makes it manageable. They then progress to the Radial and eventually on to the Olympic-class rig.

There are great choices in the twelve- to fifteen-foot range for adults interested in racing. For single-handed dinghy racing, the easy to rig and transport Laser is a tough act to beat. Its popularity also ensures much competition. The JY 15 and Vanguard 15 are also quite popular in the two-person racing scene. Both are also easy to rig and launch and perform well in a wide range of conditions.

Day sailers

If racing is not your thing, there are other learning options. For very good reason, the Sunfish has remained popular for the last fifty years. Besides being actively raced—with the resale spin-off that this lends—it's simple to rig, easy to sail, and spacious enough for two. Although not as stable as the Optimum, Sabot, JY, or catamaran, the Sunfish is easy for a small sailor to handle as long as the breeze remains under fifteen knots. And, in the event it does capsize, it's quite easy to right—and it has a self-bailing cockpit.

Other vessels of this variety that are all good beach-launching vessels are the Sunflower, the Expedition 12.5, and 14.5, the Capri Wave, and the Escape.

Catamarans are fast and quick. In addition, they're extremely versatile in terms of conditions they can handle. They make great leisure or racing craft and are very easy to launch.

Sailing tenders

Beyond being great for ferrying you in from your large keelboat, sailing tenders can be fun little sailing vessels in a class of their own. They can be rowed or rigged and can get in and out of tight areas with limited draft.

Physical Inspection

It is possible to hire a marine surveyor who will do a professional inspection of a boat. It's like having a home inspector before buying a house. But here are some tips on what you should look for. Though portions of this section may well be applicable to smaller vessels, it's mainly applicable to the larger overnight keelboats.

Take a walk around the boat—outside, around the deck, and inside—getting an overall impression and recording your comments as you walk. It's not necessary to have a detailed picture here—all you want to do is get that all-important overview and note issues,

Buyer's Kit

- Cassette recorder—to give yourself a quick reference where writing would be too slow or not extensive enough. Perhaps you even hear something strange in the engine and can later get an expert opinion by replaying the sound rather than describing it.
- Video camera—to get a visual to use in the same manner as the audio.
- Decibel meter—available at electronic stores—measures engine noise.
- GPS—to cross-check the accuracy of instruments on board.

both good and bad, that'll warrant later review. Besides noting details for later review, keep a running commentary of layout, aesthetics, materials, features, and general condition or appropriateness to your requirements. List the questions you have for the seller.

The issue you should constantly have in mind is how well the vessel matches up to your expectations and needs. Depending on the purpose you're buying the boat for, you'll have differently ranked criteria. Though it could go on *ad infinitum*, the following short list might trigger more questions you'd typically ask if you're purchasing a cruiser. You'd obviously adapt and expand on it to best suit your personal needs:

Accommodation quarters
- Is the main cabin adequate?
- How long and wide are the bunks? It's a good thing you've brought a tape measure with you, isn't it?
- Is there sufficient privacy?
- Is sleeping possible when others are aboard?

General
- How much headroom is there? Is this a problem?
- Are there enough hold-rails if the sea turns nasty?
- Are there any protrusions that would injure someone in rough weather?
- When the boat is heeled over, can you still move about without hindrance?
- What would change when kids are aboard (safety, space, obstructions)?
- Is there sufficient stowage space and how well designed is it?
- Beyond layout, what is the workmanship like in the hidden areas?

Galley
- Could you comfortably prepare a meal in difficult conditions?
- Will through traffic in companionways interfere with kitchen activity?
- Is the icebox sufficient, and are other facilities adequate?

Structural soundness

- What does the engine sound like?
- How does the wiring look? Is it neatly bundled and free of corrosion?
- Is there any sign of chafing to wires, especially near openings to bulkheads? If this is a new boat, there should be some kind of padding present that would dampen the effects of chafing due to engine vibrations.
- Is the battery secured with a strong hold-down provision?
- Does the battery have a heavy-duty fuse or circuit breaker installed close by?
- Is there sufficient space to install more batteries?
- Is the alternator the correct size for the battery capacity? If not, recharging the battery might mean several hours of idling the engine even while you're already at anchor.

General accessibility

- In the event the vessel started to take on water, the first check you'd make would be whether the sea cocks are the culprit. How easy are they to reach when at sea?
- What is the routing of the drinking and freshwater system? Are the valves and filters accessible? Apply these same questions to the water heating system.
- What about the fuel and oil filters? Can you reach them too?
- Are there any other drive belts, fuel injectors, or other routine maintenance sites that need to be accessed?
- Could you realistically bleed air from the fuel system while at sea?
- Would it be possible to service the shaft while at sea? Reach down and feel.

Ready to Test Sail

With all of your questions satisfactorily answered, it's time to give her a test run. You will be able to do this right away, or you may have to schedule a time that is

convenient. The more serious the seller gauges your intentions to be, the more likely you'll be able to set up a proper run. Since you have conducted yourself in a very professional manner by arriving with all the right tools and asking all the right questions, you'll probably receive red carpet treatment.

So Little Time, So Much To Do

You'll only have a relatively short time on this cruise, in only one weather and water environment, to test an awful lot about the vessel. Therefore, arriving at accurate conclusions very rapidly will be vital if the significant investment you're about to make will ultimately become an asset rather than a liability to your lifestyle. Of course, to do so you'd better have your wits about you. This section is designed to help you focus on the really important issues in order to make a rapid and valid diagnostic assessment.

The Environment

Note the weather conditions—the wind velocity, its consistency, and state of the sea. Clouds or rain won't have much of a bearing on the boat's performance, so disregard this type of element—they're not a factor in assessing the boat. What you're really attempting to do then is to exaggerate in your mind those elements that directly affect the boat and her performance.

The other element to separate the boat from is the seller or owner. Their objective is to sell her to you, so without being hostile or rude, attempt to ignore their upbeat chitchat and cloaked sales pitch.

If your test day happens to be dead still and flat calm, you'll be left with very few clues as to how the boat will react when things are a little more perky. Asking the salesperson the direct question "She's great today, but what about in 30 knots or a three-foot chop?" is not likely to illicit an absolutely accurate truth. You'll need to be a little more leading in your questions, identifying an element of handling that you believe might present a problem under different conditions. This will require a direct answer.

Questions

Obviously you won't be able to see every detail that you need to know. Besides the questions you'll be asking the seller or salesperson based on your observations, the following questions will help you to have a deeper understanding of the boat in terms of your requirements and expectations.

However, it's important to note that sellers tend to round many of these questions off with a global answer that would indicate that the boat is a panacea to your every requirement. Now, that just isn't true. No single boat can be all things to all people. Remember, every boat is a compromise.

At the very least, these questions will make the seller think that you know what you're talking about and they'll tend to keep their answers a lot more specific and closer to the truth. That's not to say they'd otherwise lie, but salespeople do have a way of leaving out details.

- Who built the boat and for what purpose was it built—profit or personal use?
- What is unique about the boat? What does it feature?
- What am I not seeing? What safety features are built in, such as flotation chambers?
- What is the construction material, how strong is it, and how easy would it be to repair if something happened?
- Are deck fittings secured properly? What is backing them and what is it made from?
- What's the vessel's top speed and cruising speed under sail and motor?
- What kind of cruising range has she got and what kind of fuel consumption will this give me?

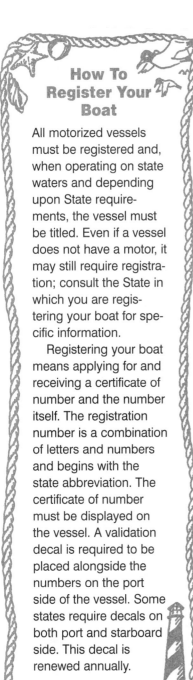

How To Register Your Boat

All motorized vessels must be registered and, when operating on state waters and depending upon State requirements, the vessel must be titled. Even if a vessel does not have a motor, it may still require registration; consult the State in which you are registering your boat for specific information.

Registering your boat means applying for and receiving a certificate of number and the number itself. The registration number is a combination of letters and numbers and begins with the state abbreviation. The certificate of number must be displayed on the vessel. A validation decal is required to be placed alongside the numbers on the port side of the vessel. Some states require decals on both port and starboard side. This decal is renewed annually.

Your Mindset

Try to remain fixed on the task. Move away from the salesperson, and if he or she follows, simply say that you need a little time to get a feel for the boat. You're the customer and you have a right to create the environment to your satisfaction.

Your Tasks

If you've got some equipment such as GPS or a decibel meter, periodically take readings and record any unusual variation. With the engine running at various speeds, check and record noise readings in all cabins and in the main saloon. Also, recheck these readings when the engine is idling and the boat is halted as this will give you an idea of what it might sound like if you have to charge the battery while at anchor.

Various yachting magazines run similar tests, and you can compare your readings to the published values for similar craft.

Activity Under Way

Take part in some of the activities to get a feel for them; other times just hang back and actively watch how the helmsman and crew work to make the boat perform.

- Is there enough room and is it reasonably easy to move about the deck while lines are being handled and fenders shipped?
- Some boats have their own little idiosyncrasies that need to be coaxed into life. Are there any special techniques involved with regard to throttle and wheel handling?
- How does the boat accelerate, handle, and turn?
- How quickly can she stop and come about?
- Do winches operate smoothly and are they geared correctly for your physique?
- Are all of the lines set up to suit your preferences? Can you reach the boom with ease?
- What are the provisions for stowing halyards and sheets?
- Do any of the winches foul?

Hands-On Testing

Make sure that you literally take the boat in hand. Handle the various lines yourself, get behind the wheel, and conduct every other aspect of the sailing routine that you typically would in all conditions. At the helm, put the boat on a close reach and ensure the following:

- Feel the wheel or tiller. How does she react to fine adjustments, rough ones, and slow carving movements?
- Try sitting and standing, and put your body in every conceivable physical position that you might ever be forced to be in. Imagine wind and spray coming over you from various angles, and imagine how you'd find shelter yet still have a sufficient view of the surroundings.
- Do there appear to be any blind spots that would mask an obstruction or other boat?
- Are all the instruments functioning well, and are they easy to monitor from your position?
- Once satisfied, sheet in and put yourself on a close haul.
- Has the boat done anything strange at all?
- How has the wheel reacted, and have there been any unusual sounds?
- If you've had variable wind, how did the boat react?
- If the wind has been steady, how has the boat reacted?
- Is there excessive motor vibration, smoke emission, or did you notice a particularly oily film on the water that might have come from the motor when you first boarded?

Steering Deficiencies

You need to know if the boat has steering deficiencies, and the best way to check this is to execute a few short tacks—as though you're going to windward while in a narrow channel.

Is This Craft Close-Winded?

In some boats, sailing to windward can be a long and slow process. To discover if this is one of those vessels, conduct the following test:

Careless, Reckless, or Negligent Operation

- It is the responsibility of the skipper to refrain from careless, reckless, or negligent operations on the water.
- Failure to operate a boat in a safe manner could endanger life, or property of other persons.
- Be courteous and exercise caution.
- The best way to become a safe and diligent boater is to use common sense. If it doesn't make sense to do something on land, it probably doesn't make sense to do it on the water.
- Don't allow passengers to ride or sit on the bow, stern, or sides of the boat while under way.

- Sail close to the wind and note the compass bearing, then come about onto the other tack.
- Maintain course awhile and note if there are any wind shifts that might be altering your speed or handling, then recheck the compass.
- Subtract the two compass headings from one another (taking any wind shifts into account). If the angle is greater than 95 degrees, then the boat is not happy sailing close to the wind.

Speed Run

Ease into a speed run by bearing off and check your maximum speed against wind speed. This will give you an idea of how efficiently the craft is performing.

Jibe

Ask the helm to turn downwind and jibe. Hopefully the conditions are moderate, and this will give you a good idea of whether the boat gives any problems.

The Acid Test

The way a boat feels is one of the main turn-ons for any sailor. This is the ultimate acid test. Forget the instruments, what the salesperson has said, and everything else for the moment. If you're not blown away and happy at this moment, then this boat isn't for you.

Heave To

Under full sail, heave to and head to the wind until the boat comes to a halt. Trim the jib over to one side and counter steer the wheel. If this boat is well behaved it should go onto an easy drift.

Unfurl the Sails

Help with unfurling the sails and see if there are any problems.

Moment of Truth

Turn the helm over—it's time to play truth or dare. Discuss your observations with the owner or representative and find out as much as you can about how the boat would have reacted under different conditions, or what the optimum sail configuration in different wind conditions is.

By now, with your hands-on experience you'll have a reasonable idea of how forthright and truthful they're being.

The Boat Post-Sail

The boat has now been stressed a little and there's probably a bit of dampness on deck, so it's time to look her over again.

- Is the antislip deck still effective at all venues?
- Are the rails and guards sufficient, well placed, and easy to use with the boat rocking in the chop?

Anchor System

- Is the anchor system well laid out and is the anchor locker sufficiently large?
- Will the existing anchor be sufficient for your needs?
- Is the bow roller appropriate to accommodate the type of anchor(s) you intend using?

Under Motor Power

Speed, range, and engine output

With the sails stowed, you can get a really good feeling of how the boat feels under power. Correlate that rpm with the speed and you'll be able to calculate what her optimum cruising speed will be. Correlate this with the seller's claims and get a feel for what your instinct says about the vibration and sound at that rpm pitch.

You'll also be able to get an idea of what the top end should be under full throttle and what your range would be if you were forced to motor somewhere in a hurry.

Proper Display of Boat Numbers

- The figures are read from left to right.
- They must be displayed on the forward half of each side of the bow of the boat.
- Numbers must be in bold, block letters of good proportion.
- Numbers must be not less than three inches high.
- They must be of contrasting color to the boat hull or background.
- They must be as high above the waterline as practical.
- No number other than the number assigned can be displayed on the forward half of the vessel.
- Letters must be separated from numbers by spaces or hyphens.
- The validation decal must be displayed within six inches of the number.

Steering

Ensure there are no obstructions, then communicate your intentions to everyone aboard. Swing the rudder hard to port and make a full circle. Repeat this to starboard. Study the wake and you'll get an idea of the boat's turning circle and its responsiveness. Most boats should make their turn in less than two-boat lengths.

Ensure that the figure eight you've made has two circles that are approximately the same size. This will give you an idea of any potential problems with the steering rig.

Stopping and handling

Pick a mark, usually a buoy or some other nonfixed object. Start by motoring slowly toward it, then engage reverse and see how quickly and accurately you can bring the boat to gently nudge it.

Now go slowly in reverse, noting the quality of steering and how accurately you can maneuver the boat. Could you put the bow or the stern right next to the reference buoy without touching it?

Next, rush the reference point and see how the boat reacts to emergency halts. If she pulls to port, inquire whether she has a starboard prop, as pulling to port will be a natural reaction when she's dragged from the starboard side.

From a standstill, see how the boat reacts to sudden reversing under full power. Running astern at full speed, reverse the halting procedure and power forward to see how the boat halts. How did the steering behave during this procedure? Did the boat try to heel, and did she ship any water or shudder in a strange way?

Precision maneuvering

By reversing and going ahead, check out how accurately you could place the boat at any relative angle and position to your reference buoy.

Docking

By now the seller is probably either totally impressed or totally peeved. Either way, it shouldn't matter, because you've been protecting your interests with perfectly acceptable trials.

If you wish, hand the docking procedure over to the seller, then participate from a position that will give you the best overall feel for how she is best brought alongside. If it's the owner at the helm, watch for the little tricks he or she might have developed to make everything go off smoothly. If it's a representative or broker, remember that they're probably fairly unfamiliar with this particular vessel and will probably be a little overly cautious.

If you notice anything odd about the way the boat handles, ask why this is so. After you've been through the docking and stowing procedure, it's probably a good time to give the seller your honest impressions and hear what their comments are and how they counter any objections you might have.

Acquiring Equipment
Don't Skimp

Before looking at the details, we'd like to be very emphatic that the reliability of sailing equipment is vital if you're to avoid worst-case safety scenarios. Because you'll pretty much get what you pay for, it's very important that you not be penny-wise and pound-foolish. Invest the extra money and get the best.

Assembling a Sail Inventory

Anyone who thinks there's no such thing as an engine without moving parts really hasn't factored sails into consideration. Since the average sailor can't simply look at a sail's specifications as he or she would a car engine and give an instant assessment of the performance, there is a certain mystery to judging whether he or she indeed likes the cut of the jib—to use a corny phrase.

Speculation aside, the average sailor certainly should realize that the sail is a big-ticket item that will be the ultimate determiner of how well his or her boat can perform, so there's also a level of anguish and frustration when a purchase selection needs to be made.

History of Yachts, II

- It may be said that yachting goes back to the ancient Romans, Greeks, and Egyptians who maintained vessels for pleasure.
- The word yachting is said to derive from the Dutch term "jaghtschip" or "jaght." The Dutch are considered to have been the first to engage in sailing as a sport.
- King Charles II of England brought the sport to the British Isles on his accession to the throne in 1660.
- The first organized yacht club, the Water Club of Cork Harbor, came about by 1720 in Ireland.

There are four main criteria upon which the sail's value will be judged:

- Its inherent design and quality of cut
- The material of construction
- Its ability to withstand abuse
- Its condition—if second-hand

Finding the Right Sail and Sailmaker

Sail making is quite a large industry and there are an awful lot of materials, designs, and makers to choose from. Depending on whether you're a weekend warrior, a serious racer, or a blue-water cruiser, you'll want to choose an appropriate specialist, design, and material.

Before getting into more detail, it's interesting to note that technology and computer-aided design have resulted in ever better sail design and material. For this reason alone, if performance is a factor, you'll probably want to look at new or fairly current designs only.

What follows is an elementary overview of sail design that should be applicable to your chosen interest. It's by no means a final word on the matter, and you should consult with various parties—though not necessarily salespeople—who can help you focus a little better on what would best suit your particular needs.

For weekend warriors

If you're mainly interested in day sailing and stick close to home, you probably won't have a big budget to spend on fancy extras. You won't need state-of-the-art designs, so pick good-quality and well-constructed sails from respected sailmakers. You're looking to buy sails in this order of priority:

- *Mainsail*: Woven-polyester crosscut—standard or economy-grade fabrics will do—with conventional battens and one reef line.

- *Headsail*: 150 percent overlap woven-polyester crosscut—again, standard or economy-grade fabric with leech and foot ultraviolet covers.
- *Cruising spinnaker:* It should be a .75-ounce radial-head cruising spinnaker with dousing sock.

For racer cruisers

You're one of the lucky among us who can take off on week-long jaunts to race or cruise over courses of hundreds of miles. So that you can cram more sightseeing into less time and get where you're going quicker, you'll need to invest a little more money in performance sails that can deliver maximum thrust over a wide range of conditions and maintain their form for a long period of time.

- *Mainsail*: Woven-polyester crosscut of standard or high-tenacity fabric, and fill-oriented, with full-length battens or at least top-two-full battens; two reefs; lazyjacks or Dutchman system (for racing) or built-in sail cover if you're into cruising.
- *Headsail*: Radial-paneled laminate or fiber-oriented if you're into racing, but if you're into cruising, 135 percent or racing-specific overlap; foam luff flattener; head and tack reefing patches or extended reinforcing; leech and foot ultraviolet covers for cruisers.
- *Cruising spinnaker*: Again a .75-ounce, though tri-radial construction, dousing sock.
- *Storm jib:* Non-overlapping roller-reefing/furling laminate jib with foam luff flattener.

For blue-water buffs

If you're into ocean crossing or spending lazy months cruising through harsh tropical regions where UV eats everything it can lay its rays on, make sail longevity your top priority. In addition, you can't afford problems out in the deep, so durability is everything. Here are some guides for a minimum sail inventory:

Hull Identification Number

Boats built since 1972 are required to have a Hull Identification Number (HIN) permanently attached to the transom on the starboard side above the waterline. This number is a serial number exclusive to your boat and is necessary to title and register it.

In 1984 a new regulation was passed which requires the HIN number to also be permanently attached in a second unexposed location.

- *Mainsail*: Woven-polyester crosscut of high-tenacity, fill-oriented fabric that is one ounce heavier than standard. Select either full-length battens if your budget can withstand a top-quality luff-car system, or, if boat performance can afford a reduction in mainsail area, go for battenless two reefs with extended two-ply head and clew areas and triple-stitched "Seam-kote" plastic-coated seams. Try to ensure extra reinforcing in batten areas, tablings, and luff and foot slides. Go for top-quality hardware; the most "bulletproof" furling system available.
- *Primary headsail*: Woven-polyester crosscut of high-tenacity fabric that is one ounce heavier than standard, with 135 percent overlap, triple-stitched "Seam-kote" seams, two-ply head and clew areas, extended patching or head and tack reefs, extra reinforcing in leech and foot tablings, and foam luff flattener.
- *Jib or staysail*: Constructed of woven-polyester crosscut of high-tenacity fabric that is one ounce heavier than standard with extra reinforcing, foam luff flattener, storm trysail and storm jib with two-ply sections along leech.
- *Cruising spinnaker*: Tri-radial construction, .75-ounce with 1.5-ounce luff panels, or entirely 1.5-ounce if possible.

Hardware Equipment

It's absolutely vital that the peripheral equipment you add to your vessel is both good quality and, where applicable, professionally installed. Some of the instruments mentioned below might be covered in other sections. The reason they appear here is because they may well be additional portable hardware that you'd like to purchase.

Here are the details of gizmos and items that'll make your sailing a lot smoother and more comfortable.

Mechanical Goodies

Winches

Because not all winches are made equal and there is such diversity in size, function, load capacity, and quality, it's quite important that you have expert advice before deciding to buy.

Blocks

A block is a pulley or a system of pulleys that is set into a casing. You've probably heard the term "block and tackle," and in nautical terms, this refers to the system whereby line is fed through a rigging of blocks in such a way that a gearing effect can be achieved. In other words, it applies the principle of leverage to roapwork in such a way that recovering ten feet of line might only move the desired object—say the boom—one foot, therefore applying a ten-fold gearing to the effort. In English, this would mean that you'd move the boom to windward by one foot with say forty pounds of pulling effort, even though you'd have to recover ten feet of line to achieve this. Of course, you'd also be hauling in four hundred pounds of pressure, which is not a task that your average sailor would relish.

With so much wind power in huge sails, it makes a lot of sense to have good-quality, purpose-built blocks installed in appropriate places. They might be carrying quite a load, and you don't want to leave any margins for error.

Finding-Your-Way Goodies

Navigation instruments

All of the fancy bells and whistles installed at the helm of a modern cockpit are generally available in portable versions. If you've got the surplus funds, it's not a bad idea to double up on some items such as a GPS, because it's something you can take with you if you're ever marooned.

Marine sextants

The name seems to conjure up images of something that the sextant is not, and the way it received such a strange-sounding

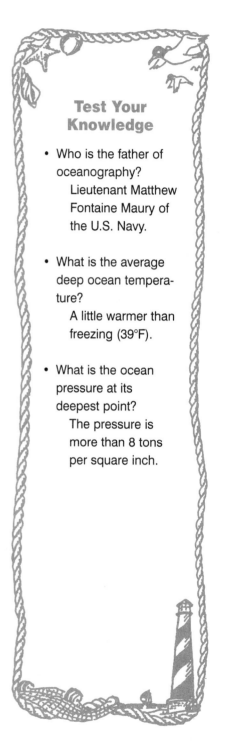

Test Your Knowledge

- Who is the father of oceanography?
  Lieutenant Matthew Fontaine Maury of the U.S. Navy.

- What is the average deep ocean temperature?
  A little warmer than freezing (39°F).

- What is the ocean pressure at its deepest point?
  The pressure is more than 8 tons per square inch.

name is a mystery. For certain, it has been around since 1730, and its function is to measure the altitude of celestial bodies from which sailors can fix their position on the globe.

Although not in common use for today's sport sailor, it's nonetheless a vital piece of hardware when our modern technology lets us down. However, without knowledge of how to use it and some hands-on experience riding out the waves while squinting through the sighting mechanism, it'll be about as much use to you as an unattached faucet fitting in the desert. If you buy one of these—and for oceangoing craft we seriously suggest that you do—ensure that you get some lessons and practice with it from time to time.

Night vision goggles

A wonderful toy and one of the latest additions to the modern sailor's array of goodies, only a half-dozen years ago night vision technology was the stuff of Hollywood sensationalism where the heroes wore cyclops-style helmets with the protruding single eye jutting from their foreheads.

These days the technology can run you anywhere from a little over $100 on up to several thousand dollars. For your money you'll get a pixilated twilight view of the world even on the blackest of nights. Of course there's an incredible application here for spotting hazards and assisting rescuers in blackout conditions, but it's still a luxury item and will probably remain so for some time into the future.

Binoculars

These need no introduction. However, because you'll generally be using them onboard a rocking and rolling platform, do consider that too narrow a field of view will seriously affect your ability to hold station on a desired object.

Navigation computers

These vary from control-room-sized monsters right down to calculator-sized LCD displays. Nobody can say exactly where this technology is headed or how fast it will get there, but based on the last ten years of observation, you can bank on there being an extraordinary time ahead for technophiles.

Other good things

Then there are all the other wonders in a box that are covered in depth elsewhere in the text. These include radios, GPS, depth-sounder, weather monitoring equipment, and compasses and other plotting tools.

Software

Not even the wide blue oceans are safe from the creeping encroachment of high technology. Modern boats bristle with gadgetry, and there are software applications to cater to your every need and whim.

Check out this brief sample selection that'll be out of date even before this book hits the printing press. You get the picture? This is such a fast-moving part of the sailing industry that it's best you ask at your local sailing and software store for applications that will suit you. Whatever we review here will shortly be redundant, as will be whatever you choose to buy.

Velocity Sailing—Velocity offers software for both performance prediction and for hull design, and also consultation on speed under sail.

Blue Peter Marine Systems—Providers of a family of hull design programs.

Nautical Technologies—The Cap'n Electronic Charting System—electronic charting system.

Nobeltec—*marine navigation software.*

Posey Yacht Design—*sailing simulators.*

ProMar Software—*provides a shareware navigation program.*

Regatta Scoring and Race Management—*a comprehensive computer program for regatta scoring and race management.*

TT Designs—*marine computing.*

Waterman Services—*computer solutions for the mariner, hardware and software.*

TopYacht Software—*provides club membership lists, race and regatta management, and handicapping and yardstick-based scoring for dinghies, trailables, and keelboats.*

Able Plotter—a fully programmed graphical pocket computer for the traditional yacht navigator.

SailMan—database of production and semi-custom sailboats from twenty feet up.

Starpath School of Navigation—radar simulator and tutorial with tides and currents prediction software.

Other interesting titles
- Ultimate Sailing Screen Saver by Sharon Green
- Virtual Passage
- DataBoat
- Kiwi Tech Marine Solutions
- OnBoard Yacht Management Software
- Posey Yacht Design Simulators
- Sail 2000 America Cup Simulation
- Sailing Interactive CD-ROM sailing simulator with video and sound Sailing Master 2

Sailing Schools
- Catamaran Charters Sailing School
  http://edumall.com/catamaransailing/school/intro.htm
- Chapman School of Seamanship
  http://www.chapman.org/
- Cooper Boating Center
  http://www.cooper-boating.com/index.html
- CYOA Yacht Charters
  http://www.usvi.net/vimi/cyoa/houston
- International Sail and Power Association
  http://www.axionet.com/ispa/
- Island Yachting Centre Inc.
  http://www.islandyc.com/
- J. World Sailing School
  http://www.sailjworld.com
- Joysail
  http://www.joysail.com/
- Kolius Sailing Schools
  http://www.kolius-sailing.com/
- LMI
  http://www.lmitraining.com/

- The Mariner Sailing School
  http://saildc.com/
- Martin's Sailing School & Club
  http://www.lovetosail.com/
- Mumbles Sailing School
  http://members.aol.com/sailgower/index.html
- The School of Ocean Sailing
  http://www.nlbbs.com/~svsamana/
- Offshore Sailing School
  http://www.offshore-sailing.com/
- Ottawa Sailing School
  http://www2.magmacom.com/~oss/
- Pacific Yachting and Sailing
  http://www.pacificsail.com/
- Roy Lawson's Sea Skippers Academy
  http://users.iafrica.com/s/sh/shorstop/
- Sail Training Adventures
  http://www.occsailing.com/
- Sailboats Inc.
  http://www.sailboats-inc.com/
- Sea Wing Sailing School
  http://www.seawing.com/school/
- Torresen ASA Sailing School
  http://www.torresen.com/school/school.htm

Sailor Talk

Head

The "head" aboard a Navy ship is the bathroom. The term comes from the days of sailing ships when the place for the crew to relieve themselves was all the way forward on either side of the bowsprit, the integral part of the hull to which the figurehead was fastened.

Another version of explanation claims that crew would sometimes go over the side. In consideration of their crewmates who might have their head sticking out of a porthole and in the line of fire, crew would shout "heads" before commencing the act.

DOCK 15

Sailing Schools

What follows is a list of sailing schools. At the time of writing, these details checked out, but do verify this locally.

Schools differ in terms of their focus: racing or cruising. Choose one that best suits your needs. You'll find schools that are national affiliates, for profit or non-profit, short and intense or long and comprehensive, specialized to large or small vessels only, or for the commercial license-seeking individual.

Check it out; it's all a matter of need and availability. Please remember that this list is just a smattering of what's out there. A comprehensive list could probably fill a book on its own.

Northeastern United States

Maine
- Sawyer's Sailing School
  Auburn, ME
  Tel: (800) 372-8465, (207) 783-6882
  http://www.boatshow.com/CaptainBob.html
- Bay Island Yacht Charters
  Rockland, ME
  Tel: (207) 596-7550
  Fax: (207) 594-0407
- Bay Island Sailing School of Maine
  Rockport, ME
  http://www.midcoast.com/~sailme/

Vermont
- NE Quadrant/International Sailing School
  Colchester, VT
  Tel: (802) 864-9065
  Fax: (802) 863-4016

Massachusetts
- Boston Harbor Sailing Club
  Boston, MA
  Tel: (617) 345-9202
  http://www.by-the-sea.com/bhsclub
- Boston Sailing Center
  Boston, MA
  Tel: (617) 227-4198
  Fax: (617) 227-5644

Connecticut
- Bud's North O'Newport Sailing
  Somers, CT
  Tel: (860) 763-1980
- Coastline Yacht Club
  Noank, CT
  Tel: (860) 536-2689
  Fax: (860) 572-0778
- Yachting Services of Mystic
  West Mystic, CT
  Tel: (800) 536-9980
  Fax: (860) 536-8411
  http://www.ysmystic.com
- Sail the Sounds
  Mystic, CT
  Tel: (860) 536-2689

New York
- New York Sailing Center Yacht Club
  City Island, NY
  Tel: (718) 885-0335
- Manhattan Sailing School
  New York, NY
  Tel: (212) 786-0400
  Fax: (212) 786-3318
- Port Liberte/North Cove Sailing
  New York, NY
  Tel: (800) 532-5552
  http://www.sailnyc.com
- Croton Sailing School
  Croton-on-Hudson, NY
  Tel: (914) 271-6868
  Fax: (518) 672-5046
- New York Sailing School
  New Rochelle, NY
  Tel: (914) 235-6052
  Fax: (914) 633-6429
  http://www.nyss.com

- Sigsbee Sailing
  Port Washington, NY
  Tel: (516) 767-0971
  Fax: (516) 767-0945
- South Bay Sailing School
  Holtsville, NY
  Tel: (516) 289-0077
- Oyster Bay Sailing School
  Oyster Bay, NY
  Tel: (516) 624-7900
  Fax: (516) 922-4502
- Sag Harbor Sailing School, Inc.
  Sag Harbor, NY
  Tel: (516) 725-5100
  Fax: (516) 725-8760
- Great Hudson Sailing Center Inc.
  Kingston, NY
  Tel: (914) 429-1557
- Yachting Operation Services
  Hendersen Harbor, NY
  Tel: (315) 938-5494
  Fax: (315) 938-5536
- Polish Sailing Club, Inc.
  Brooklyn, NY
  Tel: (718) 854-0100

New Jersey
- Newport Sailing School & Cruising
  Jersey City, NJ
  Tel: (201) 626-3210
  Fax: (732) 530-1567
  http://www.newportsail.com
- Philadelphia Sailing School
  Riverside, NJ
  Tel: (609) 461-3992
  Fax: (609) 461-9415
- New Jersey Sailing School
  Pt. Pleasant, NJ
  Tel: (732) 295-3450
  Fax: (732) 295-3331
  http://www.njplaza.com/sail
- Nelson Sailing Center
  Island Heights, NJ
  Tel: (908) 270-0022
- Down Easterly Sailing Adventures
  Beach Haven Park, NJ
  Tel: (609) 492-2822

Pennsylvania
- Liberty Sailing of Philadelphia
  Philadelphia, PA
  Tel: (215) 923-SAIL
  Fax: (215) 393-7559
  http://www.libertynet.org/~sailing
- Midlantic Sailing School
  Philadelphia, PA
  Tel: (215) 574-1758
  Fax: (215) 592-4677
  http://www.midsail.com

Maryland
- Havre de Grace Sailing School
  Havre de Grace, MD
  Tel: (410) 939-2869
- Getaway Sailing Ltd.
  Baltimore, MD
  Tel: (410) 342-3110
  Fax: (410) 342-5421
- Annapolis Sailing School
  Annapolis, MD
  http://www.usboat.com/annapway/
  home.html
- Chesapeake Sailing School
  Annapolis, MD
  Tel: (410) 269-1594
  Fax: (410) 268-1049
- The Maryland School of Sailing &
  Seamanship
  Rock Hall, MD
  Tel: (410) 639-7030
  Fax: (410) 639-7038
  http://www.mdschool.com
- Upper Bay Sailing School
  Worton, MD
  (888) 302-SAIL
  http://www.upperbaysailing.com

Southeastern United States

Virginia
- Norton's Yacht Sales Inc.
  Deltaville, VA
  Tel: (804) 776-9211
  Fax: (804) 776-9044
  http://www.nortonyachts.com

- Trident Charters
  Norfolk, VA
  Tel: (757) 588-2022
  Fax: (757) 427-0249
- Lake Sailing Academy
  Huddleston, VA
  Tel: (888) SAIL SML

North Carolina
- North Beach Sailing Inc.
  Duck, NC
  Tel: (919) 261-6262
- Water Ways
  Wilmington, NC
  Tel: (910) 256-4282
  Fax: (910) 256-9330
- Broadreach
  Raleigh, NC
  Tel: (919) 833-1907
  Fax: (919) 833-1979
- Down Easterly Sailing Adventure
  Oriental, NC
  Tel: (919) 249-1650

Georgia
- Kingdom Yachts Sailing Club
  Cumming, GA
  Tel: (770) 887-7966
  http://www.andrews.com/kysc
- Windsong Sailing Academy
  Lilburn, GA
  Tel: (404) 256-6700
  http://www.windsongsail.com
- Lanier Sailing Academy
  Bufford, GA
  Tel: (800) 684-9463, (770) 945-8810
  Fax: (770) 945-4507
  http://www.mindspring.com/~laniersail
- Dunbar Sails Inc.
  St. Simons Island, GA
  Tel: (912) 638-8573
  Fax: (912) 638-6905

Florida
- Adventure Sailing Cruises
  Panama City, FL
  Tel: (904) 233-5499

- Sailing South
  Destin, FL
  Tel: (904) 654-1518
- Sailing School at Sandestin
  Destin, FL
  Tel: (850) 650-4412
  http://www.saildestin.com/
- St. Augustine Sailing
  St. Augustine, FL
  Tel: (800) 683-SAIL, (904) 829-0648
- Windward Sailing School, Inc.
  Fernandina Beach, FL
  Tel: (904) 261-9125
  http://www.windwardsailing.com/
- Diamond 99 Marina
  Melbourne, FL
  Tel: (407) 254-1490
- Chapman School of Seamanship
  Stuart, FL
  Tel: (561) 283-8130
  Fax: (561) 283-2019
  http://www.chapman.org/
- Vinoy Charters & Sailing School
  St. Petersburg, FL
  Tel: (800) 879-2244
- Ft. Myers Yacht Charters
  Cape Coral, FL
  Tel: (813) 540-8050
  Fax: (941) 549-4901
- The Sailing Academy, Inc.
  Indian Rocks Beach, FL
  Tel: (813) 593-8374
- Florida Sailing and Cruising School
  North Ft. Myers, FL
  Tel: (941) 656-1339
  Fax: (813) 656-2628
- Vacation Yachts Inc.
  Ft. Myers, FL
  Tel: (941) 437-2800
  Fax: (904) 469-8116
- International Sailing School
  Punta Gorda, FL
  Tel: (800) 824-5040, (941) 639-7492
  Fax: (941) 639-0085
  http://www.IntlSailSch.com/
- Gulf Wind Yachting Inc.
  Naples, FL
  Tel: (813) 775-7435

- Island Yachting Centre Inc.
  Palmetto, FL
  Tel: (941) 729-4511
  Fax: (941) 722-7677
- Tropical Diversion
  Hollywood, FL
  Tel: (954) 921-1044
- Island Sailing
  Ft Lauderdale, FL
  Tel: (305) 525-5956
- Ahoy Marine & Charters
  Ft. Lauderdale, FL
  Tel: (954) 564-0199
  Fax: (305) 563-8828
  http://www.ahoycharters.com/
- Southeast Yachting School & Charter
  Ft. Lauderdale, FL
  Tel: (954) 523-BOAT
- Blue Water Sailing School
  Ft. Lauderdale, FL
  Tel: (800) 255-1840, (954) 763-8464
  Fax: (954) 768-0695
  http://www.bwss.com/
- Florida Yacht Charters
  Miami Beach, FL
  Tel: (800) 537-0050, (305) 532-8600
  Fax: (305) 672-2039
- Florida Sailing Club
  Palm City, FL
  Tel: (305) 361-3611
- The Catamaran Company
  Miami Beach, FL
  Tel: (800) 262-0308, (305) 538-9446
  Fax: (305) 538-1556
- Go Native Yacht Charters
  Plantation, FL
  Tel: (800) 359-9808, (954) 791-4692
  http://www.gnyc.com
- International Sailing Center
  Key Largo, FL
  Tel: (305) 451-3287
  Fax: (305) 453-0255
- Little Palm Island Sailing St School
  Little Torch Key, FL
  Tel: (305) 872-1226

Central United States

Ohio

- Ohio Sailing Club
  Vermilion, OH
  Tel: (216) 967-0260
  Fax: (216) 967-0297
- Adventure Plus Yacht Charters
  Sandusky, OH
  Tel: (419) 625-5000
  Fax: (419) 625-4428
  http://www.visitohio.com/adventureplus
- North Coast Sailing School
  Cleveland, OH
  Tel: (216) 861-6250
- Great Lakes Sailing Academy
  Lorain, OH
  Tel: (440) 239-9379

Illinois

- Fairwind Sail Charters Inc.
  Chicago, IL
  Tel: (312) 427-1525
  Fax: (312) 567-0366

Wisconsin

- Fox River Marina Inc
  Oshkosh, WI
  Tel: (920) 236-4220
  Fax: (920) 236-4226

Michigan

- Lake St. Clair School of Sailing
  St. Clair Shores, MI
  Tel: (810) 772-5475
  Fax: (810) 776-4267
- Torresen Marine Inc
  Muskegon, MI
  Tel: (616) 759-8596
- Bay Breeze Yacht Charters
  Traverse City, MI
  Tel: (616) 941-0535
  Fax: (616) 941-9548

Missouri

- St. Louis Sailing Center
  Bridgeton, MO
  Tel: (314) 298-0411
  Fax: (314) 298-7194
- Sailing Charters & Academy
  Branson, MO
  Tel: (417) 739-5555
  Fax: (417) 324-3071

Tennessee

- Sail Tennessee
  Jefferson City, TN
  Tel: (423) 475-4009

Kentucky

- Lighthouse Landing Sailing School
  Grand Rivers, KY
  Tel: (502) 362-8201

Louisiana

- Murray Yacht Sales Inc.
  New Orleans, LA
  Tel: (504) 283-2507
- Ship to Shore Co
  Lake Charles, LA
  Tel: (318) 474-0730

Mississippi

- Southern Cross Sailing
  Long Beach, MS
  Tel: (601) 863-6880

Arkansas

- Sailing Charters of Arkansas
  Paron, AR
  Tel: (501) 594-5424
  http://www.maxpages.com/sailingcharter

Oklahoma

- Britt Sails
  Oologah, OK
  Tel: (918) 712-7245
  Fax: (918) 443-2859
- Redbud Sailing School
  Claremore, OK
  Tel: (918) 341-5190
  Fax: (918) 341-9166

Texas

- Southwest Sailing Academy
  Amarillo, TX
  Tel: (806) 351-0188
- Nautica Boat Club
  Denison, TX
  Tel: (903) 463-7245
  Fax: (903) 463-3294
- North Texas Sailing School
  Rockwall, TX
  Tel: (972) 771-2002
  Fax: (972) 771-6029
- Magellan Sailing Center, Inc.
  Dallas, TX
  Tel: (214) 827-8990
  http://www.TheSailboat.com
- Dallas/Ft. Worth Sailing School
  Grape Vine, TX
  Tel: (817) 481-4099
- Sailing Center on Joe Pool Lake
  Fort Worth, TX
  Tel: (817) 921-0343
  Fax: (817) 921-4040
  http://www.flash.net/~jplsail
- Cedar Mills Marina
  Gordonville, TX
  Tel: (903) 523-4222
  Fax: (903) 523-4077
- Bay Charter Inc.
  Kemah, TX
  Tel: (281) 334-3597
  Fax: (281) 474-7420
  http://www.baycharter.com
- Houston Marine Training Services
  http://www.houstonmarine.com/marine/
  hm_index.htm
- Corpus Christi Sailing Center, Inc.
  Corpus Christi, TX
  Tel: (512) 881-8503
  Fax: (512) 881-8504
  http://www.constant.com/sailing

Western United States

Washington

- Island Sailing Club
  Kirkland, WA
  Tel: (425) 822-2470
- Northwest Cruising Academy
  Seattle, WA
  Tel: (206) 623-8123
- Seattle Sailing Club
  Seattle, WA
  Tel: (206) 782-5100
- San Juan Sailing
  Bellingham, WA
  Tel: (800) 677-SAIL, (360) 671-4300
  Fax: (360) 671-4301
  http://www.sanjuansailing.com
- Bellhaven Charters
  Bellingham, WA
  Tel: (800) 542-8812, (360) 733-6636
  http://www.pacificrim.net/~belhaven
- Puget Sound Sailing Institute
  Tacoma, WA
  Tel: (800) 487-2454, (253) 383-1774
  Fax: (253) 274-8703

Oregon

- Bubba Louie's West Winds Sailing
  Hood River, OR
  Tel: (800) 880-0861, (541) 386-4222
  http://www.bubbalouie.com
- Portland Sailing Center
  Portland, OR
  Tel: (503) 281-6529
- Island Sailing Club
  Portland, OR
  Tel: (503) 285-7765
  Fax: (503) 286-9370

Idaho

- The Sail Loft
  Bayview, ID
  Tel: (208) 683-7245

Nevada

- Sailing Ventures
  Zephyr Cove, NV
  Tel: (702) 884-4144
  Fax: (916) 542-1691
  http://www.sailtahoe.com

Colorado

- Dillon Marina
  Dillon, CO
  Tel: (970) 468-5100
- Victoria Sailing School
  Morrison, CO
  Tel: (303) 697-7433
  http://www.victoriasailingschool.com
- The Anchorage
  Lyons, CO
  Tel: (970) 823-6601

California

- Sailing Ventures
  South Lake Tahoe, CA
  Tel: (530) 542-1691
  http://www.sailtahoe.com
- Martin's ASA Sailing School of
  Sacramento
  Sacramento, CA
  Tel: (916) 369-7700
  http://www.lovetosail.com/
- Live & Learn School of Sailing
  Sonora, CA
  Tel: (209) 533-4437
- Safe Passage Sailing Center
  Foster City, CA
  Tel: (415) 715-0252
- Spinnaker Sailing School
  Redwood City, CA
  Tel: (415) 363-1390
  Fax: (415) 363-0725
- Spinnaker Sailing School
  San Francisco, CA
  Tel: (415) 543-7333
  Fax: (415) 543-7405
  http://www.baysail.com/spinnaker

- Club Nautique
  Alameda, CA
  Tel: (510) 865-4700
  Fax: (510) 865-3851
- Tradewinds Sailing Center
  Pt. Richmond, CA
  Tel: (510) 232-7999
  Fax: (510) 232-8188
  http://www.sfsailing.com/tradewinds/
  try.html
- Modern Sailing Academy
  Sausalito, CA
  Tel: (415) 331-6266
  Fax: (415) 331-7065
  http://www.modernsailing.com
- Club Nautique
  Sausalito, CA
  Tel: (415) 332-8001
- Pacific Yachting School
  Santa Cruz, CA
  Tel: (408) 423-7245
  Fax: (408) 423-4260
- Sailing Center of Morro Bay
  Morro Bay, CA
  Tel: (805) 772-6446
  Fax: (805) 772-6818
- Sailing Center of Santa Barbara
  Santa Barbara, CA
  Tel: (805) 962-2826
  Fax: (805) 966-7435
  http://www.sbsailctr.com
- California Sailing Academy
  Marina del Rey, CA
  Tel: (310) 821-3433
  Fax: (310) 821-4141
  http://www.insidewla.com/csa/
- Marina Sailing MDR
  Marina del Rey, CA
  Tel: (310) 822-6617
  Fax: (310) 823-5568
- Pacific Sailing
  Marina del Rey, CA
  Tel: (310) 823-4064
- Sea Mist Skippers of M.D.R.
  Marina del Rey, CA
  Tel: (310) 398-8830
  Fax: (310) 391-8110
  http://www.seamist-skippers.com/mdr

- Marina Sailing Long Beach
  Long Beach, CA
  Tel: (310) 432-4672
  Fax: (310) 432-0369
- Oceanside Sailing Club & School
  Vista, CA
  Tel: (619) 722-2518
- Harbor Sailboats
  San Diego, CA
  Tel: (800) 854-6625, (619) 291-9568
  Fax: (619) 291-1473
  http://www.harborsailboats.com
- San Diego Sailing Academy
  San Diego, CA
  Tel: (800) 441-8672, (619) 299-9247
  Fax: (619) 296-3389
  http://www.sdsa.com
- Seaforth Boat Rentals
  San Diego, CA
  Tel: (619) 223-1681
- San Diego Sailing Club & School
  San Diego, CA
  Tel: (619) 298-6623
  Fax: (619) 298-6625
- Harbor Island Yacht Club
  San Diego, CA
  Tel: (619) 291-7245
  Fax: (619) 296-2482
- Marina Sailing of San Diego
  San Diego, CA
  Tel: (619) 221-8286
  Fax: (619) 221-8263
- Sailing Solution
  San Diego, CA
  Tel: (619) 225-8225
- Marina Sailing NP
  Newport Beach, CA
  Tel: (714) 673-7763
  Fax: (714) 673-7763
- Blue Dolphin Sailing Club
  Balboa Island, CA
  Tel: (714) 644-2525
  http://www.bluedolphinsc.com
- Offshore Island Sailing Club
  Oxnard, CA
  Tel: (805) 985-3600
  Fax: (805) 985-3350

- Marina Sailing Channel Island
  Oxnard, CA
  Tel: (805) 985-5219
- Pacific Sailing, Ventura
  Oxnard, CA
  Tel: (805) 658-6508

International

- United Kingdom Sailing Academy
  http://www.uk-sail.org.uk/
- Westabout Adventures
  http://www.webcraft.co.uk/westbound/
- Britannia Sailing School
  http://www.semaphore.co.uk/britannia/

Youth Sailing Summer Camps and Programs

Sailing programs for children and adolescents are the largest of all specialized programs. Nearly every yacht club has a youth sailing program; many community organizations and sailing clubs have regular or special summer programs. In addition, the Boy Scouts, the Girl Scouts, and other youth-oriented groups offer sailing to junior members.

- Boy Scouts of America
  Tel: (214) 580-2359
- Cass' Marina Junior Sailing Program
  Tel: (415) 332-6789
- Community Boating, Inc.
  Tel: (617) 523-1038
- Courageous Sailing Center
  Tel: (617) 242-3821
- Girl Scouts of the USA, Inc.
  Toll free: (800) 223-0624
- Lake Merritt Adapted Boating Program
  Tel: (510) 238-2290
- Sarasota Youth Sailing Program
  Tel: (813) 955-0181
- US Sailing
  Tel: (401) 849-5200

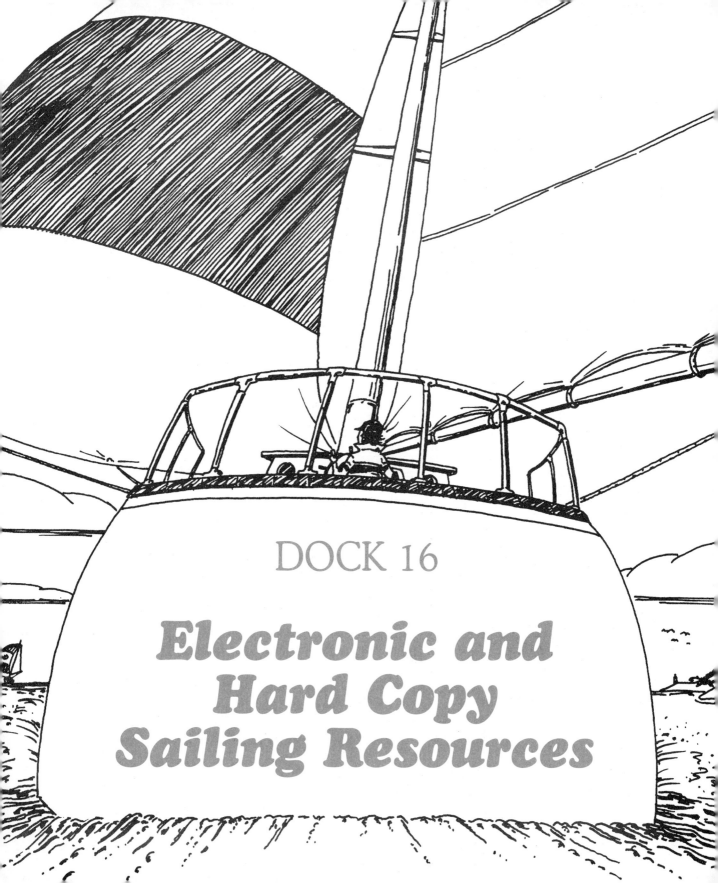

DOCK 16

Electronic and Hard Copy Sailing Resources

Sailing Catalogs

- IMP
  IMP Mail Order
  64 Market Street
  South Normanton, Derbyshire (United Kingdom) DE5 2EL
  http://www.imp-sail.u-net.com/home.htm#topofpage
- She Sails, Inc.
  Toll free: (888) She-Sails (743-7245)
  http://www.aztec.com/shesails/

Sailing Software and CD-ROMs

Buying a boat

- So Many Sailboats, Ovation Digital Productions.

General boating

- Databoat International Ltd.
- Chapman Piloting: Hands-On Powerboating on CD-ROM
- Get Your Captain's License (CD-ROM)
- Learn to Sail with Little Pines
- Power & Sail Collection Screen Saver
- Starpath NavRules for WinHelp
- Starpath Radar Trainer for Windows
- Starpath Weather Trainer

Specialized Books of Interest

Basic Sailing Books

- *Basic Keelboat.* Monk Henry, Rob Eckhardt (Illustrator), Kim Downing (Illustrator). U.S. Sailing Association.
- *Colgate's Basic Sailing.* Steve Colgate. Offshore Shore Sailing School.
- *Competent Crew*, 2nd ed. Malcolm McKeag. Fernhurst Books.
- *Complete Sailor: Learning the Art of Sailing.* David Seidman. International Marine Publishing.
- *Learning to Sail: The Annapolis Sailing School Guide for All Ages.* Diane Goodman & Ian Brodie. International Marine Publishing.
- *Royce's Sailing Illustrated: The Sailors Bible Since '56.* Patrick M. Royce. Royce Publishing.
- *Sailing: A Parent's Handbook for Junior Sailing.* Susan D. Artof, Johi Palmer, Paul Artof. Center Press.
- *Sailing for Kids.* Gary & Steve Kibbie. Fernhurst Books.
- *Sailor's Start-Up.* Doug Werner. Tracks Pub.

- *Start Sailing Right!* Derrick Fries, Burt Bilbrey. United States Sailing Association.

General Sailing Books

- *Born To Sail (On Other Peoples Boats).* Jennifer P. Stuart. Sheridan House.
- *Cruising With Children.* Gwenda Cornell. Sheridan House.
- *Laser Sailing for the 1990's.* Dick Tillman. International Marine Publishing.
- *High Performance Sailing.* Frank Bethwaite. International Marine Publishing.

Marine Electrical and Electronics System Manuals

Equipment fails. The more you can fix yourself, the better off you'll be.

- *Boat Electrics.* James Yates. Helmsman Books.
- *The Boat Owner's Guide to Marine Engine Installation.* Peter F. Caplen. Crowood Press.
- *Boat owner's Illustrated Handbook of Wiring.* Charlie Wing. International Marine Publishing.
- *GMDSS for Small Craft.* Alan Clemmetsen. Fernhurst Books.
- *Independent Energy Guide.* Kevin Jeffrey. Chelsea Green Pub Company.
- *Managing 12 Volts.* Harold Barre. Summer Breeze Pub.
- *Marine Electrical & Electronics Bible.* John C. Payne. Sheridan House.
- *Marine Electronics Handbook.* Colin Jones. Motorbooks International.
- *Marine SSB Operation; A Small Boat Guide to Single Sideband Radio.*
- *J. Michael Gale.* Fernhurst Books.

Modeling Books

If you simply can't leave your passion for sailing in the water, bring it home to the dining table.

- *How to Make Clipper Models.* E. Armitage McCann. Dover Pubns.
- *Building a Working Model Warship.* William Mowll. United States Naval Inst.
- *The Dory Model Book.* Harold "Dynamite" Payson. Wooden Boat Pub.
- *Period Ship Handbook 2.* Keith Julier. United States Naval Inst.
- *Ship Modeling From Scratch.* Edwin B. Leaf. Intl Marine Pub.

Navigation & Piloting Books
- *Basic Coastal Navigation.* Frank J. Larkin. Sheridan House.
- *Chapman Piloting, 62nd Ed.* Elbert S. Maloney. Hearst Books.

Coastal Navigation
- *GPS Made Easy: Using GPS in the Outdoors.* Lawrence Letham. Mountaineers Books.
- *How to Avoid Huge Ships.* John W. Trimmer. Cornell Maritime Press.
- *Primer of Navigation.* George W. Mixter, ed. Herrold Headley. W.W. Norton & Company.

Celestial Navigation Books
Remember, fancy modern equipment does fail from time to time. At that point, your only hope of coming home lies in the sky.

- *Celestial Navigation: A Programmed Learning Course.* Gerry Smith. Sheridan House.
- *One Day Celestial Navigation.* Otis Brown. Washington Book Distributors.
- *100 Problems in Celestial Navigation.* Leonard Gray. Paradise Cay Publications.
- *Soap Operas of the Skies.* Jeannie Kuich. Cruising Guide Pubns.

Boat Buying Books
We've done a pretty good job, but these specialty books take you to the next level.

- *ABC's of Boat Camping.* Gordon and Janet Groene. Sheridan House.
- *Boatwatch: Master Guide to Powerboats.* Max Wade Averitt. Boatwatch.
- *Boatwatch: Master Guide to Sailboats of the World.* M.W. Everett. Boatwatch.

Childrens' Sailing Books
Sailing is fun, but with children aboard it can be both dangerous and sometimes taxing. These books will give you some useful insight.

- *Adrift! Boating Safety for Children*, Colleen Politano & Joan Neudecker.
- *Beneath the Sea*, Mark Blum.
- *Birdie's Lighthouse*, Deborah Hopkinson.

- *Bluewater Journal—The Voyage of the Sea Tiger*, Loretta Krupinski.
- *Braving the North Atlantic*, Delno West and Jean West.
- *Captain Jonathan Sails the Sea*, Wolfgang Slawski.
- *Draw 50 Sharks, Whales and Other Sea Creatures*, Lee J. Ames with Warren Budd.
- *Edward and the Pirates*, David McPhail.
- *Flying Ship*, Andrew Lang, illustrated by Dennis.
- *Ghost Canoe*, Will Hobbs.
- *Hide and Seek in the Ocean*, Dawn Apperley & Kate Burns.
- *Inside the Titanic: A Giant Cutaway Book*, Ken Marschall.
- *Into the Sea*, Brenda Z. Guiberson.
- *Letters from the Sea*, Deborah Shapiro.
- *Little Rabbit and the Sea*, Gavin Bishop.
- *The Maggie B.*, Irene Haas.
- *O is for Orca*, Andrea Helman.
- *Ocean Paper Chains*, Stewart and Sally Walton.
- *Origami Sea Life*, John Montroll and Robert Lang.

Handy Cookbooks
When you get a huge appetite but have limited storage, you need to make the most of what you've got.

- *Alaska Heritage Seafood Cookbook*, Ann Chandonnet.
- *Care and Feeding of Sailing Crew*, Lin Pardey with Larry Pardey.
- *Chesapeake Bay Restaurant Guide & Recipe Book*, Charles and Susan Eanes.
- *Coasting and Cooking*, Barbara Williams.
- *Cruising Cuisine*, Kay Pastorius.
- *Cruising K.I.S.S. Cookbook*, Corinne C. Kanter.
- *Galley Collection*, Ann Wilson.
- *Good Food Afloat*, Joan Betterley, Registered Dietitian.
- *The Great Cruising Cookbook*, John C. Payne.
- *The Portable Baker*, Jean and Samuel Spangenberg.
- *Seafood Twice a Week*, Evie Hansen and Cindy Synder.
- *Skagit Valley Fare*, Lavone Newell.

Cruising and Travel Guides
Get the inside scoop on areas you'd love to visit.

- *Adventuring in the Caribbean*, Carrol B. Fleming.
- *Adventuring in the Pacific*, Susanna Margolis.
- *Alaska's Glacier Bay: A Traveler's Guide*, Karen Jettmar.
- *Atlantic Pilot Atlas*, 2nd ed., James Clarke.
- *Bahamas Cruising Guide*, Mathew Wilson.
- *Baja Bash*, Capt. Jim Elfers.

- *Bali Handbook*, 2nd ed., Bill Dalton.
- *California Boating and Water Sports*, Tom Stienstra.
- *The Coast of New England*, Stan Patey.
- *Cruise   Fax: Morro Bay to San Diego*, Jev Haugen.
- *Cruising Guide to Cuba*, 2nd ed., Simon Charles.
- *Cruising Guide to the Leeward Islands, 5th ed.*, Chris Doyle.
- *Cruising Guide to Nova Scotia*, Peter Loveridge.
- *Cruising Guide to Puerto Rico & Spanish Virgin Islands*, Bruce Van Sant.
- *Cruising Guide to Sea of Cortez*, Simon and Nancy Scott.
- *Cruising Guide to Trinidad & Tobago*, 2nd ed., Chris Doyle.
- *Cruising Guide to Venezuela & Bonaire*, Chris Doyle.
- *Docks and Destinations*, Peter Vassilopoulos.

Boat Design Books

When the building and renovation bug bites, or if you'd simply like to play a "what if" game and toy with getting into a new vessel, check these out.

- *American Fishing Schooners 1825-1935*, Howard I. Chapelle.
- *Cruising Designs*, Jay Benford.
- *Cruising Multi-hull*, Chris White.
- *Cruising Sailboat Kinetics: The Art, Science & Magic of Cruising Boat Design*, Danny Greene.
- *Great American Boat Design Collection*, Ken Hankinson Assoc.
- *Guide to Vessel Designs in the Rudder: 1891-1950*, Norman B. Clarke.
- *How To Design a Boat*, 2nd ed., John Teale.
- *Of Yachts and Men*, William Atkin.
- *100 Boat Designs Reviewed*, Peter H. Spectre.
- *Practical Junk Rigboat*, H.G. Hasler and J.K. McLeod.
- *Sail Performance*, C.A. Marchaj.
- *Sailing Yacht Design*, Capt. Richard Miller and Karl Kirkman.
- *Seaworthiness: The Forgotten Factor*, C.A. Marchaj.

Boat Maintenance and Repair

- *Canvas Work and Sail Repair*, Don Casey.
- *Complete Book of Yacht Care*, 3rd ed., Michael Verney.
- *Diesel Troubleshooter*, Don Deddon.
- *Do it Yourself Yacht Improvements*, Reg Minel.
- *Outboard Engines: Troubleshooting, Maintenance, & Repair*, Ed Sherman.
- *Sailboat Hull and Deck Repair*, Don Casey.
- *Shopping for Safer Boat Care*, Neil Smith and Phil Troy.

Medical and Survival Books

Hopefully you'll never need them, but if you do, these are recommended.

- *Advanced First Aid Afloat*, Peter F. Eastman.
- *Bugs, Bites and Bowels: Healthy Travel*, Jane Wilson Howarth.
- *Onboard Medical Handbook*, Paul G. Gill, Jr. MD.
- *Your Offshore Doctor*, Dr. Michael H. Beilan.

Seamanship Books

The more you know, the better you'll make your equipment perform. There are infinite ways you can improve your sailing technique.

- *Barging in Europe*, Roger Van Dyken.
- *Cruising 101, Avoiding the Pitfalls of Paradise*, Amy L. Sullivan, Kevin J. Donnelly.
- *Dockside: Handling Troubles Afloat*, John Mellor.
- *How to Cope with Storms*, Dietrich von Haeften.
- *Marine Salvage*, George H. Reid.

Outfitting and Equipment Books

- *Advice to the Sealorn*, Herb Payson.
- *Care and Repair of Small Marine Diesels*, Chris Thompson.
- *The Innovative Yacht*, Andrew Simpson.
- *Intricate Art of Living Afloat*, Clare Allcard.
- *Offshore Cruising Encyclopedia*, 2nd ed., Steve and Linda Dashew.
- *Safety Preparations for Cruising*, Jeremy R. Hood.
- *Why Didn't I Think of That?*, John and Susan Roberts.
- *Wind Vane Self Steering*, Bill Belcher.

Knots and Ropework Books

Get more detail and step-by-step photos of the insider tricks to rope tying.

- *Complete Book of Knots*, Geoffrey Budworth.
- *The Complete Rigger's Apprentice*, Brion Toss.
- *Nautical Knots & Lines Illustrated*, Paul and Arthur Snyder.

Weather Books

Learn to avoid trouble and make your sailing a pleasant experience by outsmarting the weather.
- *Instant Weather Forecasting*, Alan Watts.
- *Sailor's Weather Guide*, Jeff Markell.

Boat Videos

Sailing and Cruising Videos

Most sailing videos are published by Bennett Marine Video

Around Cape Horn
1980, B&W, 37 min.
Synopsis: Captain Irving Johnson narrates this chronicle of his own passage around the stormy Cape aboard the three-masted windjammer *Peking* in 1929.

Improve Your Sailing Skills
1992, Color, 60 min.
Synopsis: Set sail off the coast of California with some of the nation's top racers as they demonstrate moves that turn the novice into an expert. You'll learn draft control, reefing, spinnaker handling, tacking and jibing, anchoring, and trimming the sails.

Sailing With Confidence
1993, Color, 90 min.
Synopsis: Designed for the novice, the program covers helmsmanship and maneuvers, heavy weather sailing, and flying spinnakers.

Setting Sail—The Star of India Goes to Sea
Sports/Recreation, English, 1991, Color, 30 min.
Synopsis: Walter Cronkite narrates as the magnificent bark *Star of India* sets sail onto the open sea.

The Sixty Minute Sailor
1991, Color, 60 min.
Synopsis: Graphics and computer animation make the essentials of sailing easy to understand.

Airborne
1987, Color, 135 min.
Synopsis: A video that enables the viewer to cross the Atlantic with William F. Buckley, Jr. as he navigates his yacht, *Cyrano*. Demonstrates how to weather storms, how to heave to, how knock downs occur, and how emergencies are handled.

Bill Harmon's Cruising Guide to the British Virgin Islands
1994, Color, 70 min.
Synopsis: A complete video guide for mariners including navigation information, reefs, anchorages, sport areas, and more.

By Way of Cape Horn
1986, Color, 52 min.
Synopsis: Sir Anthony Quayle narrates this video coverage of the Whitbread Round the World Yacht Race, the greatest race in the world.

Cruising With Lin & Larry Pardey
1994, Color, 56 min.
Synopsis: Lin and Larry share more than 25 years of experience in fitting out and cruising their boats with a wealth of useful hints and innovations.

Voyage of Eros—Cruising Fiji "Crossroads of the Pacific"
1991, Color, 51 min.
Synopsis: The crew of the *Eros* explores the islands of Fiji and attends a Sevu Sevu ceremony with a village chief. Tips for cruising near coral.

Cruising the British Virgin Islands
English, 1991, Color, 46 min.
Synopsis: The popular cruising and chartering destination reviewed on video.

Voyage of Eros—First Bluewater Crossing
1988, Color, 46 min.
Synopsis: A video cruise to the South Pacific aboard the *Eros*

Guide to Weekend Cruising
1990, Color, 60 min.
Synopsis: Sid Neal discusses weather, destination, safety equipment, below deck prep, topside prep, personal gear, undocking, leaving harbor, under way, anchoring, weighing anchor.

Boat Maintenance Videos

Basic Yacht Maintenance—Fiberglass
1990, Color, 45 min.
Synopsis: Easy-to-follow instructional video demonstrates how to make routine maintenance tasks simple, inexpensive, and enjoyable. Techniques for varnishing, painting, cleaning or minor hull and engine repairs are demonstrated on a variety of power and sailing yachts.

Basic Yacht Maintenance—Steel
1990, Color, 45 min.
Synopsis: Easy-to-follow instructional video demonstrates how to make routine maintenance tasks simple, inexpensive, and enjoyable. Techniques for varnishing, painting, cleaning or minor hull and engine repairs are demonstrated on a variety of power and sailing yachts.

Basic Yacht Maintenance—Wood
1990, Color, 45 min.
Synopsis: Easy-to-follow instructional video demonstrates how to make routine maintenance tasks simple, inexpensive and enjoyable. Techniques for varnishing, painting, cleaning or minor hull and engine repairs are demonstrated on a variety of power and sailing yachts.

Going Aloft
1993, Color, 60 min.
Synopsis: Safety procedures for climbing the mast and rig in rough weather.

Inspecting Your Rig
1993, Color, 60 min.
Synopsis: The most overlooked and yet important aspect of sailing is the rigging. This video shows how to inspect the rigging before something goes wrong.

The Brightside of Interlux
1993, Color, 15 min.
Synopsis: Application instructions for "Bright Side" urethane system from International Paint.

Boat Safety Videos

All About Fire Prevention on Your Boat
1992, Color, 20 min.
Synopsis: Boat owners learn how to prevent onboard fires and efficiently extinguish fires from different source. Includes instruction on proper testing and storage. Produced in association with "Sea Fire Extinguishers."

The Medical Emergency Video
1993, Color, 31 min.
Synopsis: Six of the deadliest medical emergencies are dramatized and the techniques an average person can use to save a life are demonstrated by emergency room physician Dr. Magruder and paramedic Kyle Vaught. Emergencies include heart attack, choking, drowning, poison/overdose, burns, and bleeding/shock.

All About Personal Flotation Devices
1992, Color, 20 min.
Synopsis: This program demonstrates correct selection, usage, and storage of this important safety equipment. Responsibilities and requirements are discussed in detail including tips on how to use ordinary clothing as a personal flotation device if necessary.

All About Visual Distress Signals
1992, Color, 20 min.
Synopsis: This program demonstrates correct usage of flares applied to emergency situations. These life-saving methods on flare signalling are important knowledge for the boat owner and crew. Includes important proper handling and storage information of these potentially explosive devices.

Boat Handling Videos

Power Boating —V.1—Twin Screw Boat Handling
1987, Color, 50 min.
Synopsis: Step-by-step approach to operating a twin screw power boat. Also includes the use of controls, basic maneuvering, wind and currents, docking, and emergency procedures.

The Cruiser's Guide to Sailboat Handling Under Power
1992, Color, 40 min.
Synopsis: A must for all sailboaters, this video covers crucial topics including approaching and leaving docks and slips, backing into slips, use of lines, maneuvering under power, optimal turning, compensating for prop walk, crew teamwork and responsibility.

Sailboat Racing Videos

1987 America's Cup—The Official Film
1987, Color, 60 min.
Synopsis: Viewers share the sailing excitement as the Americans avenge their 1983 loss to the Australians in this official film of yachting's most famous race. Contains highlights of the qualifying races, the opening ceremonies, the race itself, an interview with Captain Dennis Conner, and the concluding ticker-tape parade.

Merit-Whitbread 89/90
1990, Color, 65 min.
Synopsis: This dramatic video documents the 33,000-mile, nine-month saga of the Merit Challenge to capture the fifth Whitbread, acknowledged as the most grueling and prestigious of all around-the-world races.

Steinlager Challenge, The—How New Zealand Won the Whitbread 1989/90 Round the World Race
1991, Color, 60 min.
Synopsis: Here is the unforgettable saga of one of the most breath-taking triumphs in the annals of ocean racing as the truly magical *Steinlager 2,* captained by New Zealand's legendary Peter Blake, pounds its way to victory across the finish line.

The Whitbread Round the World Race 1993/1994
1994, Color, 60 min.
Synopsis: Gary Jobson hosts this video covering the 32,000-mile Whitbread Round the World Race, nine months of sailboat racing 24 hours a day in often grueling conditions.

Winning With Lawrie Smith
1994, Color, 60 min.
Synopsis: Lawrie Smith, accomplished veteran of the Whitbread Round the World Race, the America's Cup and Olympic sailing competitions shares techniques to increase boat speed in competition as well as pre-race preparations for serious sailers.

Yachting in the '30s
1983, B&W and Color, 45 min.
Synopsis: A documentary of the "Weetamoe," a 1930 film of the Herreshoff-built J-boat and other short films.

Sailing Publishers

Contact these and find out what interesting sailing titles are in their lists.

- Atlantis Technical Services
  Atlantean House
  Dingwall Business Park
  Dingwall, IV15 9XB
  Scotland, UK
  Tel: +44 1-(349) 864-816
  Fax: +44 1-(349) 862-379
  E-mail: atlantis@btinternet.com

- Fernhurst Nautical Books
  East Shore Sailing
  1000 East Shore Drive
  Ithaca NY 14850
  Tel: (607) 387-6347
  Fax: (607) 387-6353
  E-mail: 73563.3345@compuserve.com
- Paradise Cay Publications
  E-mail: idefendm@msn.com
- Seaworthy Publications, Inc.
  507 Sunrise Drive
  Port Washington, WI 53074
  Tel: 1-(800) 444-0138
  Fax: 1-(800) 777-3966
  Outside the US:
  Tel: (414) 268-9250
  Fax: (414) 268-9208
  E-mail: info@seaworthy.com

Sailing Magazines On-line
- *Atlantic Coastal Kayaker*
  http://www.qed.com/ack/ack/index.htm
- *Beachcomber*
  http://www.cnconnect.com/beachcomber/
- *Behind the Boat (magazine of boat-towed sports)*
  http://www.behindtheboat.com/
- *Blue Water Sailing*
  http://www.bwsailing.com/
- *Boardhead.com*
  http://www.pilot.infi.net/~tox/
- *Boat Trader Online*
  http://vision.traderonline.com/boat/
- *Boatshopper Magazine*
  http://www.boatshoppermagazine.com/
- *Boating For Women*
  http://yachtworld.com/bfw/
- *By-The-Sea*
  http://www.by-the-sea.com/
- *Canadian Yachting Online*
  http://www.canyacht.com/canyacht/
- *Chesapeake Bay Internet Nautical News*
  http://www.waterw.com/~weidner/cbinn.htm
- *Classic Boat*
  http://www.marinedata.co.uk/classic/index.html
- Cruise Industry News
  http://www.cruiseindustrynews.com/

- *Cruising World and Sailing World*
  http://www.cruisingworld.com/
- *Diver*
  http://www.divernet.com/divermag.htm
- *DIY Boat Owner Online*
  http://www.diy-boat.com/
- *Great Lakes Cruiser*
  http://www.cris.com/~Glcruise/
- *Heartland Boating*
  http://www.iwol.com/iww/customers/onlinemagazines/
  Heartland/
- *Internet Yachts*
  http://www.iyachts.com/
- *Latitude 38*
  http://www.latitude38.com/
- *Liveaboard Magazine*
  http://www.liveaboardmagazine.com/
- *Mainsheet*
  http://paw.com/sail/mainsheet/
- *Messing About In Boats*
  http://www.mims.com/maib/
- *Motor Boats Monthly*
  http://www.marinedata.co.uk/mbm/index.html
- *Nautica Magazine Online*
  http://www.nautica.it/magazine/
- *The Nautical Research Journal*
  http://www.naut-res-guild.org/journal.html
- *No Quarter Given*
  http://www.discover.net/~nqgiven/index.htm
- *PassageMaker*
  http://www.passagemaker.com/
- *Power & Motor Yacht On-Line*
  http://yachtworld.com/pmy_online/
- *Professional Boatbuilder*
  http://media4.hypernet.com/~PROBOAT/proboat.htm

- *Sailing New Zealand*
  http://www.sailing.co.nz/
- *The Sailing Source*
  http://www.paw.com/sail/
- *A Salty Dog*
  http://www.seakayaker.com/
- *Sea*
  http://www.iwol.com/iww/customers/onlinemagazines/sea/
- *The Sea History Archive*
  http://www.marineart.com/nmhs/seahistory.html
- *Semaphore World Sailing*
  http://www.semaphore.co.uk/sailing/
- *Sennit—A Great Lakes Literary Journal*
  http://members.aol.com/jj3858/greatlks.htm
- *The Shetland News Shipping Pages*
  http://www.shetland-news.co.uk/shipping/shipping.html
- *Tall Ships International*
  http://www.tallship.co.uk/tallship/index.html
- *Underwater Sports World*
  http://www.uwsports.ycg.com/
- *The Wave Length Paddling Magazine Network*
  http://www.wie.com/~wavenet/
- *The WestCoast Fisherman* (Western Canada commercial
  fishing magazine)
  http://www.west-coast.com/fish_hom.html
- *The WestCoast Mariner*
  http://www.west-coast.com/mar_hom.html
- *Wooden Boat*
  http://media4.hypernet.com/~WOODENBOAT/wb.htm
- *Yachting Net*
  http://www.yachtingmag.com/
- *Yachts & Yachting Online*
  http://sailing.org/sailweek/

DOCK 17

Glossary of Important Sailing Terms

aback. Wind on the wrong side of the sails.

abaft. Behind the boat.

abeam. At a right angle to the length of the boat.

abreast. Off the side, even with the boat.

admeasure. Formal measurement of a boat for documentation.

admiralty law. The law of the sea.

adrift. Not under control, floating free with the currents and tides.

aerodynamic. Having a shape reduce wind drag increases efficiency.

aft; after. Toward the stern of the boat.

after bow spring line. A mooring line fixed to the bow of the boat and leading aft where it's attached to the dock.

aground. When the boat's bottom is resting on the ground.

aid to navigation. Any fixed object that a navigator may use to find his/her position.

amas. The outboard hulls of a trimaran.

anchor bend. A type of knot used to fasten an anchor to its line.

anchor light. A white light, usually on the masthead, visible from all directions; used when anchored.

anchor locker. A locker used to store the anchor rode and anchor.

anchor windlass. A windlass used to assist raising the anchor.

anchor. A heavy metal object designed such that its weight and shape will help to hold a boat in its position when lowered to the sea bottom on a rode or chain. The act of using an anchor.

anchorage. A place where a boat anchors.

anemometer. A device that measures wind velocity.

aneroid barometer. A mechanical barometer used to measure air pressure for warnings of changing weather.

astern. Toward the stern of a vessel.

athwart; athwartships. Lying along the ship's width, at right angles to the vessel's centerline.

auxiliary. A second method of propelling a vessel.

aweigh. To raise an anchor off the bottom.

backing (wind). The changing of the wind direction; opposite of veering.

backsplice. A method of weaving the end of a rope to keep it from unraveling.

backwinded. When the wind pushes on the wrong side of the sail, causing it to be pushed away from the wind.

bail. To remove water from a boat.

ballast. A weight at the bottom of the boat to help keep it stable. Ballast can be place inside the hull of the boat or externally in a keel.

bar. A region of shallow water usually made of sand or mud and running parallel to the shore.

barge. A long vessel with a flat bottom used to carry freight on rivers.

barograph. An instrument used to keep a record of atmospheric pressure.

barometric pressure. Atmospheric pressure as measured by a barometer

batten. (1) A thin strip of hard material, such as wood or plastic. (2) Battens are attached to a sail to stiffen it to a more preferred shape. They are placed in pockets sewn into the sail called batten pockets.

batten pockets. Pockets in a sail where battens can be placed to stiffen the sail.

bay. An enclosed body of water with a wide mouth leading to the sea.

beam reach. Sailing on a point of sail such that the apparent wind is coming from the beam (side) of the boat

at about a 90° angle. A beam reach is usually the fastest point of sail. A beam reach is a point of sail between a broad reach and a close reach.

beam. The widest part of a boat.

bear away; bear off. To fall off. A boat falls off the wind when it points its bow further from the eye of the wind. The opposite of heading up.

beating. Tacking; to sail against the wind by sailing on alternate tacks (directions).

Beaufort wind scale. A method of measuring the severity of the force of wind, named after Admiral Beaufort who created the system.

becket. A loop at the end of a line.

bend. A type of knot used to connect a line to a spar or another line. Also the act of using such a knot.

berth. (1) A place for a person to sleep. (2) A place where the ship can be secured. (3) A safe and cautious distance.

binnacle. The mount for the compass, usually located on the wheel's pedestal.

binocular. A pair of small telescopes, one for each eye, used to magnify distant objects.

bitt. A sturdy post mounted on the bow or stern to which anchor or mooring lines may be attached.

bitter end. The end of a line. Also the end of the anchor rope attached to the boat.

block and tackle. A combination of one or more blocks and the associated tackle necessary to give a mechanical advantage. Useful for lifting heavy loads.

block. One or more wheels with grooves in them (pulleys) designed to carry a line and change the direction of its travel. A housing around the wheel allows the block to be connected to a spar, or another line. Lines used with a block are known as tackle.

boatswain. A crew member responsible for keeping the hull, rigging, and sails in repair.

bolt rope. A line (rope) sewn into the luff of a sail. The bolt rope fits in a notch in the mast or other spar when the sail is raised.

boom vang. Any system used to hold the boom down.

bow and beam bearings. A set of bearings taken from an object with a known position, such as a landmark, to determine the ship's location.

bow. The front of the boat.

Bowditch. A reference book named after the original author, Nathaniel Bowditch. Updated versions contain tables and other information useful for navigation.

bowline. A knot used to make a loop in a line. Easily untied, it's simple and strong. The bowline is used to tie sheets to sails.

brace. A line used to control the movement of the object at the other end, such as a spar.

breakers. A wave that approaches shallow water where the wave height exceeds the depth of the water and "trips" and falls over.

breast line. A line attached laterally from a boat to a dock preventing movement away from the dock.

bridge. (1) The room from which a ship is controlled. If it's outside, it's known as a cockpit. (2) A man-made structure crossing a body of water, usually for the use of automobiles or train.

brightwork. Pieces of wood trim and any polished metal on a vessel.

broach to. An undesirable position in which a vessel is turned to expose its side to the oncoming waves.

broaching. The unplanned turning of a vessel to expose its side to the oncoming waves.

broad on the beam. The position of an object that lies off to one side of the vessel.

bulkhead. An interior wall in a vessel.

burgee. A type of flag used to identify a boater's affiliation with a yacht club or boating organization.

cabin. A room inside a boat.

cam cleat. A mechanical cleat used to automatically hold a line. It uses two spring loaded cams that come together to clamp their teeth on the line, which is placed between them.

camber. The curvature of an object such as a sail, keel, or deck. Usually used when referring to an object's aerodynamic or hydrodynamic properties.

can buoy. A cylindrical buoy painted green and having an odd number; used in the United States as a navigational aid. At night they may have a green light. Green buoys should be kept on the left side when returning from a larger body of water to a smaller one.

canal. A man-made waterway used to connect bodies of water that do not connect naturally.

canoe stern. A pointed stern.

canvas. Tightly woven cloth used for sails, covers, dodgers, and biminis. Typically made from cotton, hemp, or linen. Modern sails are made out of synthetic materials generally known as sail-cloth.

capsize. When a boat falls over in the water, a.k.a. a "pop-side-down" adventure.

captain. The person who's in charge of a vessel and legally responsible for it and its occupants.

car. A sliding fitting that attaches to a track allowing for the adjustment of blocks or other devices attached to the car.

cardinal points. The points of north, south, east, and west as marked on a compass rose.

carlins. Structural pieces running fore and aft between the beams.

carrick bend. A knot used to tie two lines together.

catamaran. A twin-hulled boat.

catboat. A sailboat rigged with one mast and one sail.

catenary. The sag in a line strung between two points.

caulking. Material used to seal the seams in a wooden vessel, making it watertight.

celestial navigation. A method of using the stars, sun, and moon to determine one's position. Position is determined by measuring the apparent altitude of one of these objects above the horizon using a sextant and recording the times of these sightings with an accurate clock. That information is then used with tables in the **Nautical Almanac** to determine one's position.

celestial sphere. An imaginary sphere surrounding the globe that contains the sun, moon, stars, and planets.

center line. The imaginary line running from bow to stern along the middle of the boat.

certificate. A legal paper or license of a boat or its captain.

chafing gear. Tape, cloth, or other materials placed on one or more parts that rub together.

chain locker. Storage for the anchor chain.

channel. A navigable route on a waterway, usually marked by buoys.

chart datum. The water level used to record data on a chart. Usually the average low tide water level.

chart table. A table designated as the area in the boat where the navigator will study charts and plot courses.

cheek block. A block with one end permanently attached to a surface.

chine. The location where the deck joins the hull of the boat.

chockablock. When a line is pulled as tight as is can go, as when two blocks are pulled together.

chop. Small, steep disorderly waves.

cleat. A fitting to which lines can be easily attached.

close reach. Sailing with the wind coming from the direction forward of the beam of the boat. A close reach is the point of sail between a beam reach and close hauled.

close up. A flag hoisted to the top of a flagpole.

clove hitch. A type of knot typically used when mooring. It's easily adjustable, but it may work loose.

club. A boom on a jib or staysail.

Coast Pilots. Books covering information about coastal navigation, including navigational aids, courses, distances, anchorages, and harbors.

coastal navigation. Navigating near the coast, allowing one to find one's position by use of landmarks and other references.

cockpit sole. The floor of the cockpit.

cockpit. The location from which the boat is steered, usually in the middle or the rear of the boat.

cold front. Used in meteorology to describe a mass of cold air moving toward a mass of warm air.

cold molding. A method of bending a material into an appropriate shape without heating or steaming to soften the material first.

colors. The national flag and/ or other flags.

compass card. A card labeling the 360 degrees of the circle and the named directions such as north, south, east, and west.

compass course. The course as read on a compass. The compass course has added the magnetic deviation and the magnetic variation to the true course.

compass rose. A circle on a chart indicating the direction of geographic north and sometimes also magnetic north. Charts usually have more than one compass rose. In that case the compass rose nearest to the object being plotted should be used as the geographic directions and magnetic variations may change slightly in different places on the chart.

composite construction. An object made with more than one type of material.

continental shelf. A region of relatively shallow water surrounding each of the continents.

cordage. Any rope or line.

counter. The part of the stern aft of where it leaves the waterline.

course. (1) The direction the boat is traveling or intends to travel. (2) A path which racing boats are to follow.

courtesy flag. A smaller version of the flag of the country being visited. It's flown from the starboard spreader.

cowls. Scoop-like devices used to direct air into a boat.

CQR anchor. Also called a plow anchor, short for coastal quick release anchor. An anchor that is designed to bury itself into the ground by use of its plow shape.

crest. The top of a wave.

cringle. A fitting in a sail that allows a line to fasten to it.

crosstrees. Spreaders; small spars extending toward the sides from one or more places along the mast. The shrouds cross the end of the spreaders, enabling the shrouds to better support the mast.

cunningham. A line used to control the tension along a sail's luff in order to maintain proper sail shape.

current. The movement of water due to tides, river movement, and circular currents caused by the motion of the earth.

cutter. (1) A single-masted, fore-and-aft-rigged sailing vessel with two or more headsails and a mast set somewhat farther aft than that of a sloop. (2) A ship's boat, powered by a motor or oars and used for transporting stores or passengers.

dacron. A synthetic polyester material.

daggerboard. Similar to a centerboard except that it's raised vertically. Like a keel, daggerboards are used to prevent a sailboat being pushed sideways by the wind.

danforth anchor. A brand of lightweight anchor. It has pivoting flukes that dig into the ground as tension is placed on the anchor. It does not have a stock.

davit. A device that projects beyond the side of the boat to raise objects from the water. Typically a single davit is used on the bow of a vessel to raise an anchor, and a pair are used on the side or stern of the vessel to raise a dinghy.

daybeacon; daymark. A navigational aid visible during the day. In the United States and Canada, square red daybeacons should be kept on the right and triangular green daybeacons should be kept on the left when returning from a larger to smaller body of water.

daysailer. A small boat intended to be used only for short sails or racing.

dayshape. Black diamond, ball, and cone shapes hoisted on vessels during the day to indicate restricted movement ability or type.

dead ahead. A position directly in front of the vessel.

dead reckoning. A method of determining position by making an educated guess based on the last known position, speed, and currents.

deadlight. Fixed ports that do not open; placed in the deck or cabin to admit light.

deadrise. The measurement of the angle between the bottom of a boat and its widest beam.

deck stepped. A mast that is stepped (placed) on the deck of a boat rather than through the boat and keel stepped. The mast of a deck-stepped boat is usually easier to raise and lower and is usually intended for lighter conditions than keel-stepped boats.

deckhead. The underside of the deck, viewed from below.

depth sounder. An instrument that uses sound waves to measure the distance to the bottom.

deviation. See **magnetic deviation** or **compass error**.

dismast. The loss of a mast on a boat.

displacement speed. Also hull speed. The theoretical speed that a boat can travel without planing based on the shape of its hull. This speed is 1.34 times the length of a boat at its waterline. Since most monohull sailboats cannot exceed their hull speed, longer boats are faster.

displacement. The weight of a boat measured as the weight of the amount of water it displaces. A boat displaces an amount of water equal to the weight of the boat, so the boat's displacement and weight are identical.

distance made good. The distance traveled after correction for current, leeway, and other errors that may not have been included in the original distance measurement.

distress signals. Any signal that is used to indicate that a vessel is in distress. Flares, smoke, audible alarms, and electronic beacons are all types of distress signals.

dividers. (1) A navigational tool used to measure distances on a chart. (2) The act of entering a dock.

dolphin. A group of piles used for mooring or as a channel marker.

downwind. (1) In the direction the wind is blowing. (2) A term describing the amount of curvature designed into a sail.

drag. The resistance to movement.

drawbridge. A bridge that can be raised vertically to allow boats to pass underneath.

drogue. Any object used to increase the drag of a boat. Typically shaped like a parachute or cone when opened underwater, drogues slow a boat's motion in heavy weather.

dry dock. A dock where a boat can be worked on out of the water.

dry storage. Storing on land.

ducts. Tubes used to move air, such as to ventilate an enclosed area.

DWL. For **design waterline**. Also length waterline or load waterline (LWL). This is the length of the boat where it meets the water when loaded to its designed capacity.

ease. To slowly loosen a line while maintaining control, such as when loosening the sails.

ease the sheets. To loosen the lines that control the sails.

east. One of the four cardinal compass points. East is at 90 degrees on a compass card.

east wind; easterly wind. A wind coming from the east.

ebb; ebb tide. The falling tide when the water moves out to the sea and the water level lowers.

echo sounder. An electrical fish finder or depth sounder that uses sound echoes to locate the depth of objects in water.

electronic navigation. The use of echo sounders, radio, and various electronic satellite and land-based position finders to determine the location of a boat.

emergency tiller. A tiller that's designed to be used in the event that wheel steering fails.

EPIRB. For **emergency position indicating radio beacon**. An emergency device that uses a radio signal to alert satellites or passing airplanes to a vessel's position.

equator. An imaginary line around the center of the world at Ø degrees of latitude.

estimated position. A position based on dead reckoning estimations of a boat's position using estimated speed, currents, and the last known position (fix) of the boat.

eye splice. A splice causing a loop in the end of a line by braiding the end into itself or similar methods. It may or may not be reinforced by a metal fitting known as a thimble.

fair. Good weather condition.

fairlead. A fitting designed to control the direction of a line with minimal friction.

fall off. Also bear away or bear off. A boat falls off the wind when it points its bow further from the eye of the wind. The opposite of heading up.

fastening. An item such as a nail, screw, rivet, or other device used to fasten objects together.

fathometer. A brand name for a depth measuring device.

FCC rules. Federal Communications Commission rules governing radio equipment and operation in the United States.

feathering. A propeller that can have the pitch of its blade changed to reduce drag when not in use.

feet. More than one foot. A foot is a unit of measurement used primarily in the United States. One foot equals 30.48 centimeters.

fender. A cushion hung from the sides of a boat to protect it from rubbing against a dock or another boat.

fetch. (1) The distance that wind and seas (waves) can travel toward land without being blocked. (2) The act of sailing to a location accurately and without having to tack.

fid. A pointed tool used to separate strands of rope.

fiddle. A small rail on tables and counters used to keep objects from sliding off when heeled or in heavy seas.

figure eight. A type of knot that can be used to stop a line from passing through a block or other fitting.

fin keel. A keel that is narrow and deeper than a full keel.

finger pier. A small pier that projects from a larger pier.

fisherman anchor. Kedge anchor, a traditionally shaped anchor having flukes perpendicular to the stock of the anchor and connected by a shank.

flake. To fold a sail in preparation for storage.

flame arrester. A device used to prevent or stop unwanted flames.

flashing. Blinking on and off in regular patterns.

flotsam. Debris floating on the water surface.

following sea. A sea with waves approaching from the stern of the boat.

foot. (1) The bottom edge of a sail. (2) Sailing slightly more away from the wind than close hauled to increase the boat speed.

fore and aft sail. The more common position of the sail with its length running along the ship's length as opposed to a sail such as a square sail, which is mounted across the width of the vessel.

fore. Toward the bow (front) of the vessel.

forecabin. The cabin toward the front of the vessel.

forecast. A weather prediction.

forecastle. The most forward below-deck area of a vessel.

foremast. The forward mast of a vessel with two or more masts.

foresail. A sail placed forward of the mast, such as a jib.

forestay. A line running from the bow of the boat to the upper part of the mast designed to pull the mast forward. A forestay that attaches slightly below the top of the mast can be used to help control the bend of the mast. The most for-

ward stay on the boat is also called the headstay.

forestaysail. A sail attached to the forestay, as opposed to a jib, which is attached to the headstay.

foretriangle. The space between the mast, the deck, and the headstay.

fractional rig. A type of rig where the jib attaches below the top of the mast.

fronts. Used in meteorology to describe boundaries between hot and cold air masses.

full keel. A keel that runs the length of the boat.

fully battened. A sail having battens that run the full horizontal length of the sail.

fully stayed. A mast supported by the use of lines known as stays and shrouds.

gaff sail. A four-sided sail used instead of a triangular main sail. Used on gaff-rigged boats.

gaff. (1) A spar that holds the top of a four-sided gaff sail. (2) A pole with a hook at the end used to get a fish on board.

gale. A storm with a wind speed between 34 to 40 knots.

gale force winds. Wind speeds strong enough to qualify the storm as a gale.

galley. The kitchen area on a boat.

gallows frame. A frame used to support the boom.

gasket. Ties used to tie up the sails when they are furled.

gennaker. A large sail that is a cross between a spinnaker and a genoa. Hoisted without a pole, the tack is attached at the bottom of the headstay.

genoa. A large jib that overlaps the mast. Also known as a jenny.

geographic position. The position of a boat on a chart.

Global positioning system (GPS). A system of satellites that allows one's

position to be calculated with great accuracy by the use of an electronic receiver.

GMT. Time measured in Greenwich mean time. Coordinated universal time is a newer standard—a time standard that is not affected by time zones or seasons.

go about. To tack.

grab rail. See **hand rail**.

great circle route. A course that is the shortest distance between two points, following a great circle.

green buoy. A can buoy.

green daymark. A navigational aid used in the United States and Canada to mark a channel. Green triangular daymarks should be kept on the left when returning from a larger to smaller body of water. Red daymarks mark the other side of the channel.

grommet. A ring or eyelet normally used to attach a line, such as on a sail.

ground swells. Swells that become shorter and steeper as they approach the shore due to shallow water.

ground tackle. The anchor and its rope or chain and any other gear used to make the boat fast.

gunkholing. Cruising in shallow water and spending the nights in coves.

guy. Also called a brace. A line used to control the movement of the object at the other end, such as a spar.

gybe. Spelled jibe. To change direction when sailing in a manner such that the stern of the boat passes through the eye of the wind and the boom changes sides.

gyres. A large circular ocean current.

hail. To attempt to contact another boat or shore, either by voice or radio.

half hitch. A simple knot usually used with another knot or half hitch.

halyard. A line used to hoist a sail or spar. The tightness of the halyard can affect sail shape.

hand. Someone who helps with the work on a boat.

hand-bearing compass. A small portable compass.

hand lead. A weight attached to a line used to determine depth by lowering it into the water.

hand rail. A hand hold, usually along the cabin top or ladder.

handsomely. To do something carefully and in the proper manner, such as when stowing a line.

handy-billy. A movable block and tackle.

hanging locker. (1) A locker big enough to hang clothes. (2) Using such slips to attach a sail to a stay.

harbormaster. The individual who is in charge of a harbor.

hard-a-lee. A command to steer the boat downwind.

hard-chined. A hull shape with flat panels that join at sharp angles.

hatch. A sliding or hinged opening in the deck, providing people with access to the cabin or space below.

haul out. Remove a boat from the water.

hauling part. The part on the object which is hauled upon.

hawse hole. A hole in the hull for mooring lines to run through.

hawsepipes. Pipes to guide lines through the hawse hole. On large vessels anchors are stored with their shanks in the hawsepipes.

hawser. A rope that is very large in diameter, usually used when docking large vessels.

hazard. An object that might not allow safe operation.

head. (1) The front of a vessel. (2) The toilet and toilet room in a vessel.

head seas. Waves coming from the front of the vessel.

head up. To turn the bow more directly into the eye of the wind. The opposite of falling off.

headsail. Any sail forward of the mast, such as a jib.

headway. The forward motion of a vessel through the water.

heaving to. Arranging the sails in such a manner as to slow or stop the forward motion of the boat, such as when in heavy seas.

heavy seas. When there are large or breaking waves in stormy conditions.

heavy weather. Stormy conditions, including rough, high seas and strong winds.

heeling error. The error in a compass reading caused by the heel of a boat.

hemisphere. half of a sphere. On the globe, hemispheres are used to describe the halves of the earth north or south of the equator.

high tide. The point of a tide when the water is the highest. The opposite of low tide.

hiking stick. An extension to the tiller allowing the helmsman to steer while moving about cockpit. This may be desired for improved visibility or stability.

hitch. A knot used to attach a line to a cleat or other object.

holding ground. The type of bottom that the anchor is set in, as in, "Good **holding ground**."

holding tank. A storage tank where sewage is stored until it can be removed to a treatment facility.

horizon. Where the water and sky or ground and sky appear to intersect.

horseshoe buoy. A flotation device shaped like a U and thrown to people in the water in emergencies.

hull. The main structural body of the boat, not including the deck, keel, mast, or cabin. The part that keeps the water out of the boat.

hurricane. A strong tropical revolving storm of force 12 or higher in the Northern Hemisphere. Hurricanes revolve in a clockwise direction. In the Southern Hemisphere these storms revolve counterclockwise and are known as typhoons.

hydrography. The study of the earth's waters.

ICW. For **Intracoastal Waterway**. A system of rivers and canals along the Atlantic and Gulf coasts of the United States allowing boats to travel along them without having to go offshore.

in irons. A sailboat with its bow pointed directly into the wind, preventing the sails from filling properly; the boat cannot move.

inboard cruiser. A motorboat with an inboard engine.

inboard. (1) Toward the center of the boat. (2) An engine that is mounted inside the boat.

inches of mercury. A unit used when measuring the pressure of the atmosphere. Inches of mercury are used because some barometers use the height of mercury in a sealed tube as a measuring device.

inflatable. A dinghy or raft that can be inflated for use or deflated for easy stowage.

International Code of Signals. A set of radio, sound, and visual signals designed to aid in communications between vessels without language problems. It can be used with Morse code, with signal pennants, and by spoken code letters.

isobars. Lines drawn on a weather map indicating regions of equal pressure. When the lines are close together, this indicates a rapid change in air pressure accompanied by strong winds.

isogonic lines. A line connecting points of equal magnetic variation on a map.

jack line; jack stay. A strong line, usually of flat webbing, or a wire stay running fore and aft along the sides of a boat to which a safety harness can be attached.

Jacob's ladder. A rope ladder.

jam cleat. A cleat designed to hold a line in place without slipping. It consists of two narrowing jaws with teeth in which the line is placed. **Also see cam cleat**.

jaws. A fitting holding a boom or gaff to the mast.

jenny. A genoa jib. A large jib that overlaps the mast.

jetty. A man-made structure projecting from the shore. May protect a harbor entrance or aid in preventing beach erosion.

jib netting. A rope net to catch the jib when it's lowered.

jib stay. The stay that the jib is hoisted on, usually the headstay.

jib topsail. A small jib set high on the headstay of a double headsail rig.

Jibe or **gybe.** To change direction when sailing in a manner such that the stern of the boat passes through the eye of the wind and the boom changes sides.

jiffy reefing. A method of lowering the sail in sections so that it can be reefed quickly.

junction buoy. Also known as a preferred channel buoy. A red and green horizontally striped buoy used in the United States to mark the separation of a channel into two channels. The preferred channel is indicated by the color of the uppermost stripe. Red on top indicates that the preferred channel is to the right as you return; green indicates the left. **Also see can** and **nun buoys**.

jury rig. A temporary repair using improvised materials and parts.

kedging. (1) To kedge off; a method of pulling a boat out of shallow water when it has run aground. A dinghy is used to set an anchor, then the boat is pulled toward the anchor. Those steps are repeated until the boat is in deep enough water to float. (2) A traditionally shaped anchor having flukes perpendicular to the stock of the anchor and connected by a shank.

keel. A flat surface built into the bottom of the boat to prevent and reduce the leeway caused by the wind pushing

against the side of the boat. A keel also usually has some ballast to help keep the boat upright and prevent it from heeling too much. There are several types of keels, such as fin keels and full keels.

keel stepped. A mast that is stepped (placed) on the keel at the bottom of the boat rather than on the deck. Keel-stepped masts are considered sturdier than deck-stepped masts.

keelson. A beam attached to the top of the floors to add strength to the keel on a wooden boat.

ketch. A sailboat with two masts. The shorter mizzen mast is aft of the main mast but forward of the rudder post. A similar vessel, the yawl, has the mizzen mast aft of the rudder post.

king plank. The center plank on a wooden deck.

king spoke. The top spoke on a wheel when the rudder is centered.

knocked down. A boat that has rolled so that she is lying on her side or even rolled completely over. A boat with appropriate ballast should right herself after being knocked down.

knot. (1) A speed of one nautical mile per hour. (2) A method of attaching a rope or line to itself, another line, or a fitting.

labor. Heavy rolling or pitching while under way.

lacing. A line used to attach a sail to a spar.

laid up. A boat in a dry dock.

land breeze. A wind moving from the land to the water due to temperature changes in the evening.

landlocked. Surrounded by land.

landmark. A distinctive reference point that can be used for navigation.

lanyard. A line attached to a tool.

lash. To tie something with a line.

lateral resistance. The ability of a boat to keep from being moved sideways by the wind. Keels, daggerboards, center-

boards, and leeboards are all used to improve a boat's lateral resistance.

launch. (1) To put a boat in the water. (2) A small boat used to ferry people to and from a larger vessel.

lay. The position of an item.

lazarette. A small aft storage space for spare parts and other items.

lazy guy. A line attached to the boom to prevent it from accidentally jibing.

lazy sheet. A line led to a sail but not currently in use. The line currently in use is known as the working sheet. Usually the working and lazy sheets change when the boat is tacked.

lead line. A line with a weight on the end used to measure depth. The lead is dropped into the water and marks on the line are read to determine the current water depth. The lead usually has a cavity to return a sample of the bottom type (mud, sand, etc.).

leading marks. Unlit navigational aids for use during the day. Like leading lights, they mark a bearing to a channel when they are lined up one above the other.

league. Three nautical miles.

leech. The aft edge of a fore and aft sail.

leech line. A line used to tighten the leech of a sail, helping to create proper sail shape.

leecloths. Cloths raised along the side of a berth to keep the occupant from falling out.

leeward. The direction away from the wind; opposite of windward.

leeway. The sideways movement of a boat away from the wind, usually unwanted. Keels and other devices help prevent a boat from having excessive leeway.

licensed pilot. A pilot with a license stating that he or she is qualified to guide vessels in a particular area.

lie. (1) Where an object is. (2) To put an object in place.

life boat. A small boat used for emergencies such as when the parent boat is sinking.

life jacket. A device used to keep a person afloat. Also called a life preserver, life vest, or personal flotation device (PFD).

lifeline. A line running between the bow and the stern of a boat to which the crew can attach themselves to prevent them from being separated from the boat.

life raft. An emergency raft used in case of serious problems to the parent vessel, such as sinking.

light. A lit navigational aid such as a lighthouse that can be used at night or in poor visibility.

light list. A list of lights arranged in geographical order.

lightship. A light placed on a ship; the ship remained in a fixed position. Most lightships have been replaced by lit buoys or other structures.

linestoppers. A device used to keep a line from slipping, such as a jam cleat.

liquid petroleum gas. LPG or propane for short, propane is a common fuel used for cooking and heating. CNG (natural gas) is considered safer because propane is heavier than air and will sink into the bilge if it leaks, creating the potential for an explosion. Propane is more easily available throughout the world than CNG, however, so it's used for most boats outside of North America.

list. A leaning to one side when not under way. Usually the result of an improperly loaded boat. Heeling is different from a list because it's caused by the forces of wind acting upon a sailboat that is under way. When a boat changes tacks, the direction of the heel will change sides, whereas a list is a continual leaning to the same side under any condition.

log. A device used to measure the distance traveled through the water. The distance read from a log can be affected by currents, leeway, and other factors, so those distances are sometimes corrected to a distance made good. Logs can be electronic devices or paddle wheels mounted through the hull of the boat or trailed behind it on a line.

longitude. Imaginary lines drawn through the North and South Poles on the globe used to measure distance east and west.

lookout. A person designated to watch for other vessels and hazards.

Loran. An electronic instrument using radio waves from various stations to find one's position.

lubber line. A mark on a compass used to read the heading of a boat.

luff. The edge of a sail toward the bow of a boat.

lugs. Metal or plastic pieces attached to a sail's luff that slide in a mast track to allow easy hoisting of the sail.

lying ahull. A boat that is letting herself be subjected to prevailing conditions without the use of sails or other devices.

magnetic bearing. The bearing of an object after magnetic variation has been considered, but without compensation for magnetic deviation.

magnetic course. The course of a vessel after magnetic variation has been considered, but without compensation for magnetic deviation.

magnetic deviation. Compass error; the difference between the reading of a compass and the actual magnetic course or bearing due to errors in the compass reading.

magnetic north. The direction to which a compass points. Magnetic north differs from true north because the magnetic fields of the planet are not exactly in line with the North and South Poles.

magnetic variation. The difference between magnetic north and true north,

measured as an angle. Magnetic variation is different in different locations, so the nearest compass rose to each location on a chart must be used.

main mast. The tallest (or only) mast on a boat.

main topsail. A topsail on the main mast.

mainsail. The main sail that is suspended from the main mast.

mainsheet. The line used to control the mainsail.

make fast. To attach a line to something so that it will not move.

make way. Moving through the water.

marina. A place where boats can find fuel, water, and other services. Marinas also contain slips where boats can stay for a period of time.

marl. To wrap a small line around another.

marline. A small line used for whipping, seizing, and lashing.

marlinespike. A pointed tool used to separate the strands of a rope or wire.

mast boot. A protective cover wrapped around the mast at the deck on a keel-stepped boat to prevent water from entering the boat.

masthead. The top of a mast. Wind direction indicators and radio antennas usually collect on the masthead.

masthead light. Also known as a steaming light. The masthead light is a white light that is visible for an arc extending across the forward 225 degrees of the boat. When lit the masthead light indicates that a vessel is under power, including sailboats with engines running. Masthead lights are usually located halfway up the mast rather than at the top.

mast step. The place that supports the bottom of the mast.

mast track. A track or groove in the back of the mast to which the sail is attached by means of lugs or the boltrope.

Mayday. An internationally recognized distress signal used on a radio to indicate a life-threatening situation. Mayday calls have priority over any other radio transmission and should only be used if there is an immediate threat to life or vessel.

mean low water. A figure representing the average low tide of a region.

measured mile. A course marked by buoys or ranges measuring one nautical mile. Measured miles are used to calibrate logs.

Mediterranean berth. A method of docking with a boat's stern to the dock.

messenger. A small line used to pull a heavier line or cable.

midchannel buoy. A red and white vertically striped buoy used in the United States to mark the middle of a channel. Midchannel buoys may be passed by on either side.

midships. A place on a boat where its beam is the widest.

millibar. A unit of pressure used to measure the pressure of the atmosphere. One millibar equals 0.03 inches of mercury.

mizzen sail. The sail on the aft mast of a ketch or yawl-rigged sailboat.

monkey fist. A large heavy knot usually made in the end of a heaving line to aid in accurate throwing.

moor. To attach a boat to a mooring, dock, post, anchor, etc.

mooring. A place where a boat can be moored. Usually a buoy marks the location of a firmly set anchor.

mooring line. A line used to secure a boat to an anchor, dock, or mooring.

motor. (1) An engine. (2) The act of using an engine to move a boat.

mount. An attachment point for another object.

mushroom anchor. A type of anchor with a heavy inverted mushroom-shaped head. Mushroom anchors are used to anchor in mud and other soft ground.

natural gas. Short for compressed natural gas or CNG. A type of compressed gas used as fuel for stoves and heaters. CNG is stored in metal cylinders prior to use. CNG is considered safer than other types of fuel such as propane (LPG) because it's lighter than air and may rise into the sky in the event of a leak. Caution should still be used as CNG can collect near the cabin ceiling, potentially causing an explosion. Propane is available in more areas around the world than CNG so CNG is not often used outside of North America.

Nautical Almanac. An annually published book that contains information about the position of the sun, moon, planets, and stars. This information is used for celestial navigation.

nautical mile. Distance at sea is measured in nautical miles, which are about 6067.12 feet, 1.15 statute miles, or exactly 1852 meters. Nautical miles have the unique property that a minute of latitude is equal to one nautical mile (there is a slight error because the earth is not perfectly round). Measurement of speed is done in knots where one knot equals one nautical mile per hour. A statute mile is used to measure distances on land in the United States and is 5280 feet.

nautical. Having to do with boats, ships, or sailing.

navigable water. Water of sufficient depth to allow a boat to travel through it.

navigation. The act of determining the position of a boat and the course needed to safely move the boat from place to place.

navigation lights. Lights on a boat help others determine its course, position, and what it's doing.

navigational aid. Any fixed object that a navigator may use to find his position, such as permanent land or sea markers, buoys, radio beacons, and lighthouses.

neap tide. The tide with the least variation in water level, occurring when the moon is one-quarter and three-quarters full. The lowest high tide and the highest low tide occur at neap tide. The opposite is the spring tide.

noon sight. A sighting taken for celestial navigation at noon when the sun is at its highest point in the sky.

North Pole. The "top" point of the line about which the earth rotates.

North Star. Polaris, the North Star, is visible in the Northern Hemisphere and indicates the direction of north. In the Southern Hemisphere the Southern Cross is used to find the direction of south.

north wind; northerly wind. Wind coming from the north.

north. One of the four cardinal compass points. North is the direction toward the North Pole and is at zero degrees on a compass card.

oar. A stick with a blade at the end used to row a rowboat. Oars are different than paddles because they have a provision to be secured to the rowboat for rowing, such as an oarlock.

oarlock. A device to attach oars to a rowboat, allowing the operator to row rather than paddle the boat.

observed position. A position or fix determined by observing landmarks or other objects to find the position.

occulting lights. A navigational light which turns on and off in a regular pattern, but is on more than it's off. The opposite of a blinking light.

off the wind. Sailing with the wind coming from the stern or quarter of the boat.

offshore. Away from land, toward the water.

on the bow. To the bow of the boat, forward of the beam.

on the wind. Sailing close hauled. Sailing toward the wind as much as possible with the wind coming from the bow.

open. A location that is not sheltered from the wind and seas. An open location would not make a good anchorage.

outboard. On the side of the hull that the water is on. Outboard engines are sometimes just called outboards.

outhaul. A line used to tension the foot of a sail, used to maintain proper sail shape.

out of trim. Sails that are not properly arranged for the point of sail that the boat is on. The sails may be luffing or have improper sail shape, or the boat may be heeling too much. These conditions will slow the boat down.

outrigger. A flotation device attached to one or both sides of the hull to help prevent a capsize.

overboard. In the water, outside of the vessel.

overfall. Dangerously steep and breaking seas due to opposing currents and wind in a shallow area.

overhang. The area of the bow or stern that hangs over the water.

owner's flag. A boat owner's private pennant.

pad eye. A small fitting with a hole used to guide a line.

paddle. (1) A stick with a blade at the end of it used to propel a small boat through the water. (2) The act of using a paddle to propel a boat.

painted waterline. A painted line on the side of a boat at the waterline. The color usually changes above and below the waterline as the boat is painted with special antifouling paint below the waterline.

painter. A line attached to the bow of a dinghy and used to tie it up or tow it.

palm. A tool worn on the hand with a thimble-shaped structure on it and used when sewing sails.

Pan pan. An urgent message used on a radio regarding the safety of people or property. A Pan pan message is not used when there is an immediate threat to life or property, instead the Mayday call is used. Pan pan situations may develop into Mayday situations. As with a Mayday, Pan pan messages have priority on the radio channels and should not be interrupted. In the case of a less urgent safety message, such as a hazard to navigation, the appropriate signal to use is Securite.

parachute. Sometimes used to describe a spinnaker.

parachute flare. An emergency signal flare that will float down on a parachute after launch, hopefully improving its visibility.

parallax error. Error that can be introduced when not reading an instrument directly from its front, due to the separation of the indicator and the scale being read.

parallels. Latitude lines.

partners. Supporting structures used to support areas where high loads come through openings in the deck, such as at the mast boot.

passage. A journey from one place to another.

pay out. To let out a line.

pedestal. The column that the wheel is mounted on.

pelorus. A card marked in degrees and having sightings on it that is used to take bearings relative to the ship, rather than magnetic bearings as taken with a compass.

pennant. (1) A small flag such as can be used for signaling. Flags can be used together to spell words or individually as codes, such as the quarantine flag. (2) A small line attached to a mooring chain, sometimes called a pendant.

PFD. For **personal flotation device**. A device used to keep a person afloat. Also called a life jacket, life preserver, or life vest.

Pile; piling. A pole embedded in the sea bottom and used to support docks, piers, and other structures.

pilot. An individual with specific knowledge of a harbor, canal, river, or other waterway qualified to guide vessels through the region.

pitch poled. When a boat's stern is thrown over its bow.

planing. A boat rising slightly out of the water so that it's gliding over the water rather than plowing through it.

planing speed. The speed needed for a boat to begin planing.

planking. Wood strips used to cover the deck or hull of a wooden vessel.

plug. A tapered device, usually made from wood or rubber, which can be forced into a hole to prevent water from flowing through it.

point. To sail as close as possible to the wind.

Polaris. See the **North Star.**

pole. (1) A spar, such as a pole used to position a sail. (2) One of the two points around which the earth spins, known as the North and South Poles.

poop deck. A boat's aft deck.

pooped. A wave that breaks over the stern of the boat.

port. The left side of the boat from the perspective of a person at the stern of the boat and looking toward the bow. The opposite of starboard.

porthole. A window in the side of a boat, usually round or with rounded corners.

pram. A type of dinghy with a flat bow.

preferred channel buoy. Also known as a junction buoy. A red and green horizontally striped buoy used in the United States to mark the separation of a channel into two channels. The preferred channel is indicated by the color of the uppermost stripe. Red on top indicates that the preferred channel is to the right as you return.

prevailing winds. The typical winds for a particular region and time of year.

privileged vessel. The vessel that is required to maintain its course and speed when boats are approaching each other according to the navigation rules. Also known as the stand on vessel.

prop. Slang for propeller.

propeller. An object with two or more twisted blades that is designed to propel a vessel through the water when spun rapidly by the boat's engine.

prow. The part of the bow forward of where it leaves the waterline.

pulpit. A sturdy railing around the deck on the bow.

pump out. Removing waste from a holding tank.

purchase. Two or more blocks connected to provide a mechanical advantage when lifting heavy objects.

quadrant. A device connected to the rudder that the steering cables attach to.

quarantine flag. The quebec pennant is flown when first entering a country indicating that the people on the ship are healthy and that the vessel wants permission to visit the country.

quarter. The side of a boat aft of the beam. There are both a port quarter and a starboard quarter.

quartering sea. A sea that comes over the quarter of the boat.

quarters. Sleeping areas on the boat.

quick flashing light. A navigational aid with a light that flashes about once per second.

radar. For *radio detection and ranging*. An electronic instrument that uses radio waves to find the distance and location of other objects. Used to avoid colli-sions, particularly in times of poor visibility.

radar arch. An arch to mount the radar, usually at the stern of the boat.

radar reflector. An object designed to increase the radio reflectivity of a boat so that it's more visible on radar. Many small boats are made with fiberglass and other materials that do not reflect radar very well on their own.

radio. An instrument that uses radio waves to communicate with other vessels. VHF (very high frequency) radios are common for marine use but are limited in range. Single sideband (SSB) radios have longer ranges.

radio beacon. A navigational aid that emits radio waves for navigational purposes. The radio beacon's position is known and the direction of the radio beacon can be determined by using a radio direction finder.

radiowaves. Invisible waves in the electromagnetic spectrum that are used to communicate (radio) and navigate (radar, RDF.).

raft. A small flat boat, usually inflatable.

rail. The edge of a boat's deck.

rake. (1) A measurement of the top of the mast's tilt toward the bow or the stern. (2) The difference between high and low tides.

ratlines. Small lines tied between the shrouds to use as a ladder when going aloft.

RDF. For *radio direction finder*. An instrument that can determine the direction that a radio transmission is coming from. The RDF is used with a radio beacon to find a radio bearing to help determine the vessel's position.

reaching. Any point of sail with the wind coming from the side of the boat. If the wind is coming from directly over the side, it's a beam reach. If the boat is pointed with its bow more directly into the wind it's a close reach. If the wind is coming from over the quarter, it's called a broad reach.

reciprocal. A bearing 180 degrees from the other. A direction directly opposite the original direction.

red buoy. A nun buoy. A conical buoy with a pointed top painted red and having an even number used in the United States for navigational aids. At night they may have a red light. These buoys should be kept on the right side of the boat when returning from a larger body of water to a smaller one such as a marina. Can buoys are used on the opposite side of the channel. *Also see green* and *red daymarks.*

reef cringles. Reinforced cringles in the sail designed to hold the reefing lines when reefing the sail.

reef knot. Also known as the square knot. This knot is an unreliable knot used to loosely tie lines around the bundles of sail that are not in use after reefing.

reef points. (1) Points where lines have been attached to tie the extra sail out of the way after reefing.(2) A line of rock and coral near the surface of the water.

reefing lines. Lines used to pull the reef in the sail. The reef line will pass through reef cringles, which will become the new tack and clew of the reefed sail.

reeve. Passing a line through a block or other object.

relative bearing. A bearing relative to the boat or another object rather than a compass direction.

rhumb line. A line that passes through all meridians at the same angle. When drawn on a Mercator chart, the rhumb line is a straight line. However, the Mercator chart is a distortion of a round globe on a flat surface, so the rhumb line will be a longer course than a great circle route.

rig. A combination of sails and spars.

roach. A curve out from the aft edge (leech) of a sail. Battens are sometimes used to help support and stiffen the roach.

roller furling. A method of storing a sail usually by rolling the jib around the headstay or the mainsail around the boom or on the mast.

roller reefing. A system of reefing a sail by partially furling it. Roller furling systems are not necessarily designed to support roller reefing.

rope. Traditionally a line must be over one inch in size to be called a rope.

row. A method of moving a boat with oars.

rowboat. A small boat designed to be rowed by use of its oars.

rudderpost. The post that the rudder is attached to. The wheel or tiller is connected to the rudderpost.

Rules of the Road. The rules concerning which vessel has the right of way if there is a possibility of collision between two or more boats.

run aground. To take a boat into water that is too shallow for it to float in.

running backstay. Also known as runners. Adjustable stays used to control tension on the mast.

running bowline. A type of knot that tightens under load. It's formed by running the standing line through the loop formed in a regular bowline.

running fix. (1) A fix taken by taking bearings of a single object over a period of time. By using the vessel's known course and speed, the location of the vessel can be found. (2) Used to describe a line that has been released and is in motion.

safe overhead clearance. A distance that needs to be kept between the mast and overhead electrical lines to prevent electrical arcing.

safety harness. A device worn around a person's body that can be attached to jack lines to help prevent a person from becoming separated from the boat.

safety pin. (1) Any pin that is used to prevent a fitting from falling open. (2) A pin used to keep the anchor attached to its anchor roller when not in use.

sail. A large piece of fabric designed to be hoisted on the spars of a sailboat in such a manner as to catch the wind and propel the boat.

sailboat. A boat that uses the wind as its primary means of propulsion.

sailcloth. A fabric, usually synthetic, used to make sails.

sail shape. The shape of a sail with regard to its efficiency. In high winds a sail would probably be flatter, in low winds rounder. Other circumstances can cause a sail to twist. Controls such as the cunningham, boom vang, outhaul, traveler, halyards, leech line, sheets, and the bend of the mainmast all can affect sail shape.

sail track. A slot into which the bolt rope or lugs in the luff of the sail are inserted to attach the sail. Most masts and roller reefing jibs use sail tracks. Systems with two tracks can allow for rapid sail changes.

sampson post. A strong post used to attach lines for towing or mooring.

scend. The rising movement of a ship on a wave or swell.

schooner. A sailboat with two or more masts. The aft mast is the same size or larger than the forward one(s).

scow. A boat with a flat bottom and square ends.

screw. A propeller.

scupper. An opening through the toerail or gunwale to allow water to drain back into the sea.

scuttlebutt. Gossip.

sea. A body of salt water; a very large body of fresh water.

sea buoy. The last buoy as a boat heads to sea.

sea cock. A valve used to prevent water from entering at a through hull.

sea kindly. A boat that is comfortable in rough weather.

sea level. The average level of the oceans, used when finding water depths or land elevations.

seamanship. The ability of a person to motor or sail a vessel, including all aspects of its operation.

sea room. Room for a boat to travel without danger of running aground.

secondary port. A port that is not directly listed in the tide tables but for which information is available from a nearby standard port.

sector. An arc of a circle in which certain types of navigational lights known as sector lights are visible.

secure. To make fast; to stow an object or tie it in place.

semaphore. A method of signaling using two flags held in position by the signaler.

separation zone. A region drawn on a chart to separate two lanes that have shipping vessels moving in opposite directions.

shake out. To remove a reef from a sail.

she. All boats are referred to as female.

sheathing. A covering to protect the bottom of a boat.

sheepshank. (1) A knot used to temporarily shorten a line. (2) A sudden change of course.

ship. (1) A large vessel. (2) To take an object aboard such as cargo or water. (3) To put items such as oars on the boat when not in use.

shoal. (1) Shallow water. (2) An underwater sand bar or hill that has its top near the surface.

shore. The edge of the land near the water.

shroud. Part of the standing rigging that helps to support the mast by running from the top of the mast to the side of the boat. Sailboats usually have one or more shrouds on each side of the mast.

side lights. Green and red lights on the starboard and port sides of the boat required for navigation at night. Each light is supposed to be visible through an arc of 112.5 degrees beginning from directly ahead of the boat to a point 22.5 degrees aft of the beam.

sideslip. The tendency of a boat to move sideways in the water instead of along its heading due to the motion of currents or leeway.

single sideband. A type of radio carried on a boat to transmit long distances.

sink: To cause an object to go to the bottom of the water.

skiff. A small boat.

slide. (1) Also called a lug. Metal or plastic pieces attached to a sail's luff that slide in a mast track to allow easy hoisting of a sail. (2) The act of using such lines to hoist heavy or awkward objects. (3) Ropes used to secure the center of a yard to the mast.

sloop. A style of sailboat characterized by a single mast with one mainsail and one foresail.

slot. The opening between the jib and the mainsail.

snap hook. A metal fitting with an arm that uses a spring to close automatically when connected to another object.

snatch block. A block that can be opened on one side allowing it to be placed on a line that is already in use.

snub. To suddenly stop or secure a line.

sound. Signals required by navigation rules describing the type of vessels and their activities during times of fog.

south. One of the four cardinal compass points. South is the direction toward the South Pole and is at 180 degrees on a compass card.

south wind; southerly wind. Wind coming from the south.

spar. A pole used as part of the sailboat rigging, such as masts, booms, and gaffs.

spar buoy. A tall buoy used as a navigational aid.

spherical buoy. A ball-shaped buoy marking a navigational hazard.

spill the wind. To head up into the wind or loosen a sail, allowing the sail(s) to luff.

spindle buoy. A tall, cone-shaped navigational buoy.

spinnaker. A very large lightweight sail used when running or on a broad reach.

spinnaker halyard. A halyard used to raise the spinnaker.

spinnaker pole lift. Also spinnaker lift. A line running from the top of the mast used to hold the spinnaker pole in place.

splice. The place where two lines are joined together end to end.

spreader. Small spars extending toward the sides from one or more places along the mast. The shrouds cross the end of the spreaders, enabling the shrouds to better support the mast.

spring line. Docking lines that help keep the boat from moving fore and aft while docked.

square-rigged. A sailboat having square sails hung across the mast.

stability sail. A vertical pole on which flags can be raised.

stall. To stop moving.

standing rigging. The rigging of a boat that does not normally need to be adjusted.

starboard. The right side of the boat from a perspective of a person at the stern of the boat and looking toward the boat.

starboard tack. A sailboat sailing on a tack with the wind coming over the starboard side and the boom on the port side of the boat. If two boats under sail are approaching, the one on port tack must give way to the boat on starboard tack.

steadying sail. Also stability sail or riding sail. Any small sail set to help the boat maintain its direction without necessarily moving, as when at anchor or in heavy weather.

steep seas. Tall and short waves caused by water current and wave directions being opposite to the direction of the wind.

steerage way. The speed necessary for the rudder to be able to properly steer the boat.

stem. (1) The forward edge of the bow. On a wooden boat the stem is a single timber. (2) The act of placing the foot of the mast in its step and raising the mast.

stepped. (1) A mast that is in place. (2) Where the mast is stepped, as in **keel stepped** or **deck stepped**.

stern. The aft part of a boat.

stern line. A line running from the stern of the boat to a dock when moored.

stern pulpit. A sturdy railing around the deck at the stern.

stiff. A boat that resists heeling.

stock. A crossbeam at the upper part of an anchor.

stopper knot. A knot used in the end of a line to prevent the end from running through a block or other narrow space. Stopper knots prevent a line that slips from unthreading and getting lost.

storm trysail. A very strong sail used in stormy weather. It's loose footed, being attached to the mast but not the boom. This helps prevent boarding waves from damaging the sail or the rigging.

stow. To put something away.

strike. To lower.

stuffing box. A fitting around the propeller shaft to keep the bearing lubricated and to keep water out of the boat.

superstructure. Cabins and rooms above the deck of a ship.

swab. A mop made from rope.

swinging bridge. A bridge that swings away from the waterway so that boats may pass beside it.

swinging circle; swinging room. The distance a boat can move around its anchor. Swinging room is important because if other boats or objects are within a boat's swinging circle they may collide.

swivel. A rotating fitting used to keep a line from tangling.

tabernacle. A hinged support for the bottom of a mast so that the mast can be easily lowered when passing under bridges.

tachometer. A gauge that measures engine revolutions per minute.

tack. (1) The lower forward corner of a triangular sail. (2) The direction that a boat is sailing with respect to the wind.

tacking. (1) To change a boat's direction, bringing the bow through the eye of the wind. (2) To tack repeatedly, as when trying to sail to a point upwind of the boat.

tackle. Lines used with blocks in order to move heavy objects.

taffrail. A rail around the stern of a boat.

tail. (1) The end of a line. (2) To gather the unused end of a line neatly so that it does not become tangled.

take in. (1) To remove a sail. (2) To add a reef to a sail.

tall buoy. Also called a Dan buoy. A float with a flag at the top of a pole used to mark a position such as for a race or a man overboard.

tang. A metal fitting on the mast that the spreaders are attached to.

telltale. A small line free to flow in the direction of the breeze. It's attached to sails, stays in the slot, and in other areas enabling the helmsman and crew to see how the wind is flowing. Proper use of the telltales can help sailors improve their sail trim.

tenon. The bottom of the mast, with a shape designed to fit into the mast step.

throat. The forward upper corner of a four-cornered sail known as a gaff-rigged sail.

thwart. A seat running across the width of a small boat.

thwartships. Across the width of a boat.

tidal atlas. Small charts showing tidal stream directions and rate of flow.

tidal range. The difference of a tide's high and low water levels.

tide. The predictable, regular rising and lowering of water in some areas due to the pull of the sun and the moon.

toe rail. A small rail around the deck of a boat. The toe rail may have holes in it to attach lines or blocks. A larger wall is known as a gunwale.

tonnage. The weight or displacement of a ship.

top mast. A mast on top of another mast.

topping lift. A line running from the end of the boom to the top of the mast used to keep the boom from falling when the sail is not set.

topsail. A triangular sail set above the gaff on a gaff-rigged boat.

topsides. The sides of the hull above the waterline and below the deck.

tow. (1) To pull a boat with another boat, such as a tugboat towing a barge. (2) A rail to which a sliding car is attached for easy adjustment of the position of blocks and lines.

trailing edge. The aft edge of a sail, more commonly called the leech.

transit. Also called a range. Two navigational aids separated in distance so that they can be aligned to determine that a boat lies on a certain line.

transits can be used to determine a boat's position or guide it through a channel.

trapeze. A belt and line used to help a crew hike out beyond the edge of a boat to counteract the boat's heel. Usually used on small vessels for racing.

triatic stay. A stay leading from one mast to another, such as from the main mast to the mizzenmast.

tricolor light. A running light allowed on some sailboats instead of the normal bow and stern lights. The tricolor light contains the red and green sidelights and the white stern light in a single fitting that is attached to the top of the mast.

trim tab. (1) An adjustable section of the rudder that allows the rudder to be corrected for lee helm or weather helm. (2) Sail trim; properly trimmed sails. (3) A properly balanced boat that floats evenly on its waterline.

trip line. A line attached to the end of an anchor to help free it from the ground.

tropics. The region around the equator between the Tropic of Cancer and the Tropic of Capricorn.

trough. The bottom of a wave, the valley between the crests.

truck. A cap for the top of the mast.

true wind. The speed and direction of the wind. The motion of a boat will cause the wind to appear to be coming at a different direction and speed, which is known as apparent wind.

turtle. A bag in which a spinnaker or other large sail can be stowed with the lines attached so that it can be rapidly raised.

twine. Small line used for whipping cords and other light duties.

two half hitches. A knot with two half hitches (loops) on the standing part of the line.

typhoon. A strong tropical revolving storm of force 12 or higher in the Southern Hemisphere. Typhoons revolve in a counterclockwise direction. In the Northern Hemisphere these storms revolve clockwise and are known as hurricanes.

under bare poles. Having no sails up. In heavy weather the windage of the mast and other spars can still be enough to move the boat.

under the lee. On the lee side of an object, protected from the wind.

under way. A vessel in motion.

undertow. Strong offshore current extending to the shore.

unfurl. To unfold or unroll a sail. The opposite of furl.

upwind. To windward, in the direction of the eye of the wind.

USCG. United States Coast Guard.

vane. A flat device that is affected by the wind. Vanes are used in wind direction indicators and some self-steering gear systems.

vang. A hydraulic ram or block and tackle used to hold the end of the boom down.

variable pitch. A type of propeller that has adjustable blades for varying speeds or directions, and may be able to reduce drag when under sail.

variation. See magnetic variation.

vector. A line drawn to indicate both the direction and magnitude of a force, such as leeway or a current.

veer. A shifting of the wind direction, opposite of backing. Clockwise in the Northern Hemisphere, counterclockwise in the Southern Hemisphere.

velocity made good (VMG). Actual boat speed after adjusting for such factors as current and leeway.

vertical clearance. The distance between the water level at chart datum and an overhead obstacle such as a bridge or power line.

VHF. For **very high frequency** radio waves. Radios that transmit in the VHF range are the most common communications radios carried on boats, but their range is limited to "line of sight" between the transmitting and receiving stations.

visual fix. A fix taken by visually observing the location of known landmarks.

wake. Waves generated in the water by a moving vessel.

watch. (1) A division of crew into shifts. (2) The time each watch has duty.

waterline. The line where the water comes to on the hull of a boat.

waterline length. The length of the boat at the waterline.

waterlogged. Completely filled with water.

waterway. A river, canal, or other body of water that boats can travel on.

way. The progress of a boat. If a boat is moving it's considered to be making way.

weather helm. The tendency of a boat to head up toward the eye of the wind. The opposite of lee helm.

west. One of the four cardinal compass points. West is at 270 degrees on a compass card.

west wind; westerly wind. Wind coming from west.

wet locker. A locker equipped with a drain so that wet clothes can be stored in it without damaging other objects in the boat.

whip. To bind the strands of a line with a small cord.

whistle buoy. A navigational buoy with a whistle.

wide berth. To avoid something by a large distance.

windlass. A mechanical device used to pull in a cable or chain, such as an anchor rode.

wind scoop. A funnel used to force wind into a hatch to ventilate the below-decks area.

wing and wing. A method of running before the wind with two sails set. Usually the mainsail is on one side and a headsail on the other, or one headsail is on each side.

working sheet. The sheet that is currently taut and in use to control a sail. The opposite of the lazy sheet.

yacht. A sailboat or powerboat used for pleasure.

yard. A spar attached to the mast and used to hoist square sails.

yaw. Swinging off course, usually in heavy seas.

yawl. A two-masted sailboat with the shorter mizzenmast placed aft of the rudderpost. A ketch is similar, but its mizzenmast is forward of the rudderpost.

zenith. The point of the celestial sphere directly overhead.

zephyr. A gentle breeze; the west wind.

zulu. Used to indicate times measured in coordinated universal time; a successor to Greenwich mean time.

Index

We Have

EVERYTHING!

Available wherever books are sold!

Everything **After College Book**
$12.95, 1-55850-847-3

Everything **Astrology Book**
$12.95, 1-58062-062-0

Everything **Baby Names Book**
$12.95, 1-55850-655-1

Everything **Baby Shower Book**
$12.95, 1-58062-305-0

Everything **Barbeque Cookbook**
$12.95, 1-58062-316-6

Everything® **Bartender's Book**
$9.95, 1-55850-536-9

Everything **Bedtime Story Book**
$12.95, 1-58062-147-3

Everything **Beer Book**
$12.95, 1-55850-843-0

Everything **Bicycle Book**
$12.95, 1-55850-706-X

Everything **Build Your Own Home Page**
$12.95, 1-58062-339-5

Everything **Casino Gambling Book**
$12.95, 1-55850-762-0

Everything **Cat Book**
$12.95, 1-55850-710-8

Everything® **Christmas Book**
$15.00, 1-55850-697-7

Everything **College Survival Book**
$12.95, 1-55850-720-5

Everything **Cover Letter Book**
$12.95, 1-58062-312-3

Everything **Crossword and Puzzle Book**
$12.95, 1-55850-764-7

Everything **Dating Book**
$12.95, 1-58062-185-6

Everything **Dessert Book**
$12.95, 1-55850-717-5

Everything **Dog Book**
$12.95, 1-58062-144-9

Everything **Dreams Book**
$12.95, 1-55850-806-6

Everything **Etiquette Book**
$12.95, 1-55850-807-4

Everything **Family Tree Book**
$12.95, 1-55850-763-9

Everything **Fly-Fishing Book**
$12.95, 1-58062-148-1

Everything **Games Book**
$12.95, 1-55850-643-8

Everything **Get-a-Job Book**
$12.95, 1-58062-223-2

The ultimate reference for couples planning their wedding!

- Scheduling, budgeting, etiquette, hiring caterers, florists, and photographers
- Ceremony & reception ideas
- Over 100 forms and checklists
- And much, much more!

$12.95, 384 pages, 8" x 9 1/4"

Personal finance made easy—and fun!

- Create a budget you can live with
- Manage your credit cards
- Set up investment plans
- Money-saving tax strategies
- And much, much more!

$12.95, 288 pages, 8" x 9 1/4"

**For more information, or to order, call 800-872-5627
or visit www.adamsmedia.com/everything**
Adams Media Corporation, 260 Center Street, Holbrook, MA 02343

EVERYTHING

The Everything Golf Book
by Rich Mintzer and Peter Grossman

Trade paperback, 304 pages
1-55850-814-7, $12.95

Packed with information about the game of golf, its rich history, the great players and outstanding personalities, tour and tournaments, proper etiquette, as well as anecdotes, trivia, and jokes, *The Everything Golf Book* really does have it all!

Whether you are an avid player or an enthusiastic spectator, this book has something for you!

The Everything Bicycle Book
by Roni Sarig

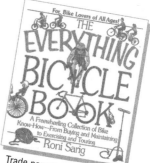

Trade paperback, 304 pages
1-55850-706-X, $12.00

Whether you're thinking about buying your first bike, or considering whether to enter the Tour de France, *The Everything Bicycle Book* has all the information you need to steer you right! You'll learn about different types of bicycles and how to choose one that's right for you.